## SECTION 5 — HOME AND ENVIRONMENT

## SECTION 6 — EDUCATION AND WORK

## SECTION 7 — GRAMMAR

Published by CGP

Contributors:
Angela Billington
Chris Dennett
Lindsay Jordan
Hannah-Louise Nash
Sam Norman
Rachael Powers
Katherine Stewart
Claire Thompson
Jennifer Underwood
Tim Wakeling
James Paul Wallis

With thanks to Helen Smith, Cheryl Robinson & Glenn Rogers
for the proofreading.

No corny clichés about French people were harmed in the making of this book.

ISBN: 978 1 84762 283 9

Groovy website: www.cgpbooks.co.uk
Jolly bits of clipart from CorelDRAW®
Printed by Elanders Ltd, Newcastle upon Tyne.

Based on the classic CGP style created by Richard Parsons.

Photocopying — it's dull, grey and sometimes a bit naughty. Luckily, it's dead cheap, easy and
quick to order more copies of this book from CGP — just call us on 0870 750 1242. Phew!

# Numbers and Amounts

Welcome to page one. On the count of three — get cracking.

## Un, deux, trois — One, two, three...

**1** It all starts off easy enough. Learn <u>nought to ten</u> — no problem.

| | |
|---|---|
| 0 | zéro |
| 1 | un |
| 2 | deux |
| 3 | trois |
| 4 | quatre |
| 5 | cinq |
| 6 | six |
| 7 | sept |
| 8 | huit |
| 9 | neuf |
| 10 | dix |

| | |
|---|---|
| 11 | onze |
| 12 | douze |
| 13 | treize |
| 14 | quatorze |
| 15 | quinze |
| 16 | seize |
| 17 | dix-sept |
| 18 | dix-huit |
| 19 | dix-neuf |

**2** 11 to 16 all end in '<u>ze</u>'. But 17, 18 and 19 are '<u>ten-seven</u>' etc.

| | | | |
|---|---|---|---|
| 20 | vingt | 60 | soixante |
| 30 | trente | 70 | soixante-dix |
| 40 | quarante | 80 | quatre-vingts |
| 50 | cinquante | 90 | quatre-vingt-dix |

**3** Most 'ten-type' numbers end in 'nte' (except '<u>vingt</u>') — but <u>70</u> is '<u>sixty-ten</u>' and <u>80</u> is '<u>four-20s</u>'. <u>90</u> is '<u>four-20-ten</u>' — phew!

**4** The in-between numbers are like English — just remember '<u>et un</u>' for numbers ending in 1. For the <u>70s</u> and <u>90s</u>, add the <u>teens</u> to 'soixante' or 'quatre-vingt'.

Before words which are <u>feminine</u>, like 'fille' or 'voiture', the 'un' or 'et un' changes to '<u>une</u>' or '<u>et une</u>'.

*soixante-treize* = seventy-three

| | | |
|---|---|---|
| 21 vingt et un | 71 soixante et onze | 82 quatre-vingt-deux |
| 22 vingt-deux | 72 soixante-douze | 95 quatre-vingt-quinze |
| 23 vingt-trois | 79 soixante-dix-neuf | 98 quatre-vingt-dix-huit |

**5** When you get to hundreds and thousands, just put cent, deux cent, mille (etc.) before the number.

| | |
|---|---|
| 100 | cent |
| 101 | cent un |
| 623 | six cent vingt-trois |
| 1000 | mille |
| 1.000.000 | un million |

*mille neuf cent quarante-sept* = 1947

1000    900    40    7

The French put <u>full stops</u> or spaces between digits in <u>long numbers</u>, rather than commas, so ten thousand would be 10.000.

## Add -ième to the number to get second, third, etc...

These are easy — just add '<u>ième</u>' to the number. But '<u>1st</u>' is 'premier' (masc.) or 'première' (fem.).

| | | | |
|---|---|---|---|
| 1st | premier, première | 7th | septième |
| | | 8th | huitième |
| 2nd | deuxième | 9th | neuvième |
| 3rd | troisième | 10th | dixième |
| 4th | quatrième | 20th | vingtième |
| 5th | cinquième | 21st | vingt et unième |
| 6th | sixième | 100th | centième |

Watch out for the spellings in <u>blue</u>. And words ending in '<u>e</u>' (like quatre) lose the 'e' (quatrième).

*Prenez là* deuxième *rue à gauche.*

= Take the <u>second</u> street on the left.

1st is written 1er, or 1ère. 2nd is written 2ème, etc.

## Your days are numbered — today's the 20th...

You're bound to know a bit about numbers already — which is cool. And it means you can spend more time checking that you know the rest of the page. Learn <u>all</u> of these words about numbers. The <u>best</u> way to check is to cover up the page and then try to write them down — right now.

# Times and Dates

You **need** to be able to tell the <u>time</u> and understand what time things happen — so if you can't, <u>learn</u> it now.

## Quelle heure est-il? — What time is it?

Just like there are <u>loads</u> of ways of saying the time in English, so there are in French too.
Of course, you have to <u>learn all</u> of them.

| Quelle heure est-il? | = What time is it? |

1) Something o'clock:

| *It's 1 o'clock:* | Il est une heure |
| *It's 2 o'clock:* | Il est deux heures |
| *It's 8 pm:* | Il est vingt heures |

2) Quarter to and past, half past:

| *(It's) quarter past two:* | (Il est) deux heures <u>et quart</u> |
| *(It's) half past two:* | (Il est) deux heures <u>et demie</u> |
| *(It's) quarter to three:* | (Il est) trois heures <u>moins le quart</u> |

3) '... past' and '... to':

| *(It's) twenty past seven:* | (Il est) sept heures <u>vingt</u> |
| *(It's) twelve minutes past eight:* | (Il est) huit heures <u>douze</u> |
| *(It's) ten to two:* | (Il est) deux heures <u>moins dix</u> |

4) The <u>24-hour clock</u>:
They use it a lot in France
— and it's easier, too.

| *03:14:* | (Il est) trois heures quatorze |
| *20:32:* | (Il est) vingt heures trente-deux |
| *19:55:* | (Il est) dix-neuf heures cinquante-cinq |

## You use 'le' for all the days of the week

More '<u>vital basics</u>' — they'll gain you simple marks in the exams.

| lundi | mardi | mercredi | jeudi | vendredi | samedi | dimanche |
|---|---|---|---|---|---|---|
|  |  |  |  |  | 1 | 2 |
| 3 | 4 | 5 | 6 | 7 | 8 | 9 |
| 10 | 11 | 12 | 13 | 14 | 15 | 16 |
| 17 | 18 | 19 | 20 | 21 | 22 | 23 |
| 24 | 25 | 26 | 27 | 28 | 29 | 30 |

### DAYS OF THE WEEK

| *Monday:* | lundi |
| *Tuesday:* | mardi |
| *Wednesday:* | mercredi |
| *Thursday:* | jeudi |
| *Friday:* | vendredi |
| *Saturday:* | samedi |
| *Sunday:* | dimanche |

Days of the week are all <u>masculine</u>, with <u>no capital letters</u>. If you want to say '<u>on Monday</u>', it's '<u>lundi</u>' — but '<u>on Mondays</u>' is '<u>le lundi</u>'.

Je pars mardi .

= I'm going away <u>on Tuesday</u>.

### SOME USEFUL WORDS ABOUT THE WEEK

| *today:* | aujourd'hui |
| *tomorrow:* | demain |
| *yesterday:* | hier |
| *the day after tomorrow:* | après-demain |
| *the day before yesterday:* | avant-hier |
| *week:* | la semaine |
| *weekend:* | le week-end |
| *on Mondays:* | le lundi |

Je fais les courses le mardi .

= I go shopping <u>on Tuesdays</u> (every Tuesday).

## He's Caesar? — No, I said, 'Il est six heures'...

In the mark schemes they make a point of how <u>megatastically important</u> it is to be able to understand all things <u>clock-</u> and <u>calendar-related</u>. So you absolutely have to know the <u>days of the week</u> and things like '<u>tomorrow</u>' or '<u>weekend</u>' inside out. So find the time... and <u>get down to it</u>.

# Times and Dates

You can <u>bet</u> your bottom dollar you'll find this stuff on dates and times really useful.
These essentials will make your sentences sound a whole lot more interesting. It's <u>guaranteed</u>.

## Janvier, février, mars, avril...

French months bear a striking resemblance to the English ones — make sure you <u>learn</u> what's <u>different</u>.

| | | | |
|---|---|---|---|
| *January:* | janvier | *July:* | juillet |
| *February:* | février | *August:* | août |
| *March:* | mars | *September:* | septembre |
| *April:* | avril | *October:* | octobre |
| *May:* | mai | *November:* | novembre |
| *June:* | juin | *December:* | décembre |

*Il part* en juillet . = He's leaving <u>in July</u>.

Months and seasons are <u>masculine</u>, with no capital letters.

| | |
|---|---|
| *winter:* | hiver |
| *spring:* | printemps |
| *summer:* | été |
| *autumn:* | automne |

You say '<u>au printemps</u>' for <u>in spring</u>. But you use '<u>en</u>' in front of all the other seasons.

## You say "the 3 May" instead of "the 3rd May"

Here's how to say <u>the date</u> in French. This is <u>bound to come up</u> somewhere in your <u>exam</u> — and the examiners won't be impressed if you can't understand what the date is.

Check out p.1 for help with the numbers.

1) In French, they don't say "the <u>third of</u> May" — they say "the <u>three</u> May". Weird, huh?

*J'arrive le trois octobre.* = I am coming on the 3rd of October.

2) The <u>first</u> is the odd one out, because it's like English. They say "<u>the first May</u>" ("<u>le premier mai</u>").

*Je suis né(e) le premier mars mille neuf cent quatre-vingt-treize.*

= I was born on the first of March 1993.

3) And this is how you <u>write the date</u> in a letter:

*Londres, le 5 mars 2009*

See p.10-11 for letters.

= London, 5th March 2009

4) And here are some other useful bits:

| | |
|---|---|
| *in the year 2000:* | en l'an deux mille |
| *in 2009:* | en deux mille neuf |

**NOT** 'deux mille <u>et</u> neuf'

## Ce matin — This morning... Ce soir — This evening

You'll use these phrases <u>all the time</u> — they're <u>great</u> for making loads of <u>arrangements</u>.

*Je fais* souvent *du ski.* = I <u>often</u> go skiing.

| | |
|---|---|
| *always:* | toujours |
| *sometimes:* | quelquefois |
| *(quite) often:* | (assez) souvent |
| *(quite) rarely:* | (assez) rarement |

See p.106 for how to say you <u>never</u> do something.

| | |
|---|---|
| *this morning:* | ce matin |
| *this afternoon:* | cet après-midi |
| *this evening/tonight:* | ce soir |
| *tomorrow morning:* | demain matin |
| *this week:* | cette semaine |
| *next week:* | la semaine prochaine |
| *last week:* | la semaine dernière |
| *the weekend:* | le week-end |

*Qu'est-ce que tu fais* ce soir ? = What are you doing <u>tonight</u>?

# Dates — better at the cinema than in French...

It doesn't come much more <u>crucial</u> than this. This is fairly basic stuff, but it <u>will</u> get you more marks, so don't forget to learn it. It's not that hard, either. Just learn the phrase '<u>Qu'est-ce que tu fais ce soir?</u>', and then learn all the different words you can slot in instead of 'ce soir'.

# Asking Questions

Curiosity may have killed the cat, but you've <u>got</u> to be able to <u>understand</u> and <u>ask questions</u> — so <u>learn this</u>.

## Quand — When... Pourquoi — Why... Où — Where

| | |
|---|---|
| *when?* | *quand?* |
| *why?* | *pourquoi?* |
| *where?* | *où?* |
| *how?* | *comment?* |
| *how much/many?* | *combien de...?* |
| *at what time...?* | *à quelle heure...?* |
| *who/whom?* | *qui?* |
| *which...?* | *quel(le)...?* |

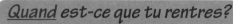

Learn these question words — they're pretty important.

*Quand est-ce que tu rentres?*

= <u>When</u> are you coming back?

Grammar fans: These are interrogative adverbs.

*Qui a cassé la fenêtre?*   = <u>Who</u> broke the window?

*Quelle est la date?*   = <u>What</u> is the date?

'Quel' is a tricky question word. It has different meanings in English <u>and</u> has to agree with the object it's talking about. It has masc., fem., singular and plural forms.

which...? what...?:
quel...?     quels...?
quelle...?   quelles...?

*Quels vêtements allez-vous porter?*

= <u>Which</u> clothes are you going to wear?

## 1) Use Est-ce que to start questions

To turn a statement into a <u>yes-no question</u>, put 'Est-ce que' onto the beginning of the sentence.

*Est-ce que tes bananes sont jaunes?*   = Are your bananas yellow?

To answer <u>yes</u> to a question containing a <u>negative</u>, use 'si'.

*Est-ce que tu n'as pas soif?*   = Aren't you thirsty?     *Si.*   = Yes.

If your question starts with '<u>What...</u>', use '<u>Qu'est-ce que</u>'.

*Qu'est-ce que tu manges le soir?*   = What do you eat in the evening?

OR...   *Que manges-tu le soir?*   You can start the question with '<u>Que</u>' — but the verb (manger) and the subject (tu) <u>switch places</u> in the question and you add a <u>hyphen</u>.

## 2) Ask a question by putting the verb first

In English, you change '<u>I can go</u>' to '<u>Can I go</u>?' to make it a <u>question</u> (swapping the subject and verb round) — it's exactly the same in French except you need to add a hyphen between the subject and the verb.

*Est-elle partie?*   = Has she gone?     *Peux-tu m'aider?*   = Can you help me?

## 3) Ask a question by changing your tone of voice

You can say a <u>normal sentence</u> but just raise your voice at the end to show it's a question.

*Tu as des frères ou des sœurs?*   = Do you have any brothers or sisters?   (<u>Literally</u>: You have brothers or sisters?)

## If you have a question for her — why not 'est-ce que'...

This page is full of question words — start by <u>learning them all</u>. Shut the book and <u>write down all the question words</u> at the top of the page. <u>Look back</u> for the ones you missed and <u>try again</u> till you get them <u>all</u>. Then, all you need to do is <u>remember</u> the <u>three</u> main ways to <u>ask a question</u>.

# Being Polite

OK, you may know all of the French covered so far, but it won't look good if the first thing you say to an actual French speaker is "Hello Bogface" — try opening with these superb gems of politeness instead.

## Bonjour — Hello

Learn these phrases — they're crucial. Nuff said.

| | | | |
|---|---|---|---|
| Bonjour: | Hello | Bon voyage: | Have a good trip |
| Salut: | Hi | Bon anniversaire: | Happy birthday |
| Bienvenue: | Welcome | Bon week-end: | Have a good weekend |
| Bonsoir: | Good evening | Bonne fête: | Have a good party |
| Bonne nuit: | Good night | Bonne année: | Happy New Year |
| Au revoir: | Goodbye | Bonne chance: | Good luck |

Bonjour.

## Comment ça va? — How are you?

Keeping a conversation going is easy if you use a few of these lil' sparklers.

**Comment ça va?** = How are you?   **Et toi?** = And you? (Informal)

**Comment allez vous?** = How are you? (Polite)   **Et vous?** = And you? (Polite)

'Tu' and 'vous' both mean 'you' in French. If you're talking to someone older than you, or to a stranger, you usually use 'vous'. Only use 'tu' if you're talking to friends, family or other young people.

**Other possible answers**

| | |
|---|---|
| Not good: | Ça ne va pas bien. |
| Not bad: | Pas mal. |
| I don't know: | Je ne sais pas. |
| Great!: | Super! |
| I feel fantastic: | Je me sens fantastique. |
| I feel good: | Je me sens bien. |
| I feel awful: | Je me sens affreux / affreuse. |
| OK: | Comme ci comme ça. |

**Ça va bien, merci.** = (I am) fine, thanks.

You can just say 'Bien, merci' (you might get more marks for the whole thing, though).

See p.22 if you're not well and you need to explain why.

## Puis-je vous présenter Chewbacca?

Other useful stuff you should know...

### — May I introduce Chewbacca?

**Voici Chewbacca.** = This is Chewbacca.

**Enchanté(e).** = Pleased to meet you. (Literally 'enchanted')

**Entre. Assieds-toi.** = Come in. Sit down. (Familiar, singular)

**Entrez. Asseyez-vous.** = Come in. Sit down. (Formal or plural)

**Merci bien. C'est très gentil.** = Thank you. That's very kind.

Thirty years on and this celebrity lookalike thing is really working out for me.

# Awfully sorry, but I don't know how to be polite...

It's a bit boring, I know. But grin, bear it, and most of all learn it, and you'll be fine. It'll be worth it when you can sit there wafting your A* in the air — this is all guaranteed to improve your marks.

# Being Polite

Minding your Ps and Qs (whatever that means). You'll be expected to use appropriate language, so if I can't get away with saying, 'Oh just get on and learn this, Hairy-toes', then you can't get away with rude-isms either.

## Je voudrais — I would like

It's more polite to say 'je voudrais' (I would like) than 'je veux' (I want).

Here's how to say you would like a thing:

Here's how to say you would like to do something:

Je voudrais du pain. = I would like some bread.

Je voudrais voyager en Europe.

She would like: Elle voudrait

= I would like to travel in Europe.

Here's how to ask for something:
The way to say 'May I' is 'Puis-je'.

Puis-je avoir du pain?

= May I have some bread?

See p.4 for other ways to ask questions, p.107 for more info on the conditional, and p.14-15 for help on asking for things at the dinner table.

## S'il vous plaît — Please... Merci — Thank you

Easy stuff — maybe the first French words you ever learnt. Don't forget them.

s'il vous plaît = please (formal)

merci = thank you

This is for when you're calling the person 'vous'. If you call them 'tu', you need to say: 's'il te plaît'. See p.5.

You're welcome: De rien

I'm really sorry Jabba... Can I help it if the cameras love me more?

## Je suis désolé(e) — I'm sorry

Here are a couple of ways to apologise — learn them both, and how they're used.

Je suis désolé(e). = I'm sorry.

Use this one if you're talking to a friend or someone you know well. → Pardon. = I'm sorry.

Add an 'e' here if you're female.

## Est-ce que je peux...? — May I...?

'Est-ce que je peux' is another way of saying 'May I' (used more commonly than 'Puis-je').

Excusez-moi... = Excuse me... (Polite)

have something to drink: avoir quelque chose à boire

go to the toilet: aller aux toilettes

You can also use this if you want to ask someone the way.

...est-ce que je peux m'asseoir? = ...may I sit down?

# Merci? — you'll get none of that from us...

These little beauties are just the ticket for excelling as a social butterfly in France... absolutely vital. A really common mistake is to say 's'il vous plaît' to someone who you're calling 'tu'. Tsk. That kind of thing is really important to get right in your speaking and writing assessments.

# Opinions

It pays to have an opinion.  <u>Learn how</u> to say what you think... in many different ways.  Genius.

## Say what you think — it'll sound impressive...

You'll often be asked what <u>you</u> <u>think</u> of stuff.  So get learning these handy phrases.

*J'aime le tennis de table, mais le football ne me plaît pas.*

| LIKING THINGS | |
|---|---|
| *I love...* | J'adore... |
| *I like/love...* | J'aime... |
| *I like...* | ...me plaît |
| *I'm interested in...* | Je m'intéresse à... |
| *I find ... great* | Je trouve ... chouette |
| *I like ... a lot* | J'aime bien... |

= <u>I like</u> table tennis, but <u>I don't like</u> football.

| DISLIKING THINGS | |
|---|---|
| *I don't like...* | Je n'aime pas... |
| *I don't like...* | ...ne me plaît pas |
| *...doesn't interest me* | ...ne m'intéresse pas |
| *I find ... awful* | Je trouve ... affreux/affreuse |

See p.106 for more on how to say what you <u>don't</u> like and <u>don't</u> do.

| OTHER USEFUL PHRASES | |
|---|---|
| *It's all right:* | Ça va |
| *I don't mind / care:* | Ça m'est égal |
| *I prefer...* | Je préfère... |

<u>Watch out</u> — 'J'aime Pierre' can mean 'I love Pierre'.  To say you like him, try 'Je trouve Pierre sympathique' *(I think Pierre's nice)*.

## Qu'est-ce que tu penses de...? — What do you think of...?

<u>All</u> these nifty phrases mean pretty much the <u>same thing</u> — 'What do you think of ...?'.
If you can use all of them, your French will be <u>wildly fascinating</u> — and that means <u>more marks</u>.

| FINDING OUT SOMEONE'S OPINION | |
|---|---|
| *What do you think of...?:* | Qu'est-ce que tu penses de...? |
| *What's your opinion of...?:* | Quel est ton avis de...? |
| *What do you think?:* | Qu'est-ce que tu penses? |
| *How do you find...?:* | Comment trouves-tu...? |
| *Do you find him/her nice?:* | Est-ce que tu le/la trouves sympa? |

| I THINK... | |
|---|---|
| *I think that... :* | Je pense que... |
| *I think that... :* | Je crois que... |
| *I think ... is ... :* | Je trouve ... ... |

*Qu'est-ce que tu penses de mon petit ami?*

= <u>What do you think of</u> my boyfriend?

*Je pense qu'il est fou.*

= <u>I think that</u> he's mad.

## Quelqu'un — Someone

You might need to know the word '<u>someone</u>', at some point, somewhere, in something.  So here it is...

*Quelqu'un m'a dit que tu n'aimes pas le football.*

= <u>Someone</u> told me that you don't like football.

*J'ai vu quelqu'un dans le jardin.*

= I saw <u>someone</u> in the garden.

## Comment dit-on 'dunno' en français...

Never underestimate the power of <u>opinions</u>.  It might seem hard to believe, but they really <u>do want</u> you to say what <u>you think</u>.  Make sure you learn <u>one way</u> to say '<u>I like</u>' and '<u>I don't like</u>' first.  They're the <u>absolute basics</u> — you'll get nowhere without them.  <u>Then</u> cram in all the <u>fancy bits</u>.

# Opinions

Don't <u>just</u> say that you like or hate something — really blow your teacher away by explaining <u>why</u>. Go for it — and knock their <u>socks</u> clean off.

## Use these words to describe things

Describing words are <u>adjectives</u>. See p.85-87 for more on this.

Here's a whole load of words to describe things you like or don't like. They're dead easy to use, so it really is worth learning them.

| | | | | | |
|---|---|---|---|---|---|
| *good:* | bon(ne) | *fantastic:* | formidable / fantastique | *marvellous:* | merveilleux / merveilleuse |
| *great:* | super / chouette | *interesting:* | intéressant(e) | *bad:* | mauvais(e) |
| *beautiful:* | beau / belle | *brilliant:* | génial(e) / super | *awful:* | affreux / affreuse |
| *friendly:* | amical(e) | *nice (person):* | sympa / sympathique | | |
| *splendid:* | magnifique | *nice / kind:* | gentil(le) | | |

**Bob est super .**

= <u>Bob</u> is <u>great</u>.

**Les filles sont affreuses .**

= <u>The girls</u> are <u>awful</u>.

## For 'because' say 'parce que'

To make your opinion more convincing, give a <u>reason</u> for it. The best way to do that is to use the handy phrase '<u>parce que</u>' — 'because'.

*J'aime bien ce film, <u>parce que</u> les acteurs sont formidables.*

= I like this film a lot, because the actors are fantastic.

*Je trouve ce film affreux, <u>parce que</u> l'histoire est ennuyeuse.*

= I think this film is awful, because the story is boring.

*J'adore jouer du violon, <u>parce que</u> je trouve la musique classique très belle.*

= I love playing the violin, because I find classical music very beautiful.

*Le rugby me plaît beaucoup, <u>parce que</u> l'ambiance dans mon équipe est très amicale.*

= I really like rugby, because the atmosphere in my team is very friendly.

Extra marks for style

## If you hear the word 'car', it means 'because'

It's handy to know that '<u>car</u>', like 'parce que', means '<u>because</u>' (or 'for'). Nothing to do with cars at all.

*Elle est très fatiguée, <u>car</u> elle travaille tout le temps.*

= She is very tired, because she works all the time.

## What's your opinion of French, then...

It's not much cop <u>only</u> knowing how to ask someone else's opinion, or how to say 'I think', without being able to say <u>what</u> and <u>why</u> you think. All these phrases are easy — just <u>stick them together</u> to get a sentence. Just make sure you don't say something <u>daft</u> like 'I hate it because it's lovely'.

# What Do You Think of...?

To boost your grade, you need to give <u>your opinions</u>. 'Boost' is such a fun word, I think — it never gets enough coverage, so I'll use it again... <u>learn</u> this, <u>do well</u> and <u>boost</u> away.

## Use 'je trouve...' to give your opinion

Giving <u>opinions</u> is really important in French. It shows that you can be <u>creative</u> with the <u>language</u>.

I think it's safe...

Je trouve ce groupe magnifique .

= I think <u>this group</u> is <u>splendid</u>.

| this team: | cette équipe |
| this magazine: | ce magazine |
| this music: | cette musique |

| bad: | mauvais(e) |
| boring: | ennuyeux/ennuyeuse |
| quite good: | assez bon(ne) |

Use these <u>adjectives</u> and the others on page 8 to give your opinion.

## Est-ce que tu aimes...? — Do you like...?

You'll also need to be able to understand other people's opinions.

Est-ce que tu aimes ce groupe ?

| this film: | ce film | this book: | ce livre |
| this newspaper: | ce journal | this programme: | cette émission |

= Do you like <u>this group</u>?

it: le/la ← For more on object pronouns, see p.93.

Je n'aime pas ce groupe. Je le trouve mauvais .

= I don't like this group. I think <u>they're bad</u>.

These are <u>linked</u>. If the <u>first bit</u> is <u>masculine</u>, then the <u>second bit</u> must be masculine too. If the thing was feminine, it would be '<u>la</u>' and mauvais<u>e</u>.

Je trouve ce journal ennuyeux . Et toi?

We need a rethink, Liam.

Use any of the adjectives at the top of p.8.

= I think this newspaper is <u>boring</u>. What do you think?

This is a good way of asking informally whether somebody <u>agrees</u> with what you've just said.

Moi aussi, je le trouve ennuyeux.

= I think it's boring, too.

# But no one says "splendid" any more...

Giving your <u>opinion</u> about things gets you <u>big marks</u> in the assessments. It's quite <u>easy</u> to say why you like something, so you've got <u>no excuses</u> — you've just got to <u>learn</u> these phrases.

# Writing Informal Letters

I just know you're gonna be <u>chuffed</u> to bits when I tell you that you'll probably have to write a letter in French at some point — it could very easily be in your written assessment.

## Start a letter with 'Cher Bob' — 'Dear Bob'

Learn the <u>layout</u> of letters, and how to say 'Dear Blank...' and all that stuff. It's essential. This letter's short on content, but it shows you how to <u>start</u> and <u>end</u> it properly, and where to put the <u>date</u>.

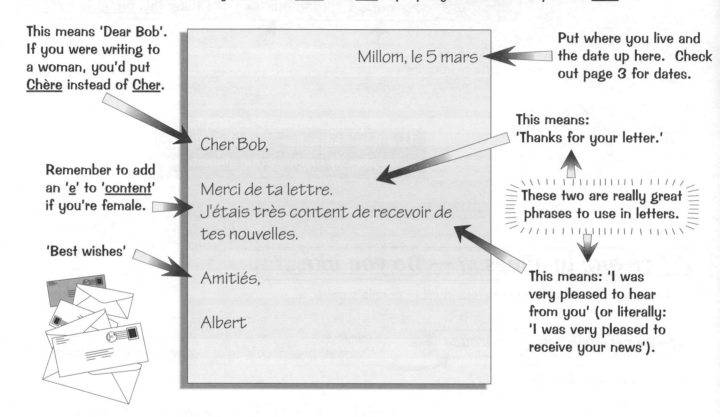

This means 'Dear Bob'. If you were writing to a woman, you'd put <u>Chère</u> instead of <u>Cher</u>.

Remember to add an '<u>e</u>' to '<u>content</u>' if you're female.

'Best wishes'

Millom, le 5 mars

Put where you live and the date up here. Check out page 3 for dates.

Cher Bob,

Merci de ta lettre.
J'étais très content de recevoir de tes nouvelles.

Amitiés,

Albert

This means: 'Thanks for your letter.'

These two are really great phrases to use in letters.

This means: 'I was very pleased to hear from you' (or literally: 'I was very pleased to receive your news').

## Use these phrases in your letters

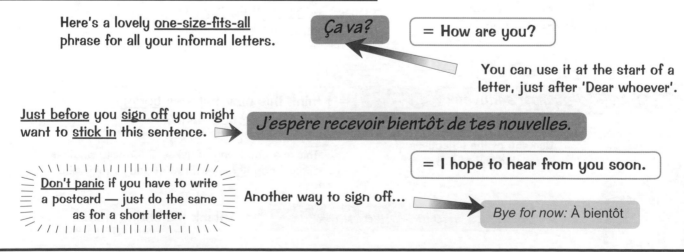

Here's a lovely <u>one-size-fits-all</u> phrase for all your informal letters.

Ça va?

= How are you?

You can use it at the start of a letter, just after 'Dear whoever'.

<u>Just before</u> you <u>sign off</u> you might want to <u>stick in</u> this sentence.

J'espère recevoir bientôt de tes nouvelles.

= I hope to hear from you soon.

<u>Don't panic</u> if you have to write a postcard — just do the same as for a short letter.

Another way to sign off...

Bye for now: À bientôt

# French letters? — let's keep it clean...

For once, some fairly <u>easy</u> stuff — hurrah. It's the <u>bread and butter</u> of your written work. Make sure you <u>know</u> the French <u>stock phrases</u> really well — then your letter will sound dead smart and <u>authentic</u>. Just write the <u>main part</u> like you would write to a friend in English. In French, obviously.

# Writing Formal Letters

You may be asked to write a __formal__ letter as well — it's a bit mean, but sadly you've __no choice__. On the plus side, you might have to write a __letter of complaint__ — who doesn't love a rant in a foreign language... Study the basic format below and practise creating some formal correspondence of your own.

## Put your name and address at the top left

Letters — they really are just as __simple__ as this...

It looks impressive if you put __your__ name and address at the top. (In French, the addresses go the __opposite__ way round to in English — __sender__ on the __left__, __recipient__ on the __right__.)

Put this if you __don't know__ the person's name or gender. If you know it's Monsieur Claude Terrier, put that above his address and write 'Monsieur' here.

This __little lot__ simply __means__: I spent two nights at the Saint Michel Hotel between the 12th and the 14th of April. The employees were great, very kind and welcoming and the room was clean.

Unfortunately, I'm not at all satisfied with my stay because the shower didn't work, the TV was broken and there was too much noise everywhere, so I didn't sleep very well.

The __name and address__ of who you're writing to goes here.

> Aleesha Thompson
> 16 Rusland Drive
> Manchester
> M14 7ZN
> Grande-Bretagne
>
> Hôtel Saint Michel
> 16, rue des Papillons
> Paris
> France
>
> le 20 avril 2010
>
> Monsieur / Madame,
>
> J'ai passé deux nuits à l'Hôtel Saint Michel entre le 12 et le 14 avril. Les employés étaient super, très agréables et accueillants, et la chambre était propre.
>
> Malheureusement, je ne suis pas du tout satisfaite de mon séjour parce que la douche n'a pas fonctionné, la télévision était cassée ct il y avait trop dc bruit partout, donc jc n'ai pas très bien dormi.
>
> Veuillez agréer, Monsieur/Madame, l'expression de mes sentiments distingués.
>
> A. Thompson
> Aleesha Thompson

Put the date here.

Yours sincerely

Check out page 50 for __problems vooab__ and pago 70 for holp writing a __job application letter__.

## Learn these ways to end a letter

This __set ending__ is quite long, I'm afraid — just __learn it__ and churn it out.

*to a woman:* Madame

> *Je vous prie d'agréer,* Monsieur, *l'expression de mes sentiments distingués.*

= Yours faithfully / sincerely

Another __useful__ phrase: *Je vous remercie d'avance.*

= Many thanks in advance.

## How to end a letter — just stop writing...

I know, I know — __letter structure__ needs a lot of __effort__ to get it firmly lodged in your brain. And then there are __set polite phrases__ for formal French letters just like there are in English — it's __essential__ to know the right ones for the __start__ and __end__. Have a go at writing some practice letters.

# Revision Summary

This section includes all the <u>absolute</u> basics... with a few lessons in <u>letter writing</u> thrown in for good measure. All the bits on your <u>opinions</u>, and on <u>dates</u> and <u>times</u> (including today, tomorrow, every week, on Mondays etc.) can make a huge <u>difference</u> to your marks. Go back over and <u>over the section</u> again until you can answer every single one of the questions here first time — sans hésitation.

1) Count out loud from 1 to 20 in French.

2) How do you say these numbers in French?  a) 22  b) 35  c) 58  d) 71  e) 112  f) 2101

3) What are these in French?  a) 1st  b) 4th  c) 7th  d) 19th  e) 25th  f) 52nd

4) Ask 'What time is it?' in French.
   How would you say these times in French?  a) 5:00  b) 10:30  c) 13:22  d) 16:45

5) Say all the days of the week in French, from Monday to Sunday.

6) How do you say these in French?  a) yesterday  b) today  c) tomorrow

7) Say all of the months of the year in French, from January to December.

8) How do you say the <u>date</u> of your birthday in French?

9) 'Qu'est-ce que tu fais <u>ce soir</u>?' means 'What are you doing <u>this evening</u>?'
   How would you say, 'What are you doing:  a) this afternoon?'  b) this morning?'  c) next week?'

10) 'Tu chantes' means 'You sing' or 'You are singing'.  What do these questions mean?
    a) Pourquoi tu chantes?  b) Où est-ce que tu chantes?  c) Qu'est-ce que tu chantes?
    d) Chantes-tu bien?  e) Quand est-ce que tu chantes?  f) Est-ce que tu chantes?

11) What's the French for?  a) Please  b) Thank you  c) How are you?  d) I'm sorry  e) May I...

12) How would you ask someone what they think of Elvis Presley?  (In French.)
    Give as many ways of asking it as you can.

13) How would you say these things in French?  Give at least one way to say each of them.
    a) I like Elvis Presley.  b) I don't like Elvis Presley.  c) I find Elvis Presley interesting.
    d) I love Elvis Presley.  e) I find Elvis Presley awful.  f) I think that Elvis Presley is fantastic.

14) To win this week's star prize, complete the following sentence in
    10 words or fewer (in French):  'I like Elvis Presley because...'

15) You like the group 'The Sheep Shearers', but you think 'James and the Infinite Monkeys'
    are brilliant.  How would you tell someone that in French? (Leave the band names in English.)

16) How would you ask your penfriend if he/she agrees?  (There are two ways.)

17) Write a letter to your friend Marie-Claire.  Write your address, say hello and tell her something
    you've done.  You would like to hear from her soon — how would you say that in your letter?

18) Which side of the page does your address go on in a formal French letter?

19) How would you end a formal letter in French?

20) What does this phrase mean: 'Je vous remercie d'avance'?  Is it for a formal or informal letter?

# Food

You need to learn the vocab for all the basic food, especially the things you like and eat often.
There's a lot of information to digest here, but the more you know, the better.

## L'épicerie et la boucherie — Greengrocer's and Butcher's

This is basic, meat and two veg vocab. You really do need to know it.

**VEGETABLES: les légumes (masc.)**

| potato: | la pomme de terre |
|---|---|
| carrot: | la carotte |
| tomato: | la tomate |
| cucumber: | le concombre |
| onion: | l'oignon (masc.) |
| cauliflower: | le chou-fleur |
| French bean: | le haricot vert |
| lettuce: | la salade / la laitue |
| mushroom: | le champignon |
| cabbage: | le chou |
| pea: | le petit pois |

**MEATS: les viandes (fem.)**

| pork: | le porc | lamb: | l'agneau (masc.) | chicken: | le poulet |
|---|---|---|---|---|---|
| sausage: | la saucisse | beef: | le bœuf | turkey: | la dinde |
| salami: | le saucisson | steak: | le bifteck | duck: | le canard |
| ham: | le jambon | veal: | le veau | goose: | l'oie (fem.) |

**SEA FOOD: les fruits de mer (masc.)**

| fish: | le poisson | oyster: | l'huître (fem.) |
|---|---|---|---|
| salmon: | le saumon | mussel: | la moule |
| trout: | la truite | crab: | le crabe |
| tuna: | le thon | prawn / shrimp: | la crevette |

## Les boissons et les desserts — Drinks and Desserts

Every decent meal needs a dessert and a drink.

**DRINKS: les boissons (fem.)**

| tea: | le thé |
|---|---|
| coffee: | le café |
| beer: | la bière |
| cider: | le cidre |
| wine: | le vin |
| coke: | le coca |
| fruit juice: | le jus de fruit |
| lemonade: | la limonade |
| mineral water: | l'eau minérale (fem.) |

**DESSERTS: les desserts (masc.)**

| cake: | le gâteau |
|---|---|
| biscuit: | le biscuit |
| ice cream: | la glace |
| pancake: | la crêpe |
| yogurt: | le yaourt |
| honey: | le miel |
| jam: | la confiture |
| chocolate: | le chocolat |
| sweets: | les bonbons (masc.) |

**FRUITS: les fruits (masc.)**

| apple: | la pomme |
|---|---|
| banana: | la banane |
| strawberry: | la fraise |
| raspberry: | la framboise |
| pineapple: | l'ananas (masc.) |
| grapefruit: | le pamplemousse |
| cherry: | la cerise |
| apricot: | l'abricot (masc.) |
| peach: | la pêche |
| pear: | la poire |
| lemon: | le citron |

## D'autres aliments — Other foods

Here are some more basic foods and some French specialities you might want to try — learn them really well.

**OTHER FOODS: d'autres aliments (masc.)**

| bread: | le pain | sugar: | le sucre | mustard: | la moutarde |
|---|---|---|---|---|---|
| milk: | le lait | salt: | le sel | soup: | le potage / la soupe |
| cream: | la crème | pepper: | le poivre | pasta: | les pâtes (fem.) |
| butter: | le beurre | vinegar: | le vinaigre | cereals: | les céréales (fem.) |
| cheese: | le fromage | flour: | la farine | chips: | les pommes frites (fem.) |
| egg: | l'œuf (masc.) | rice: | le riz | crisps: | les chips (fem.) |

**SPECIALITIES: les spécialités (fem.)**

| croissant: | le croissant | cheese and ham toastie: | le croque-monsieur |
|---|---|---|---|
| snails: | les escargots (masc.) | potatoes with cheese topping: | le gratin dauphinois |
| salad starter: | les crudités (fem.) | leg of lamb: | le gigot d'agneau |

## Learn the crêpe out of this page...

A lot of foods are easy to remember in French — like le biscuit, la crème, le café... But some aren't — you just have to learn the tricky ones. Have a good look at the French specialities too. Always order the gratin dauphinois (sliced potato baked with cream — mmm). Snails though — geesh...

# Mealtimes

You can use the vocab on this page to be polite in French, at <u>any time</u>, in <u>any situation</u>, if politeness is what's required — when you meet Monsieur le Président, for example.

## *Voudriez-vous...? — Would you like...?*

This is another form of that useful verb '<u>vouloir</u>'.

'Voudriez' is in the conditional — see p. 107.

**Voudriez-vous le sel ?**　　= Would you like <u>the salt</u>?

*the pepper:* le poivre　　*the wine:* le vin　　*the butter:* le beurre

**Est-ce que je peux vous passer une serviette ?**　　= Can I pass you <u>a napkin</u>?

*to drink:* boire

**Voudriez-vous manger ?**　　= Would you like <u>to eat</u>?

**Oui, je veux bien.**　= Yes please.　　**Non, merci.**　= No thanks.

Either '<u>Oui, je veux bien</u>' or '<u>Oui, merci</u>' sound more French than '<u>Oui, s'il vous plaît</u>'.

## *Est-ce que tu as faim ou soif? — Are you hungry or thirsty?*

Questions like these are <u>important</u>. Make <u>sure</u> you understand them, or you may go hungry... or lose marks.

**Est-ce que tu as faim ?**　　= Are you <u>hungry</u>?

*thirsty:* soif

**J'ai faim .**　　= I'm <u>hungry</u>.

*thirsty:* soif

**Non, merci. Je n'ai pas faim .**

= No thanks. I'm not hungry.

## *Pourriez-vous...? — Could you...?*

Here are two <u>dead nifty</u> phrases to <u>learn</u>. Use them <u>properly</u> and you'll be the soul of politeness.

**Est-ce que je peux avoir le sel , s'il vous plaît?**　　= May I have <u>the salt</u>, please?

*a napkin:* une serviette　　*the sugar:* le sucre

**Pourriez-vous me passer le poivre , s'il vous plaît?**

= Could you pass me <u>the pepper</u>, please?

## You'd like the salt? Just help your sel...

Make sure you remain polite in French at <u>all</u> times... You never know who might be listening... But politeness is the key to showing you've mastered the language and it's the ticket to hitting the high grades. So throw in some lovely <u>conditionals</u> where you can and you'll be laughing. Politely.

# Mealtimes

For <u>top marks</u> this stuff can be <u>really useful</u>. And it's useful in tons of different situations too. Bonus.

## Je ne mange pas de... — I don't eat...

Je suis désolé(e). Je ne mange `pas` de `petits pois`. = I'm sorry. I <u>don't</u> eat <u>peas</u>.

*always:* toujours

*no longer:* plus
*never:* jamais

*meat:* viande (fem.)
*dairy:* produits laitiers (masc.)

See p.13 for more foods.

Je mange `souvent` des fruits. J'adore les fruits. = I <u>often</u> eat fruit. I love fruit.

Je suis `végétarien(ne)` / `végétalien(ne)`. = I'm a <u>vegetarian</u> / <u>vegan</u>.

## Vous dînez en famille? — Do you eat with your family?

Now show that you can <u>link</u> the <u>family</u> and <u>food</u> topics.

See p.18 for more family members.

On mange toujours `en famille`. = We always eat <u>as a family</u>.

*at the same time:* en même temps    *separately:* séparément

`Mon père` `travaille tard`, donc il n'est pas possible de manger ensemble.

*My mother:* Ma mère
*My sister:* Ma sœur
*My brother:* Mon frère

*goes to the gym:* va au gymnase
*has a football match:* a un match de foot
*goes ice skating:* va à la patinoire

= <u>My dad works late</u>, so it's not possible to eat together.

## If you only want a little, ask for 'un peu'

These amount words are dead <u>useful</u>.

*a bit:* un peu

Je voudrais `beaucoup` de sucre, s'il vous plaît. = I would like <u>lots</u> of sugar, please.

Je voudrais `un grand morceau` de gâteau. = I would like <u>a big piece</u> of cake.

J'ai `assez` mangé, merci. = I've eaten <u>enough</u>, thanks.

*a lot:* beaucoup    *trop:* too much

Ça suffit. = That's enough.

For more quantities stuff, look at page 35.

## Est-ce que ça vous a plu? — Did you like it?

You'd get asked this question in <u>most restaurants</u> and it might pop up in your <u>listening exam</u>.

Le repas était `bon`.

*very good:* très bon
*bad:* mauvais
*very bad:* très mauvais
*delicious:* délicieux

Le repas n'était pas bon.

= The meal was <u>good</u>.

= The meal wasn't good.

# Que c'est bon, que c'est bon...

I for one <u>seriously</u> love French food. They're really big on high-quality, fresh produce. You can see that just by going round a French <u>market</u>. The fruit stalls look like a beautiful <u>Renoir painting</u>.

# Daily Routine

Chores and revision — two peas from the same pod. But unlike ironing, once done, <u>revision</u> is <u>done for ever</u>.

## Décris-moi une journée typique...

Daily <u>routine</u>. <u>Learn</u> it. <u>Work</u> it. <u>Know</u> it like it's... um... <u>routine</u>.

## — Describe a typical day to me...

Je me réveille à sept heures .

= I <u>wake up</u> at <u>seven o'clock</u>.

| | | | |
|---|---|---|---|
| *I get up:* | Je me lève | *I work:* | Je travaille |
| *I shower:* | Je me douche | *I relax:* | Je me détends |
| *I get dressed:* | Je m'habille | *I go to bed:* | Je me couche |

See page 2 for more info about time.

## Est-ce que tu fais le ménage? — Do you do the housework?

Even if you <u>never</u> help at home, <u>learn</u> these words.

Je fais la vaisselle à la maison.

= I <u>wash up</u> at home.

Je dois faire la vaisselle .

= I have to <u>wash up</u>.

| | | | |
|---|---|---|---|
| *I make my bed:* | Je fais mon lit | *make my bed:* | faire mon lit |
| *I do the laundry:* | Je fais la lessive | *do the laundry:* | faire la lessive |
| *I do the shopping:* | Je fais les courses | *do the shopping:* | faire les courses |
| *I tidy my room:* | Je range ma chambre | *tidy my room:* | ranger ma chambre |
| *I lay the table:* | Je mets la table | *lay the table:* | mettre la table |
| *I wash the car:* | Je lave la voiture | *wash the car:* | laver la voiture |
| *I do some gardening:* | Je fais du jardinage | *do some gardening:* | faire du jardinage |
| *I walk the dog:* | Je promène le chien | *walk the dog:* | promener le chien |

Je gagne de l'argent de poche pour aider à la maison .

= I earn pocket money for <u>helping at home</u>.

These verbs are all in the <u>infinitive</u> (see page 97).

## As-tu besoin de quelque chose? — Do you need anything?

In your listening exam, you might hear somone <u>asking</u> for <u>something</u> or <u>offering to help out</u>...

Est-ce que vous avez du dentifrice ?

= Do you have any <u>toothpaste</u>?

*a towel:* une serviette   *an aspirin:* une aspirine

Est-ce que je peux prendre une douche ?

= Can I <u>take a shower</u>?

*have a towel:* avoir une serviette

Est-ce que je peux faire la vaisselle ?

= Can I <u>wash up</u>?

*vacuum:* passer l'aspirateur
*lay the table:* mettre la table

Peux-tu m'aider faire la lessive ?

= Can you help me do <u>the washing</u>?

*the washing-up:* la vaisselle

Est-ce que je peux vous aider faire la lessive ?

= Can I help you do <u>the washing</u>?

## Your turn to do the housework — ménage à toi...

OK, it might not be the most <u>exciting</u> way to spend your youthful years, but it's not really hard. It's just about sitting down and learning the words. Commit them to <u>memory</u> and you're away.

# About Yourself

You might already know some of this stuff, but it's <u>ultra-important</u>, so make sure you know it back to front. Talking about yourself in your speaking or writing assessment — it's pretty much a dead cert.

## *Parle-moi de toi-même — Tell me about yourself*

These are the <u>basics</u>. <u>Learn</u> them <u>all</u>.

*What are you called?*: Comment tu t'appelles?

Je m'appelle Angela . | = I'm called <u>Angela</u>.

*How old are you?*: Quel âge as-tu?

J'ai quinze ans . | = I'm <u>15 years old</u>.

*When is your birthday?*: Quand est ton anniversaire?

Mon anniversaire est le douze décembre . | = My birthday is the <u>12th of December</u>.

See pages 60-61 for where you live, page 1 for more numbers and page 3 for more dates.

*Where do you live?*: Où habites-tu?

J'habite à Lancaster . | = I live in <u>Lancaster</u>.

*What do you like?*: Qu'est-ce que tu aimes?

J'aime le football . | = I like <u>football</u>.

You can use this to say you like anything, but be careful: 'Je t'aime' means 'I love you'.

## *Comment es-tu? — What are you like?*

You have to <u>describe</u> how gorgeous you are as well.

Je suis grand(e) . | = I am <u>tall</u>.

| short: | petit(e) |
| fat: | gros(se) |
| thin: | maigre |
| slim: | mince |

medium height: de taille moyenne

For more colours, see page 36.

J'ai les yeux marron . | = I have <u>brown</u> eyes.

| blue: | bleus |
| green: | verts |

'Marron' is a strange adjective — it doesn't need an 's' on the end even though 'yeux' is plural.

J'ai les cheveux longs . | = I have <u>long</u> hair.

| short: | courts |
| shoulder-length: | mi-longs |
| quite long: | assez longs |

| dark: | foncés | red: | roux |
| light: | clairs | black: | noirs |
| blond: | blonds | brown: | bruns |

England
Dear Simon,
I am a sixteen-year-old-girl with blackish hair, fair skin and brown eyes.

## *Comment ça s'écrit? — How do you spell that?*

You may have to <u>spell</u> your name and home town letter by letter in your <u>speaking assessments</u>. Here's how to <u>pronounce</u> the letters of the French <u>alphabet</u>. Practise going through it <u>out loud</u> — yes, you'll sound daft, but you'd sound dafter getting it wrong.

| | | |
|---|---|---|
| A — ah (like in 'car') | J — jee ('j' like 'g' in 'beige') | S — ess |
| B — bay | K — kah | T — tay |
| C — say | L — ell | U — ue (as in 'tu') |
| D — day | M — em | V — vay |
| E — eu (like in 'peu') | N — en | W — doob-le-vay |
| F — eff | O — oh | X — eex |
| G — jay ('j' like 'g' in 'beige') | P — pay | Y — ee-grek |
| H — ash | Q — kue ('ue' like in 'tu') | Z — zed |
| I — ee (like in 'me') | R — air | |

| | |
|---|---|
| é — aigu | ç — cédille |
| è — grave | ï — tréma |
| ê — circonflexe | |

For letters with accents, you just say the letter followed by the accent, so 'â' would be 'ah circonflexe'.

# *I'm tall, handsome, witty, a compulsive liar...*

<u>Learn</u> how to ask and answer questions about yourself, and make <u>darn sure</u> you know the French alphabet. It's the kind of thing that could crop up in the <u>listening</u> exam — e.g. there'll be someone saying they're from a <u>random French town</u> you won't have heard of, and then they'll <u>spell it out</u>.

# Family and Pets

You might have to talk or write about your <u>family</u> situation and your <u>pets</u> — it's best to be prepared...

## J'ai une sœur — I have one sister

To <u>describe</u> your family structure, use these sentences:

J'ai <u>deux</u> frère<u>s</u> et une sœur .    = I have two <u>brothers</u> and one <u>sister</u>.

Ils s'appellent Jack, Henry et Charlotte.    = They are called Jack, Henry and Charlotte.

'Ils' is used for a group of <u>males</u> or a <u>mixture</u> of males and females.

The average family

*a girlfriend:* une petite amie

J'ai un petit ami .    = I have <u>a boyfriend</u>.     Je suis célibataire.    = I am single.

## Ma sœur / Mon frère est... — My sister / brother is...

Remember, <u>detail</u> is key in the assessments. Use these phrases to <u>describe</u> your family in more <u>detail</u>:

Il a douze ans.    = <u>He</u>'s 12 years old.     Elle a les yeux bleus .    = <u>She</u> has <u>blue</u> eyes.

| | | | | | |
|---|---|---|---|---|---|
| *My father:* | Mon père | *My male cousin:* | Mon cousin | *My girlfriend:* | Ma petite amie/ma copine |
| *My brother:* | Mon frère | *My female cousin:* | Ma cousine | *My boyfriend:* | Mon petit ami/mon copain |
| *My sister:* | Ma sœur | *My stepmother:* | Ma belle-mère | | |
| *My mother:* | Ma mère | *My stepfather:* | Mon beau-père | | |
| *My aunt:* | Ma tante | *My grandmother:* | Ma grand-mère | | |
| *My uncle:* | Mon oncle | *My grandfather:* | Mon grand-père | | |
| *My niece:* | Ma nièce | *My wife:* | Ma femme | | |
| *My nephew:* | Mon neveu | *My husband:* | Mon mari | | |

Il est marié .    = He's <u>married</u>.

| | |
|---|---|
| *single:* | célibataire |
| *separated:* | séparé(e) |
| *divorced:* | divorcé(e) |
| *widowed:* | veuf / veuve |

Je viens d'une famille monoparentale.    = I come from a single-parent family.

## Est-ce que tu as des animaux domestiques?

## — Have you any pets?

| | | | |
|---|---|---|---|
| *a cat:* | un chat | *a guinea pig:* | un cochon d'Inde |
| *a bird:* | un oiseau | *a rabbit:* | un lapin |
| *a fish:* | un poisson | *a mouse:* | une souris |
| *a horse:* | un cheval | *a hamster:* | un hamster |

<u>Animals</u>. Always <u>useful vocab</u> to know. And oh so cute...

Non, je <u>n</u>'ai <u>pas</u> d'animaux .    = No, I don't have <u>any animals</u>.

Oui, j'ai un chien .    = Yes, I have <u>a dog</u>.

See page 36 for colours, page 17 for things like fat and thin, and page 106 for more info on <u>negatives</u>.

Mon chien s'appelle Cannelle.     Il est marron .    = He is <u>brown</u>.

= My dog is called Cannelle.     Swap in <u>any</u> descriptive word here.

## No pets — why not just make some up...

This stuff is pretty straightforward. You learn the sentence, learn the words, and just <u>slot in</u> whichever words you need. There's no excuse for not being able to do this stuff — learn it.

# Personality

It helps you connect to other people, makes or breaks that job interview, could win you a spot on X Factor or in the hearts of the nation, and it's who you are. It's personality, and it's important.

## Comment es-tu? — What are you like?

You might be asked to talk about your personality in the speaking tasks, so here goes...

*He is:* Il est  *She is:* Elle est

Je suis **magnifique** .

= I am amazing.

| nice: | agréable / sympa | friendly: | amical(e) |
|---|---|---|---|
| funny: | amusant(e) / drôle | kind: | aimable / gentil(le) |
| lively: | plein(e) de vie / animé(e) | wise: | sage |
| chatty: | bavard(e) | generous: | généreux / généreuse |
| honest: | honnête | hard-working: | travailleur / travailleuse |

*quite:* assez

Je suis **un peu** **idiot(e)**

= I am a bit stupid.

| impatient: | impatient(e) | jealous: | jaloux / jalouse |
|---|---|---|---|
| impolite: | impoli(e) | selfish: | égoïste |
| mean: | méchant(e) | proud: | fier / fière |
| boring: | ennuyeux / ennuyeuse | shy: | timide |
| lazy: | paresseux / paresseuse | sad: | triste |

## J'ai une attitude positive — I have a positive attitude

J'ai **toujours** une attitude **positive** .    = I always have a positive attitude.

*He has:* Il a...  *She has:* Elle a...

*negative:* négative

Je sais **comment faire** **rire** les gens.    = I know how to make people laugh.

*He knows:* Il sait...
*She knows:* Elle sait...

*cry:* pleurer

*in a bad mood:* de mauvaise humeur

Je suis souvent **de bonne humeur** .    = I'm often in a good mood.

*Oh we do, do we? Go on then, amuse us...*

## La personalité des autres — Other people's personalities

Talking about other people's personalities is simple — just use these celeb examples as guidelines...

J'ai beaucoup de respect pour Reese Witherspoon. Elle a le sens de l'humour. Elle est **travailleuse** , **optimiste** et **pleine de vie** . Elle est aussi une bonne mère.

= I have lots of respect for Reese Witherspoon. She has a sense of humour. She is hard-working, optimistic and lively. She is also a good mother.

You can put any of the personality traits above in these white boxes.

= I have lots of respect for Lewis Hamilton. He always has a positive attitude. He is hard-working, chatty and kind. He is also a good driver.

J'ai beaucoup de respect pour Lewis Hamilton. Il a toujours une attitude positive . Il est **travailleur** , **bavard** et **aimable** . Il est aussi un bon pilote.

## Am I decisive? Well, yes and no...

This personality vocab isn't just useful for GCSE French — it could also come in handy to describe the man or woman of your dreams if you're ever a contestant on Blind Date in France...

# Relationships and Future Plans

This page is particularly useful if you want to send a letter to a French agony aunt.

## Un bon ami doit être... — A good friend must be...

It's good to know the qualities you're looking for...

a good partner: un(e) bon(ne) partenaire

À mon avis, un(e) bon(ne) ami(e) doit ... = In my opinion, a good friend must...

| | |
|---|---|
| be honest: | être honnête |
| be trustworthy: | être fidèle |
| be kind: | être sympa |
| be understanding: | être compréhensif / compréhensive |

| | |
|---|---|
| be chatty: | être bavard(e) |
| be fun: | être amusant(e) |
| be like me: | être comme moi |
| be there for me: | être là pour moi |

## On s'entend bien ensemble... — We get on well together...

Sometimes relationships are plain sailing...

Je m'entends bien avec mon ami(e). = I get on well with my friend.

Nous sommes meilleur(e)s ami(e)s. = We are best friends.

my mother: ma mère    my sister: ma sœur    my brother: mon frère

Il me plaît. = I fancy him.

Je suis tombé(e) amoureux / amoureuse. = I've fallen in love.

On ne se comprend pas. = We don't understand each other.

Il ne m'écoute pas. = He doesn't listen to me.

Elle est trop égoïste. = She's too selfish.

She doesn't listen to me: Elle ne m'écoute pas
They don't listen to me: Ils ne m'écoutent pas

On se dispute toujours. = We argue all the time.

## Je voudrais me marier... — I'd like to get married...

It's good to have a plan. If you're not sure of your relationship plans then learn how to say so...

À l'avenir, je voudrais ... = In the future, I'd like...

| | |
|---|---|
| ... to fall in love: | tomber amoureux(euse) |
| ... to get engaged: | me fiancer |
| ... to get married: | me marier |
| ... to have children: | avoir des enfants |

Je vais attendre un(e) partenaire idéal(e). = I'm going to wait for an ideal partner.

Je peux très bien me débrouiller seul(e) — je n'ai pas l'intention de me marier tout de suite. = I can get along fine on my own — I don't intend to get married right away.

Je ne suis pas prêt(e) à y penser. = I'm not ready to think about it.

## I'd like to propose...

...that you take another look over this page so it all comes trippingly off the tongue. It's a bit embarrassing talking about relationships in French lessons, but you'll just have to get used to it.

# Social Issues and Equality

Unemployment, equal ops, gender and race issues — it's enough to make you want to wave around a big banner. Try a verse of 'We shall not, we shall not be moved' — simply superb for revision morale.

## Notre société n'est pas égale — Our society isn't equal

Certains **me traitent différemment** parce que **je viens d'Afrique** .

= Some people treat me differently because I come from Africa.

| | |
|---|---|
| *are violent:* sont violents | *I am a girl / a guy:* je suis une fille / un garçon |
| *are racist:* sont racistes | *I am younger / older:* je suis plus jeune / plus âgé(e) |
| *are mean:* sont méchant(e)s | *I am Jewish / Muslim / Christian* je suis juif / juive / musulman(e) / chrétien(ne) |

C'est **raciste** . = It's racist.

*sexist:* sexiste   *unfair:* injuste

Ce n'est pas juste de discriminer à cause **d'âge** . = It's not fair to discriminate because of age.

*of race:* de race   *of religion:* de religion

## La violence et le vandalisme — Violence and vandalism

Il y a beaucoup de **violence** dans ma ville. = There is lots of violence in my town.

*poverty:* pauvreté   *vandalism:* vandalisme

*bullied:* brutalisé(e)   *hit:* battu(e)

En rentrant à la maison une fois j'ai été **menacé(e)** . = On the way home once I was threatened.

C'est effrayant. = It's terrifying.

Je voudrais vivre sans **crainte** . = I'd like to live without fear.

*violence:* violence   *threats:* menaces

## Les effets du chômage — The effects of unemployment

Il y a beaucoup de **chômeurs** dans ma ville. = There are lots of unemployed people in my town.

*homeless people:* personnes sans abri   *disadvantaged people:* personnes défavorisées

Fromage au chômage.

Il est au chômage depuis deux ans. = He's been out of work for two years.

Sans argent, il est difficile de trouver un logement. = Without money, it's difficult to find housing.

On commence à se sentir déprimé. = You start to feel depressed.

## Sorry, a bit bleak, this page...

Hardly a barrel of laughs, was it, and quite a tricky one to boot. Try to learn some of the more complex sentences off by heart. You'll be surprised how this will help you in the assessments.

# Feeling Ill

Pain, illness and suffering — more fun and frolics from those full-of-glee examiners. I suppose if setting the exams every year is as mind-numbing as taking them, it's not surprising they aren't too chirpy.

## Comment ça va? — How are you?

**Je suis malade.**   = I feel ill.   **Je ne me sens pas bien.**   = I don't feel well.

*to the hospital:*   à l'hôpital (masc.)
*to the chemist's:* à la pharmacie

**Je dois aller voir le médecin .**   = I need to go to see the doctor.

## Où as-tu mal? — Where does it hurt?

Here's how you say what bit hurts...

You can use 'j'ai mal à' with any part of your body that's hurting...

**J'ai mal à l'estomac .**   = I have stomach ache.

*a headache:* mal à la tête   *a sore throat:*  mal à la gorge
*backache:*    mal au dos     *an earache:*     mal à l'oreille

Use 'au' for 'le' words, 'à la' for 'la' words, 'à l'' for words starting with a vowel or a silent 'h', and 'aux' for plurals.

*My head:* Ma tête
*My arms:* Mes bras (masc.)
*My ears:* Mes oreilles (fem.)

**Mon doigt me fait mal .**

*hurt (plural):* font mal

= My finger hurts / has been hurting.

**Je me suis cassé le bras.**   = I've broken my arm.

*a cough:*        une toux
*flu:*            la grippe
*seasickness:*    le mal de mer
*a temperature:*  de la fièvre

**J'ai un rhume .**

= I have a cold.

| LA TÊTE: THE HEAD | |
|---|---|
| the nose: | le nez |
| the eye: | l'œil (masc.) |
| the eyes: | les yeux (masc.) |
| the ear: | l'oreille (fem.) |
| the mouth: | la bouche |
| the teeth: | les dents (fem.) |
| the lips: | les lèvres (fem.) |
| the hair: | les cheveux (masc.) |

| LE CORPS: THE BODY | |
|---|---|
| the head: | la tête |
| the neck: | le cou |
| the throat: | la gorge |
| the back: | le dos |
| the foot: | le pied |
| the knee: | le genou |
| the leg: | la jambe |
| the finger: | le doigt |
| the hand: | la main |
| the arm: | le bras |
| the shoulder: | l'épaule (fem.) |

## Pouvez-vous me donner quelque chose? — Can you give me something?

**Pouvez-vous me donner un médicament ?**   = Can you give me some medicine?

*some plasters:* des sparadraps (masc.)
*some tablets:* des comprimés (masc.)
*some aspirin:* de l'aspirine (fem.)

**Ça va mieux.**   = I feel better.

**Ça va bien .**   = I feel well.

# What do you call the cold part of a French house...

...un rhume. This feeling ill vocab might easily come up in one of your speaking or listening tasks. Admittedly, it might not. Much in the same way that Daniel Craig may or may not propose to me this year. There's no way of knowing — so you'd best keep learning this stuff and I'll keep hoping.

# Health and Health Issues

These next two pages are a bit like PSHE in French — you lucky, lucky people. You probably have an <u>opinion</u> on this stuff already. Some of the French vocab and expressions are a bit tricky though.

## Qu'est-ce que tu fais pour rester en bonne santé?

Pour rester en bonne santé ...

### What do you do to stay healthy?

= To stay healthy ...

Je fais beaucoup de sport pour ...

= I play a lot of sport to ...

| | |
|---|---|
| I eat lots of vegetables: | je mange beaucoup de légumes. |
| I rarely eat chocolate: | je mange rarement du chocolat. |
| I drink water often: | je bois souvent de l'eau. |

| | |
|---|---|
| stay fit: | rester en forme. |
| lose weight: | perdre du poids. |

Je ne fais rien parce que ...

| | |
|---|---|
| exercising is boring: | faire de l'exercice, c'est ennuyeux. |
| I don't have time: | je n'ai pas le temps. |
| I'm already perfect: | je suis déjà parfait(e). |

= I do nothing because ...

Je suis au régime. Je ne mange que de l'alimentation saine.

= I'm on a diet. I only eat healthy food.

## L'obésité est devenue un grand problème

Here's how to give your opinion on <u>expanding waistlines</u>...

### Obesity has become a big problem

Il est triste de voir des enfants très gros.

= It's <u>sad</u> to see <u>very</u> fat children.

| | | |
|---|---|---|
| awful: affreux | depressing: déprimant | extremely: extrèmement | really: vraiment |

À mon avis, c'est la faute de la publicité.

In my opinion, it's the fault <u>of advertising</u>.

of society: de la société     of the parents: des parents

## Beaucoup de gens ne mangent pas suffisamment

...and on <u>tiny</u> waistlines. Have a look at what this tennis-playing lady has to say.

### A lot of people don't eat enough

"Il y a beaucoup de pression d'être maigre comme les mannequins. Il y a des filles qui pensent à leur poids tout le temps, mais franchement ce n'est pas sain. Il faut bien manger, et surtout il faut mener une vie active. Comme ça, les gens auraient moins de problèmes de santé."

= There's a lot of pressure to be as thin as models. There are girls who think about their weight all the time, but frankly it's not healthy. You have to eat well, and above all you have to lead an active life. That way people would have fewer health problems.

## Get your 5 a day. No, not 5 doughnuts...

Seriously, there's loads of stuff on this page that could easily come up somewhere in the <u>assessments</u>. Some of the 'opinions' stuff is quite tricky, but you need to be <u>ready for anything</u>.

# Health and Health Issues

Drugs, booze and fags. Enjoy.

## Qu'est-ce que tu penses du tabagisme?

This stuff's relevant for <u>drugs</u> and <u>alcohol</u> — so learn the <u>vocab</u> in the pale boxes too.

## What do you think of smoking?

*Je ne fume pas.* = I don't smoke.

*Alcohol:* L'alcool (masc.)    *drink:* boivent

*Fumer, c'est dégoûtant. Je déteste quand les autres fument, c'est vraiment impoli. Je ne sortirais jamais avec un fumeur / une fumeuse.*

*alcoholic:*    un/une alcoolique

= <u>Smoking</u> is disgusting. I hate it when others <u>smoke</u>, it's really impolite. I'd never go out with <u>a smoker</u>.

*J'aime fumer.* = I like smoking.

*Quand je fume, je me détends. Je sais que ce n'est pas sain, mais je pense que c'est cool.*

= When I smoke, I relax. I know it's unhealthy, but I think it's cool.

*drink:* bois

*Je fume mais je ne deviendrais jamais toxicomane. C'est trop dangereux.*

= I <u>smoke</u> but I <u>would never become a drug addict</u>. It's too dangerous.

*would never drink:* ne boirais jamais
*would never smoke:* ne fumerais jamais

*Heureusement il est interdit de fumer dans les lieux publics.*

= Thankfully it's forbidden to smoke in public places.

## J'ai arrêté de fumer il y a un an — I stopped smoking a year ago

*Pourquoi avez-vous décidé d'arrêter?* = Why did you decide to stop?

*Je commençais à avoir des problèmes de santé.* = <u>I was starting to have health problems.</u>

*I had trouble breathing, especially when doing sport:* J'avais du mal à respirer, surtout en faisant du sport.
*I couldn't afford it. There's too much tax on tobacco:* Ça me coûtait trop cher. Il y a trop de taxe sur le tabac.
*My boyfriend/girlfriend doesn't like it when I smoke/drink:* Mon copain/Ma copine n'aime pas quand je fume/bois.

## La drogue dans le sport — Drugs in sport

Often a big talking-point for the French, this. Especially when the <u>Tour de France</u> is on.

*La drogue est un problème dans le cyclisme.* = Drugs are a problem in <u>cycling</u>.

*athletics:* l'athlétisme (masc.)    *football:* le football    *athletes:* athlètes    *players:* joueurs

*Ce n'est pas juste pour la majorité des cyclistes qui ne trichent pas.*

= It's not fair for the majority of <u>cyclists</u> who don't cheat.

## Performance-enhancing revision guides are OK...

There's loads you might want to say about these <u>exciting</u> topics, but learning the stuff on this page is a <u>good</u> start. <u>Think</u> about what else you might want to say, write it down, and <u>practise</u> it.

# Revision Summary

These questions are here to make sure you <u>know your stuff</u>. Work through them and look up the answers to any tough ones you're struggling with. Keep practising them <u>all</u> again and again. Do I sound like a <u>broken record</u> yet... Hope so. I've always wondered what that might be like.

1) You're making fruit salad for a party. Think of as many different fruits as you can to put in it — and write down at least 5 in French. Make a list (in French) of 5 drinks for the party too.

2) Your hosts are offering you more chocolate cake. Decline politely, thank them for the meal, and say it was delicious. Offer to pass your hostess the milk for her coffee.

3) Write down how you'd say that you like vegetables but don't like sausages. You don't eat meat any more and you're hungry.

4) Décris-moi une journée typique.

5) You're telling your host family all about your home life. Say that you make your bed, do the shopping and lay the table. Tell them that you earn pocket money for helping out at home.

6) How would you tell your name, age and birthday to someone you've just met?

7) Describe three of your friends and say how old they are. Comment on the colour of their eyes and their marital status, and spell their names out loud.

8) Tell your penfriend what relations you have — including how many aunts, cousins etc.

9) Your animal-loving friend has six rabbits, a bird, a guinea pig and two cats. How could she say what these are in French?

10) Imagine that you are a boring, impolite, wise, funny, lively person who has a sense of humour and knows how to make people laugh. How would you say all this in French?

11) Write three sentences about the personalities of two of your favourite celebrities.

12) In your opinion, what three qualities should a good friend have? Finish the following sentence — À mon avis, un bon ami / une bonne amie doit...

13) Isabelle dit: "J'ai un petit ami qui s'appelle François. On s'entend bien. Nous sommes meilleurs amis. On ne se dispute jamais. François est honnête, fidèle et compréhensif, et il est toujours là pour moi. Je pense que je suis tombée amoureuse." (Sickening.) What did she say in English?

14) Write a short paragraph to explain your views on equal opportunity.

15) Do the same as in Q.14 but for unemployment... Sorry.

16) How would you say you have each of these ailments in French?
   a) stomach ache   b) headache   c) a cold   d) flu      e) a broken arm      f) seasickness

17) Est-ce que tu es en bonne santé? Pourquoi? Pourquoi pas?

18) Il y a un an tu fumais, mais maintenant tu ne fumes plus. Pourquoi?

# Sports and Hobbies

Examiners don't believe in couch potatoes — there's always loads in the exams about <u>sports</u> and <u>hobbies</u>.

## Est-ce que tu fais du sport? — Do you do any sport?

<u>Sports</u> and <u>hobbies</u> are a popular choice for speaking and writing assessments. Even if you're no demon on the pitch, you <u>need</u> to be good at talking about all things sport 'en français'.

**VERBS FOR SPORTS**

| | |
|---|---|
| *to go fishing:* | aller à la pêche |
| *to run:* | courir |
| *to cycle:* | faire du cyclisme |
| *to swim:* | nager |
| *to ski:* | faire du ski |
| *to play:* | jouer |
| *to walk, hike:* | faire une randonnée |
| *to ice skate:* | patiner |

**PLACES YOU CAN DO SPORTS**

| | |
|---|---|
| *sports centre:* | le centre sportif |
| *leisure centre:* | le centre de loisirs |
| *swimming pool:* | la piscine |
| *sports field:* | le terrain de sport |
| *gymnasium:* | le gymnase |
| *park:* | le parc |
| *ice rink:* | la patinoire |
| *mountains:* | les montagnes (fem.) |

**NAMES OF SPORTS**

| | |
|---|---|
| *basketball:* | le basket |
| *football:* | le foot(ball) |
| *tennis:* | le tennis |
| *table tennis:* | le ping pong |
| *horse riding:* | l'équitation (fem.) |
| *skateboarding:* | le skate |
| *swimming:* | la natation |
| *ice skating:* | le patinage |
| *snowboarding:* | le surf des neiges |
| *water sports:* | les sports nautiques |
| *winter sports:* | les sports d'hiver |

## Tu aimes regarder le sport? — Do you like watching sport?

*Je préfère participer parce que* ...

= I prefer to participate because...

| | |
|---|---|
| *I love training:* | j'adore m'entraîner. |
| *I like working in a team:* | j'aime travailler en équipe. |
| *I love the stadium atmosphere:* | j'adore l'ambiance du stade. |

*Je préfère regarder le jeu parce que* ...

= I prefer to watch the game because...

| | |
|---|---|
| *I'm injured and I can't play any more:* | je me suis blessé(e) et je ne peux plus jouer. |
| *it's expensive to play:* | ça coûte cher de jouer. |

## Est-ce que tu as un passe-temps? — Do you have a hobby?

There are <u>other things</u> to do apart from sports — that's where these <u>tasty selections</u> come into play.

**MUSICAL INSTRUMENTS**

| | |
|---|---|
| *flute:* | la flûte |
| *drum kit:* | la batterie |
| *clarinet:* | la clarinette |
| *guitar:* | la guitare |
| *trumpet:* | la trompette |
| *piano:* | le piano |
| *violin:* | le violon |
| *cello:* | le violoncelle |

**GENERAL BUT VITAL**

| | |
|---|---|
| *hobby:* | le passe-temps |
| *interest:* | l'intérêt (masc.) |
| *club:* | le club (de...) |
| *member:* | le membre |

**VERBS FOR INDOOR ACTIVITIES**

| | |
|---|---|
| *to dance:* | danser |
| *to sing:* | chanter |
| *to collect:* | collectionner |
| *to read:* | lire |

To see how to use verbs with different people, see pages 97-98.

**MUSICAL WORDS**

| | |
|---|---|
| *band, group:* | le groupe |
| *CD:* | le CD, le disque compact |
| *instrument:* | l'instrument (masc.) |
| *concert:* | le concert |

**OTHER IMPORTANT WORDS**

| | |
|---|---|
| *chess:* | les échecs (masc.) |
| *film:* | le film |
| *performance:* | le spectacle |
| *play (in a theatre):* | la pièce de théâtre |
| *reading (activity):* | la lecture |

If music's what you're into, see page 30.

## Get on your hobby-horse...

Blummin' great. Not only do you have to do sport in PE, you have to talk about it in French. Even if you hate sport and music, you'll have to <u>pretend</u> you do something. And you'll need to know the others when you hear them. Luckily most of them sound more or less like the English. Phew.

# Sports and Hobbies

What you do in your <u>free time</u> comes up somewhere in the assessments <u>every year</u>. You have to be able to write about what <u>you</u> get up to, and give <u>opinions</u> of other hobbies. It's <u>must-learn</u> stuff. Yeah it is.

## Qu'est-ce que tu fais pendant ton temps libre?
## — What do you do in your free time?

<u>Sport</u> and <u>music</u> are really big topics in the assessments.

*Je joue* au football *le week-end* .  = I play <u>football</u> <u>at weekends</u>.

*badminton:* au badminton
*tennis:* au tennis

*every day:* chaque jour
*every week:* chaque semaine
*twice a month:* deux fois par mois

For more about times, see pages 2–3.

*Je joue* du piano .  = I play <u>the piano</u>.

See previous page for more musical instruments.

*Je suis membre d'un* club de tennis .  = I'm a member of a <u>tennis club</u>.

*chess club:* club d'échecs   *squash club:* club de squash

<u>Handy hint</u>: To talk about any sports club, just put '<u>club de</u>' and the name of the sport.

If you're talking about games, use '<u>jouer à</u>', but with instruments, it's '<u>jouer de</u>'.
| à + le | = au | de + le | = du |
| à + la | = à la | de + la | = de la |
| à + l' | = à l' | de + l' | = de l' |
| à + les | = aux | de + les | = des |

Je joue au badminton.   Je joue de la clarinette.

## Est-ce que tu aimes le football? — Do you like football?

Here's how to say what you <u>think</u> of different hobbies — <u>learn</u> these phrases, even if you don't really <u>care</u>.

*Je trouve* le football *fantastique* .

*the cinema:* le cinéma
*hiking:* les randonnées

*exciting:* passionnant(e)(s)
*interesting:* intéressant(e)(s)

= I think <u>football</u> is <u>fantastic.</u>

More options on page 26.

*Oui, j'adore* le football .  = Yes, I love <u>football</u>.

*I agree:* Je suis d'accord.
*I don't agree:* Je ne suis pas d'accord.

For <u>agreeing</u> and <u>disagreeing</u> you can use these phrases.

For more about giving opinions, see pages 7-8.

*Pourquoi est-ce que tu penses cela?*  = Why do you think that?

*Je n'aime pas* courir *, parce que c'est* difficile .  = I don't like <u>running</u>, because it's <u>difficult</u>.

*music:* la musique    *boring:* ennuyeux

Always use the <u>masculine</u> form after "<u>c'est</u>".

# Free time, expensive hobbies...

There's important stuff on this page — you <u>need</u> to be able to say <u>what</u> you do in your <u>free time</u> and <u>why</u>. Make sure you remember when it's 'jouer <u>à</u>' and when it's 'jouer <u>de</u>'. While you're at it, learn all this <u>opinion</u> stuff for saying what you think about sports and hobbies. Fu-un...

# Television

Ah, the <u>telly</u>. You might have to listen to people talk about television in the exam, or you may need to talk about it in the speaking assessment. You never know, so make sure this is part of your <u>repertoire</u>.

## Qu'est-ce que tu aimes regarder à la télé?

Basically, this stuff's all really handy.

### — What do you like to watch on TV?

Quelles émissions est-ce que tu aimes regarder ?

*Which books:* Quels livres

*to read:* lire

= <u>Which TV programmes</u> do you like <u>to watch</u>?

*to listen to:* écouter          *to read:* lire

Put what you like to watch, listen to or read here.

J'aime regarder Westenders .

= I like <u>to watch</u> <u>Westenders</u>.

| *a documentary:* | un documentaire | *documentaries:* | des documentaires |
| *a soap:* | un feuilleton | *soaps:* | des feuilletons |
| *a film:* | un film | *films:* | des films |
| *a play:* | une pièce de théâtre | *plays:* | des pièces de théâtre |
| *a show:* | un spectacle | *shows:* | des spectacles |
| *an advertisement:* | une publicité | *advertisements:* | des publicités |
| | | *the news:* | les actualités (fem.) |

For more about giving opinions, see pages 7–8.

This one's always plural, like in English.

Je voudrais regarder ...

= I would like to watch ...

L'émission commence à vingt heures et finit à vingt et une heures trente .

For more info. about telling the time, see page 2.

= The programme starts at <u>8pm</u> and finishes at <u>9:30pm</u>.

## Qu'est-ce que tu as fait récemment?

This bit of <u>past tense</u> looks really impressive — and it's always good for a little bit o' <u>French banter</u>...

### — What have you done recently?

J'ai vu Amélie récemment .

= I <u>saw</u> <u>Amélie</u> <u>recently</u>.

For more about times and dates, see pages 2–3.

*heard:* écouté
*read:* lu

*the radio:* la radio
*the new song by Take This:*
la nouvelle chanson de Take This

| *last week:* | la semaine dernière |
| *two weeks ago:* | il y a deux semaines |
| *a month ago:* | il y a un mois |

## A soap set in a pâtisserie — Millefeuilleton...

The French often call TV '<u>le petit écran</u>' (= 'the small screen'), even if it's one of those 48" monster screens. So it's no surprise that sometimes they call the cinema '<u>le grand écran</u>'. Now try to say exactly what sort of programmes you like to watch, and explain <u>why</u> you like them.

# Talking About the Plot

Books, films, telly programmes — you may have to discuss things you've read, seen or heard recently.
It sounds quite daunting, even in English, but it's really simple if you learn these easy phrases...

## J'ai lu, J'ai vu, J'ai entendu... — I read, I saw, I heard...

Je viens **de lire** **un livre** **impressionnant** .    = I've just read an impressive book.

| | |
|---|---|
| *listened to:* | d'écouter |
| *watched:* | de regarder |
| *seen:* | de voir |

| | |
|---|---|
| *interesting:* | intéressant(e) |
| *surprising:* | surprenant(e) |
| *funny:* | drôle |

Yes, Emperor.

| | |
|---|---|
| *a play:* | une pièce de théâtre |
| *a show:* | un spectacle |
| *a film:* | un film |
| *a cartoon:* | une bande dessinée |

Le titre était 'Le Mariage de mon meilleur ennemi'.

= It was called 'My Best Enemy's Wedding'.

## Parle-moi de ce qui s'est passé...
## — Tell me about what happened...

Il s'agit d' **un homme** qui **portait** des lunettes et un manteau invisible.

= It's about a man who wore glasses and an invisible coat.

| | | | | | | |
|---|---|---|---|---|---|---|
| *woman:* | une femme | *boy:* | un garçon | *had:* | avait | *had lots of money:* avait beaucoup d'argent |
| *girl:* | une fille | *actor:* | un acteur | *wanted:* | voulait | *loved to travel:* adorait voyager |
| *actress:* | une actrice | *star:* | une vedette | *stole:* | volait | *was very handsome but a bit stupid:* |
| *singer:* | un chanteur / une chanteuse | | | | | était très beau mais un peu stupide. |

You can make up anything you like here. (Maybe don't mention robots if you're talking about a classical novel...) Just make sure you use the imperfect tense. For more info, see pages 103-104.

## Qu'est-ce que tu en pensais? — What did you think of it?

Opinions go down really well at GCSE French — so you need to learn this stuff... and get an opinion.

Je l'ai trouvé(e) **génial(e)** .    = I thought it was great.

For more about giving opinions, see pages 7-8.

This is quite tricky — remember to add an 'e' to the past participle and the adjective (if necessary) if the thing you are referring to is feminine, e.g. une émission, une publicité, une pièce de théâtre.

| | |
|---|---|
| *informative:* | instructif / instructive |
| *entertaining:* | amusant(e) |
| *interesting:* | intéressant(e) |
| *boring:* | ennuyeux / ennuyeuse |
| *fantastic:* | fantastique |

## Lu, vu and entendu... that's a lot of ooos...

I really should be writing song lyrics for Kylie or Take That, but I'm far too busy writing a French book. Once again, it's all about me. They'll be making a film of my life soon, called... um...

# Music

Treasons, strategems and spoils. That's what Shakespeare said you're fit for if you don't like music. Learn how to say what music you're into. If you are fit for those things, there's no harm in making it up.

## Qu'est-ce que tu aimes comme musique?

## — What kind of music do you like?

All fairly basic stuff this. You need to find interesting ways of talking about your musical tastes though.

**Mon genre musical préféré, c'est la musique jazz.**
☆ Extra marks for style

= My favourite type of music is jazz.

pop    rock    danse    classique    rap

It's really good if you can explain exactly what you like.
(And remember, it doesn't have to be true.)

**J'aime toutes les chansons qu'on entend en boîte.**

= I like all the songs you hear in clubs.

**Je trouve les symphonies de Beethoven incroyables.**

= I find Beethoven's symphonies incredible.

*songs by Take This:* les chansons de Take This
*musicals:* les comédies musicales
*pieces by Schumann:* les pièces de Schumann

*very good:* très bons / bonnes
*really great:* vraiment chouettes
*interesting:* intéressants / intéressantes

It's good to talk about any foreign music you've heard, too — you can bet your French teacher loves Europop.

## Où est-ce que tu aimes écouter de la musique?

## — Where do you like listening to music?

This bit's how to say where and how you listen to music.

**J'écoute de la musique en voiture sur mon lecteur mp3.**

= I listen to music in the car on my mp3 player.

*on the bus:* en autobus
*at home:* à la maison
*while I'm walking:* en marchant

*on the radio:* à la radio
*on my mobile phone:* sur mon téléphone portable
*on my hi-fi system:* sur ma chaîne hi-fi

You can also say 'baladeur mp3' for 'mp3 player'.

## To play an instrument is 'jouer d'un instrument'

**Je joue du piano. Je m'entraîne tous les jours.**

= I play the piano. I practise every day.

*the guitar:* de la guitare
*the keyboard:* du clavier
*the drums:* de la batterie

*once a week:* une fois par semaine
*at weekends:* le week-end

See page 26 for more musical instruments.

**Je fais partie d'un groupe de rock.**

= I play in a rock band.

## Never say never...

If music comes up in one of the assessments, and you haven't got much to say, you could try: 'J'aimerais jouer du piano' (= 'I'd like to...'), and then give a reason. Gotta be better than nothing.

# Famous People

Now this choice of topic seems a tad weird to me, but apparently you are supposed to be <u>fascinated</u> by celebs.  So much so that you want to <u>talk</u> about them in French with your <u>exchange partners</u>...

## Quelles célébrités aimes-tu? — Which celebrities do you like?

This is the same <u>straightforward</u> stuff that you use to talk about you and your family.

**WHO** ▶ *Je trouve Beyoncé Knowles fantastique.*  = I think Beyoncé Knowles is fantastic.

**WHAT** ▶ *C'est une chanteuse américaine célèbre.*  = She is a famous American singer.

**WHY** ▶ *Beyoncé est très mignonne et je pense qu'elle chante comme un ange, aussi.*  = Beyoncé is very cute and I think that she sings like an angel, as well.

## La vie des célébrités... — Celebrity life...

You may be asked to put yourself in someone else's French-speaking shoes — when you're <u>imagining</u> you're a <u>celebrity</u>, these phrases may come in useful...

My dad: Mon père
Elvis: Elvis

he was always there for me: il était toujours là pour moi.
his clothes were so cool: ses vêtements étaient si cools.

*... m'a beaucoup influencé(e) parce que ...*  = ... has influenced me a lot because ...

*Ma plus grande réussite est ...*  = My greatest achievement is ...

the support I've been able to give to international organisations: le soutien que j'ai pu donner aux organisations internationales.
my platinum disc: mon disque de platine.

*J'ai l'ambition de ...*  = My ambition is to ...

*Je voudrais ...*  = I would like to ...

travel: voyager.      help out: donner de l'aide.      win an Oscar: gagner un Oscar.

## Vous aimez être célèbre? — Do you like being famous?

If they ask you to write an <u>interview</u> with a celeb, here are some useful phrases:

*Oui, j'aime la vie de vedette parce que ...*
= Yes, I love life as a celebrity because ...

I am successful: j'ai du succès.
I have lots of money: j'ai beaucoup d'argent.
I am able to travel: je peux voyager.

*Non, je déteste la vie de vedette car ...*
= No, I hate life as a celebrity because ...

I don't have a normal life: je n'ai pas une vie normale.
people follow me everywhere: les gens me suivent partout.

> Pronounced like the English word 'fan'.

*Est-ce que vous* avez *beaucoup* de fans *?*  = Do you <u>have</u> lots <u>of fans</u>?

like having: aimez avoir

of hit records: de tubes      of money: d'argent

## I'm your number one fan...

This page gives <u>you</u> the freedom to give <u>your opinion</u> on <u>celebrities</u> and their <u>influence in society</u> — all in a <u>foreign language</u>.  It's tricky stuff, but master this and your French will be fabulous.

# New Technology

Ah, computers. They've even found their way into GCSE French.

## Je suis toujours sur l'ordinateur — I'm always on the computer

It's good to be able to give details about what you use computers for.

J'ai créé un site internet pour mon club d'échecs. = I have created a website for my chess club.

*a home page:* une page d'accueil

*my band:* mon groupe
*my orchestra:* mon orchestre

Here's some techy vocab that might come in handy in the assessments.

| | | | |
|---|---|---|---|
| *camera:* | un appareil photo | *touch screen:* | un écran tactile |
| *blogger:* | un bloggeur / une bloggeuse | *link:* | un lien |
| *button:* | un bouton | *monitor:* | un moniteur |
| *camcorder:* | un caméscope | *battery:* | une pile |
| *games console:* | une console de jeux | *CD drive:* | un lecteur CD |
| *internet café:* | un cybercafé | *network:* | un réseau |

And here are some useful expressions with verbs:

Je vais télécharger mes photos sur mon ordinateur.
Avant de les mettre en ligne, je vais les imprimer.

= I am going to download my photos onto my computer. Before putting them online, I am going to print them.

## Je vais bloguer ça — I'll put it on my blog

If you have a particularly interesting life, you might want to share your experiences on your blog. Also, they might ask you to imagine you're writing a blog for your written assessment.

Manchester        25/02/2009        19h20

Je viens de passer une journée très agréable.  Nous sommes allés en famille rendre visite à des amis au pays de Galles.

On a très bien mangé — du rôti d'agneau — et l'après-midi on s'est promené dans le petit village près de chez eux.

Il y avait des vues superbes des montagnes galloises. Je pense que j'aimerais vivre là-bas à l'avenir.

Regardez les photos en cliquant sur cette icône:

Je vous invite à laisser vos commentaires!

I've just had a very nice day.
We went with the family to visit some friends in Wales.

We ate very well — roast lamb — and in the afternoon we went for a walk in the little village near their house.

There were wonderful views of the Welsh mountains.  I think I'd like to live there in the future.

Look at the photos by clicking on this icon:

I invite you to leave your comments!

The blogger describes what he/she has done today in the perfect tense. See pages 101-102.

## Je blogue, tu blogues, il blogue...

Everyone's blogging nowadays. Even if you think it's the scourge of the digital age, and a medium for unadulterated drivel, for the sake of your French GCSE, get the contents of this page learnt.

# Email and Texting

We British are not the only ones to bask in the joy of <u>email</u> and <u>texting</u>, you know. The French do it too.

## Je voudrais envoyer un courrier électronique
## — I would like to send an email

Phew, that's long-winded...
and I thought <u>sending an email</u> was supposed to be <u>quick</u> and <u>easy</u>...

Est-ce que je peux envoyer un email à mon ami(e) d'ici?

= Can I send <u>an email</u> to my friend from here?

There are a few ways to say 'email'.
un courrier électronique
un courriel
un email

a fax: un fax

...and here are some <u>useful words</u> for when you're <u>emailing</u>...

| | | |
|---|---|---|
| *from:* de  *to:* à / pour | *(cc) copy to:* copier à | *subject:* sujet / objet |
| *send:* envoyer | *reply (to all):* répondre (à tous) | *forward:* transférer |

Je vérifie ma boîte email régulièrement.

= I check <u>my inbox</u> regularly.

If you're asked to write an email to someone you know, the most important thing is to use <u>informal</u> language:

1) You must use '<u>tu</u>' (and 's'il <u>te</u> plaît'). <u>DON'T</u> switch between 'tu' and 'vous'.
2) Start a text with '<u>Salut</u>' or '<u>Bonjour</u>'. End it with '<u>À plus tard</u>', '<u>À tout à l'heure</u>' or '<u>À bientôt</u>'.
3) Imagine you're <u>actually</u> writing to someone you <u>know</u>. Think of things you would <u>actually</u> say.

## Envoyer un texto — To send a text message

Who knows, you might be asked to read a <u>text message</u> in the reading exam. Here's an example of the kind of thing you should expect to see:

Hi Pierre. Do you want to come to the cinema tonight? Jean and I will be there around 7pm. We don't know yet which film we're going to watch. See you later, Steve

15:04

Salut Pierre. Tu veux venir au cinéma ce soir? Jean et moi y serons vers 19h00. On ne sait pas encore quel film on va regarder. À plus tard, Steve

For stuff about actually speaking on the phone, see page 80.

## Je préfère parler au téléphone — I prefer to talk on the phone

If you don't think much of emails and texting, <u>say so</u>.

Je préfère ne pas passer trop de temps sur l'ordinateur — ce n'est pas très sain.

= I prefer not to spend too much time on the computer — it's not very healthy.

Les courriels ne sont pas très personnels. Je préfère écrire une lettre.

= Emails aren't very personal. I prefer to write a letter.

Les enfants devraient faire du sport au lieu d'être devant un moniteur tout le temps.

= Children should be playing sport instead of being in front of a monitor all the time.

## Join my epost campaign...

'Mail' is American, '<u>post</u>' is British, so we should say '<u>epost</u>'. "<u>You've got epost</u>" — yes, that sounds much better. Oh, one thing I should say is that if you have to epost <u>someone you don't know</u> in one of the assessments, you'll have to use much more formal language ('<u>vous</u>', etc.).

# Shopping

This section gives you all the <u>bog-standard stuff</u> you need to know when you're out and about <u>shopping</u>.

## Où est...? — Where is...?

A <u>dead handy</u> question, this one.

Où est  la boulangerie , s'il vous plaît?

*the till point:*  la caisse

= Where is <u>the baker's</u>, please?

### D'autres magasins — Other shops

| | | | |
|---|---|---|---|
| *grocer's:* | l'épicerie (fem.) | *bookshop:* | la librairie |
| *hypermarket:* | l'hypermarché (masc.) | *cake shop:* | la pâtisserie |
| *department store:* | le grand magasin | *sweet shop:* | la confiserie |
| *newsagent:* | le kiosque à journaux | *fishmonger's:* | la poissonnerie |
| *perfume shop:* | la parfumerie | *delicatessen:* | la charcuterie |
| *jeweller's:* | la bijouterie | *butcher's:* | la boucherie |

## À quelle heure...? — What time...?

You need these useful sentences to talk about when shops are <u>open</u> or <u>closed</u>.

À quelle heure est-ce que le magasin  ouvre ?

= What time does the shop <u>open</u>?

*close:* ferme

*For times, see page 2.*

Le supermarché ouvre à  neuf heures .

= The supermarket opens at <u>9 o'clock</u>.

Tous les magasins ferment à  six heures .

= All the shops shut at <u>six o'clock</u>.

## Allons faire les magasins! — Let's go shopping!

Whether you prefer to <u>shop online</u> or fight it out in the shops for a <u>bargain</u>, this <u>vocab</u>'ll be <u>useful</u>...

Il y a  des soldes   au centre commercial .

= There are <u>sales</u> <u>at the shopping centre</u>.

*discounts:* des réductions (fem.)    *on the internet:* sur internet

*in town:* en ville

Je préfère faire du shopping  sur internet .

= I prefer to shop <u>on the internet</u>.

*easier:* plus facile    *cheaper:* moins cher
*more difficult:* plus difficile    *less fun:* moins drôle

Faire des achats sur internet, c'est  plus rapide  que dans les magasins .

= Buying things on the internet is <u>faster</u> than in the shops.

*try on:* essayer

Je préfère  voir  les choses avant de les acheter.

= I prefer to <u>see</u> things before buying them.

## Hypermarché — an excited market...

You might have to talk about <u>where things are</u> and <u>when they open</u> in your speaking assessment — you'd be daft not to learn it. If this stuff doesn't come up, then I'm a wombat. Get these sentences learnt, along with the names of <u>as many</u> shops as you can possibly squeeze up there...

# Shopping

So you reckon you'll get through your exam <u>without</u> ever having to mention (or recognise someone else mentioning) <u>buying stuff</u> — better wake yourself up, then. It's all here because you need it. Trust me.

## Est-ce que je peux vous aider? — Can I help you?

Say what you'd like using '<u>Je voudrais...</u>'

*1kg:* un kilo     *a litre:* un litre     *a packet:* un paquet

*Je voudrais* cinq cents grammes *de sucre, s'il vous plaît.*   = I'd like <u>500g</u> of sugar, please.

The <u>shop assistant</u> might say:

*Autre chose?*   = Anything else?

*C'est tout?*   = Is that everything?

<u>You</u> could reply:

*Non, merci.*   = No, thank you.

*Non, je voudrais aussi* une pomme de terre *, s'il vous plaît.*

**See page 1 for more on numbers.**

*two apples:*   deux pommes (fem.)
*three pears:*   trois poires (fem.)

= No, I'd like <u>a potato</u> as well, please.

## Est-ce que vous avez...? — Do you have...?

It's useful to know this vocab in case it pops up in your listening or speaking assessments...

*Excusez-moi, avez-vous* du pain ?   = Excuse me, do you have any <u>bread</u>?

*milk:* du lait     *cheese:* du fromage     *eggs:* des œufs (masc.) *bananas:* des bananes (fem.)

*Oui,* le *voilà.*   = Yes, there <u>it</u> is.   *Non, nous n'en avons pas.*   = No, we don't have any.

*it:* le / la

*Je voudrais* un peu de *fromage.*   = I'd like <u>a little bit of</u> cheese.

*lots of:* beaucoup de     *a slice of:* une tranche de           *several:* plusieurs

**See page 13 for more on food.**   *Je voudrais* quelques *pommes.*   = I'd like <u>some</u> apples.

## Ça fait combien? — How much is that?

French money's easy. There are <u>100 cents</u> in a <u>euro</u>, like there are 100 pence in a pound.

This is what you'd <u>see</u> on a French <u>price tag</u>:   € 5,50   *Ça fait* cinq euros cinquante .

This is how you <u>say</u> the price.   = That'll be <u>5 euros 50 cents</u>.

*by credit card:* par carte (de crédit)

*Est-ce que je peux payer* en argent ?   = Can I pay <u>with cash</u>?

# Splash out, buy a boat...

<u>Money</u> and <u>shop talk</u> are pretty important, especially for those nasty (and often embarrassing) speaking assessment thingies. Don't worry. Simply revise. And be happy. (Oh, and just in case it comes up in the listening exam — the French don't pronounce the 'f' in '<u>des œufs</u>'.)

# Shopping

Shopping for a bunch of bananas is all well and good, but shopping for clothes could pop up in your exams — when someone in the listening exam is banging on about the fab pair of socks they just purchased online.

## Je fais des économies... — I'm saving up...

Knowing this useful vocab about pocket money will make your shop talk more interesting...

Je reçois dix euros d'argent de poche par mois.

£5: cinq livres

week: semaine

= I get ten euros pocket money a month.

I'd like to buy: Je voudrais acheter

J'achète des vêtements de sport avec mon argent de poche.

make-up: du maquillage
computer games: des jeux électroniques (masc.)

= I buy sports clothes with my pocket money.

## Les vêtements — Clothing

Most of these clothes are everyday items — so you need to know them.

J'aime cette paire de chaussures. = I like this pair of shoes.

Je n'aime pas ce manteau. = I don't like this coat.

Le chapeau

Le bikini

Le tee-shirt

La jupe

| | | | |
|---|---|---|---|
| shirt: | la chemise | sock: | la chaussette |
| blouse: | le chemisier | shoe: | la chaussure |
| trousers: | le pantalon | trainer: | le basket |
| jeans: | le jean | sandal: | la sandale |
| shorts: | le short | hat: | le chapeau |
| dress: | la robe | scarf: | le foulard |
| jacket: | la veste | tie: | la cravate |
| skirt: | la jupe | glove: | le gant |
| jumper: | le pull | watch: | la montre |

| | |
|---|---|
| handbag: | le sac à main |
| purse: | le porte-monnaie |
| wallet: | le portefeuille |
| pyjamas: | le pyjama |
| raincoat: | l'imperméable (masc.) |
| hoody: | le pull à capuche |
| casual jacket: | le blouson |
| swimming costume: | le maillot de bain |

## They might ask what colour you want — quelle couleur...?

Colours crop up all over the place. Remember, the colour goes after the noun, and has to agree with it.

Je voudrais un pantalon bleu.

= I'd like a pair of blue trousers.

Je voudrais une jupe verte.

= I'd like a green skirt.

**COLOURS: les couleurs (fem.)**

| | | | |
|---|---|---|---|
| black: | noir(e) | brown: | brun(e) |
| white: | blanc(he) | orange: | orange |
| red: | rouge | pink: | rose |
| yellow: | jaune | purple: | violet(te) |
| green: | vert(e) | light blue: | bleu clair |
| blue: | bleu(e) | dark blue: | bleu foncé |

## So, how do you say "fluorescent lime PVC flares" again...

It's common sense — just don't forget your clothes. Some of them are dead easy — le pyjama, le pull, le short etc. Others need a bit more effort. It'll be worth it, though. Honestly.

# Shopping

Here's another <u>pretty important</u> page of lovely French shopping stuff — and it's not too tricky. <u>Result</u>...

## Je voudrais... — I would like...

Make sure you're really comfortable with '<u>Je voudrais</u>' — you'll be needing it <u>all the time</u>.

Je voudrais un pantalon s'il vous plaît. Je prends la taille quarante-quatre.

= I'd like <u>a pair of trousers</u> please. I'm size <u>44</u>.

**Important Bit:**
Another good way to say 'I would like' is 'J'aimerais bien...'

For clothing, see page 36.

**CONTINENTAL SIZES**

| | size: la taille |
| --- | --- |
| dress size 8 / 10 / 12 / 14 / 16: | 36 / 38 / 40 / 42 / 44 |
| shoe size 5 / 6 / 7 / 8 / 9 / 10: | 38 / 39 / 41 / 42 / 43 / 44 |

a receipt:  un reçu
an exchange:  un échange

Je voudrais un remboursement , s'il vous plaît.

= I'd like <u>a refund</u>, please.

## Je cherche... — I'm looking for...

Details are good — try to memorise these easy phrases to add a bit of <u>ooomph</u> to your <u>answers</u>.

brown: brun(e)      blue: bleu(e)

Je cherche un pull en laine rose .

= I'm looking for a <u>pink</u> <u>woollen</u> <u>jumper</u>.

a jacket: une veste      leather: en cuir      denim: en denim      cotton: en coton      silk: en soie

Est-ce que vous en avez un ?

= Do you have <u>one</u>?

The 'en' means 'of them'. See page 94.

Use '*une*' if the item requested is feminine or '*d'autres*' if you want to say 'other ones'.

It's good to talk about the <u>latest trends</u> too...

This summer: Cet été     This season: Cette saison

Cet automne tout le monde porte un pull à capuche .

= <u>This autumn</u> everyone is wearing <u>a hoody</u>.

## Est-ce que vous le prenez? — Will you be taking that?

To buy or not to buy — that is the question. <u>Learn</u> these useful phrases too:

it: le / la    Je le prends.

= I'll take <u>it</u>.

Je ne le prends pas. Je n'aime pas la couleur .

It's too small:      C'est trop petit.
It's a bit old-fashioned:  C'est un peu démodé.

= I'll leave it. <u>I don't like the colour</u>.

## Will you be taking that? — No, I was going to pay...

There's loads of <u>shopping language</u> here that'll come in really handy. <u>Learn</u> as much of this as you can. And <u>remember</u> — as long as you <u>know your stuff</u>, you'll do fine in your GCSE. <u>Simple</u>.

# Inviting People Out

A brief guide to having fun in French: 1) get someone to <u>agree</u> to do some fun stuff  2) come to a mutual <u>agreement</u> about what you're going to do  3) <u>organise a party</u> to celebrate all the fun...

## Sortons — Let's go out

These are all really <u>useful</u> phrases for the assessments, so get them <u>learnt</u>.

Using the 'nous' form here means 'let's' — see page 108.

**Allons** *à la piscine* .    = Let's go <u>to the swimming pool</u>.

*to the theatre:* au théâtre      *to the park:* au parc

*Oui, je veux bien* .   = <u>Yes, I'd love to</u>.     *Non, merci* .   = <u>No, thank you</u>.

*Good idea!:*   Bonne idée!
*Great!:*   Super!

*I'm sorry, I can't:*         Je suis désolé(e), je ne peux pas.
*I don't have enough money:*    Je n'ai pas assez d'argent.

## Je préférerais nager — I'd prefer to go swimming

To suggest an alternative activity or to talk about your dream hobby, use the <u>conditional</u>.

*Si j'étais riche,* *je ferais du ski* *tous les week-ends.*

For more on the conditional, see page 107 .

*I'd buy clothes:*   j'achèterais des vêtements
*I'd go clubbing:*   j'irais en boîte (de nuit)

= If I was rich, <u>I would go skiing</u> every weekend.

If you learn this and use it in the right way you'll score loads more marks — worth it, even though it's a bit tricky.

## J'organise une surprise-partie...

Party planning. In French. Could be <u>useful</u>...

### — I'm organising a surprise party...

*On va* *écouter de la musique* *et manger* *une pizza* .

= We're going <u>to listen to music</u> and eat a <u>pizza</u>.

*to watch movies:*   regarder des films
*to dance:*   danser

*sweets:*   des bonbons
*popcorn:*   du pop-corn

For more foods, see page 13.

*Veux-tu venir?*    = Do you want to come?

*Il nous faudra* *du chocolat* .    = We'll need <u>some chocolate</u>.

*some films:* des films    *some CDs:* des CD

*Est-ce que tu peux amener* *du pop-corn* ?    = Can you bring <u>some popcorn</u>?

## Désolé, je me lave les cheveux...

Great. Now you can invite Thierry Henry or Juliette Binoche to your <u>soirée</u> — or at least understand when they say they're washing their hair. If you <u>can't</u>, then <u>go back</u> over it until you can.

# Going Out

This stuff about <u>buying tickets</u>, <u>opening times</u> and <u>where things are</u> is essential — you need to be able to <u>talk</u> about it for your speaking assessments, or <u>understand</u> it in the listening exam.

## ...près d'ici? — ...near here?

Est-ce qu'il y a un théâtre près d'ici?　　= Is there <u>a theatre</u> near here?

*a sports field:*　un terrain de sport
*a bowling alley:*　un bowling
*a cinema:*　un cinéma

*play tennis:* jouer au tennis　　*go for walks:* se promener

Peut-on nager près d'ici?　　= Can we <u>swim</u> near here?

## Qu'est-ce qu'il y a à l'affiche? — What's on?

À quelle heure commence le spectacle ?　　= When does <u>the performance start</u>?

*finish:* finit　　*the film:* le film　　*the match:* le match

Il commence à huit heures et finit à dix heures .

= <u>It</u> starts at <u>8.00</u> and finishes at <u>10.00</u>.

## Ask how much it costs — 'combien ça coûte?'

Combien coûte l'entrée à la piscine ?　　= How much does it cost to go <u>swimming</u>?

*bowling:*　au bowling
*to the cinema:*　au cinéma

Ça coûte deux euros l'heure.　　= It costs <u>2 euros</u> per hour.

Combien coûte un billet ?　　= How much does <u>one ticket</u> cost?

*How much do two tickets cost?:*
Combien coûtent deux billets ?

Plural endings.

Un billet coûte cinq euros.　　= One ticket costs 5 euros.

*two tickets:* deux billets

Je voudrais un billet , s'il vous plaît.　　= I'd like <u>one ticket</u>, please.

## Quand est-ce que la piscine est ouverte?
## — When is the swimming pool open?

À quelle heure est-ce que la piscine est ouverte ?　　= What time is <u>the swimming pool open</u>?

*the sports centre:* le centre sportif　　*closed:* fermé(e)

Elle ouvre à neuf heures et demie et ferme à cinq heures .

For other places, see page 58.

'Il' for a masculine place.　　= <u>It</u> opens at <u>half past nine</u> and closes at <u>five o'clock</u>.

## French makes my head spin — I feel "d'ici"...

This stuff could come up in your <u>speaking assessment</u> or <u>listening exam</u> — you need to be able to <u>understand</u> it all... So don't just sit there, let's get to it — <u>get into gear</u> and get down to it.

# Going Out

Finally... something fun to stick on the French revision schedule — <u>films</u> and <u>major sporting events</u>.

## Je suis allé(e) au cinéma — I went to the cinema

There's a chance you'll have to mention what you did last weekend. Make sure you have a plausible answer.

*my parents:* mes parents    *some friends:* des ami(e)s    *in the evening:* le soir    *later:* plus tard

**J'ai regardé un film** avec *un ami* et *après* nous avons mangé au restaurant.

= <u>I watched a film</u> with <u>a friend</u> and <u>afterwards</u> we ate in a restaurant.

*I went shopping:* J'ai fait du shopping    *I went clubbing:* Je suis allé(e) en boîte (de nuit)

For more on talking about the past, see pages 101-102.

## Est-ce que le film était bon? — Was the film good?

You've got to be able to say whether <u>you thought</u> the film was any good — it's dead easy.

**Qu'est-ce que tu penses** *du film* ?

= What do you think <u>of the film</u>?

*of the performance:* du spectacle
*of the play:* de la pièce (de théâtre)
*of the concert:* du concert

To find out more about giving opinions, see pages 7-8.

**Est-ce que c'était un film** *d'horreur* ?

= Was it a <u>horror</u> film?

*romantic:* d'amour
*adventure:* d'aventures
*sci-fi:* de science-fiction
*comedy:* comique
*war:* de guerre
*detective:* policier

**Il** *était* *assez bon* .

= <u>It</u> was <u>quite good</u>.

If you're asked about something <u>feminine</u>, you need 'Elle' here. But 'le film' is masculine — so this is '<u>Il</u>'.

*very good:* très bon(ne)
*bad:* mauvais(e)

**Le film était bon, mais on était** *trop proche de l'écran* .

= The film was good, but we were <u>too close to the screen</u>.

*too far from the stage:* trop loin de la scène.

## Qui a gagné le match? — Who won the match?

It looks <u>really good</u> if you can give some <u>details</u> in the <u>past tense</u> about what you've seen...

**J'étais** très content(e) avec le résultat.

= <u>I was</u> really pleased with the result.

*I wasn't:* Je n'étais pas

*jumped:* a sauté    *passed the ball:* a passé le ballon

**Mon équipe** *a gagné* .

= My team <u>won</u>.    *lost:* a perdu

**Mon joueur préféré** *a marqué* deux fois.

= My favourite player <u>scored</u> twice.

## Et qui a gagné l'allumette?

<u>Tough</u> page — lots to learn. As long as you can give your <u>opinion</u> on whatever you've <u>seen</u> or <u>done</u>, it's a big piece of gâteau... That's all I have to say. There's no more advice at this point.

# Revision Summary

These questions are here to make sure you <u>know your stuff</u>. Work through them <u>all</u> and check the ones you couldn't do. <u>Look back</u> through the section to find the answers, then have another go at knocking those pesky troublesome ones right out of the parking lot. And (eventually) <u>voilà</u>.

1) What is the French for each of these sports? What's the French for the place where you would do them?   a) football        b) swimming    c) snowboarding       d) ice skating

2) Write down as many French words as you can to do with playing or listening to music.

3) Say that you go swimming at the weekend and that you're a member of a badminton club.

4) You like watching films and soaps on TV. Tonight you'd like to watch a documentary that starts at nine o'clock. How would you say this in French?

5) Think of a film you saw recently and one you saw a month ago, and say this in French. (You don't have to translate the film titles into French.)

6) You have just watched an interesting and surprising show. Say this in French. Remember to tell me its title and tell me what happened.

7) Your friend Paul is music mad. Ask him in French whether he listens to music on the radio, or on his MP3 player. Now pretend to be Paul and answer the question, giving a reason.

8) Nadine thinks she's fallen in love with Robbie Williams. Write a paragraph in French to her saying what you think about celebrities and what you think about him in particular.

9) Aimerais-tu être célèbre? Pourquoi? (Donnez <u>deux</u> raisons.)

10) Your French uncle wants to find out the UK weather forecast on the web, but he's not very internet savvy. Tell him there's a link on the homepage of the BBC website.

11) You check your email inbox every day. Tell the French-speaking world.

12) You're out of bread. How do you ask where the baker's is and whether it's open?

13) What are the French names for:   a) a newsagent   b) a cake shop   c) a butcher's   d) a bookshop   e) a sweet shop   f) a supermarket      g) a department store?

14) Est-ce que tu préfères faire du shopping sur internet? Pourquoi?

15) A shop assistant asks you 'Est-ce que je peux vous aider?' and later 'Voulez-vous autre chose?' What do these two questions mean in English? How would you answer them?

16) You want to buy a brown jumper, size 38, and some cotton pyjamas. How do you say this to the shop assistant?

17) Describe your perfectly planned surprise party in no more than 3 French sentences.

18) Tu veux aller au concert. Le concert commence à vingt et une heures et finit à vingt-deux heures trente. Un billet coûte cinq euros. Comment est-ce qu'on dit ça en anglais?

19) Décris-moi un spectacle, un film ou un match que tu as vu récemment. (3 phrases max.)

# Holiday Destinations

You need to know about <u>countries</u> and <u>nationalities</u> for describing yourself or your <u>holiday</u> plans in your <u>speaking</u> and <u>writing</u> tasks, or for <u>understanding descriptions</u> of people in the <u>reading</u> and <u>listening</u> papers.

## D'où viens-tu? — Where do you come from?

Learn this phrase <u>off by heart</u> — if the country you're from isn't here, check in a dictionary...

*Je viens* d'Angleterre *. Je suis* anglais(e) *.* = I come <u>from England</u>. I am <u>English</u>.

| Wales: | du pays de Galles |
| Northern Ireland: | d'Irlande du Nord |
| Scotland: | d'Écosse |

| Welsh: | gallois(e) |
| Northern Irish: | irlandais(e) du nord |
| Scottish: | écossais(e) |

**IMPORTANT BIT:**
You must add '<u>e</u>' on the end for <u>women and girls</u> (see page 85).
*Je suis anglais<u>e</u>.*

*Je suis* anglophone *.* ← *French-speaking:* francophone

= I am <u>English-speaking</u>.

*J'habite en* Angleterre *.* = I live in <u>England</u>.

*Où habites-tu?* = Where do you live?

or 'Où est-ce que tu habites?'

Use 'en' for feminine countries and masculine ones beginning with a vowel, and 'au' for all other masculine countries. For plural countries, it's 'aux'.

## Learn these foreign countries

You also need to <u>understand</u> where <u>other people</u> come from.

| Algeria: | l'Algérie (fem.) |
| America: | l'Amérique (fem.) / les États-Unis (masc.) |
| Australia: | l'Australie (fem.) |
| Austria: | l'Autriche (fem.) |
| Belgium: | la Belgique |
| Canada: | le Canada |
| China: | la Chine |
| France: | la France |
| Germany: | l'Allemagne (fem.) |
| Greece: | la Grèce |
| Holland: | la Hollande |
| Netherlands: | les Pays-Bas (masc.) |
| India: | l'Inde (fem.) |
| Italy: | l'Italie (fem.) |
| Japan: | le Japon |
| Morocco: | le Maroc |
| Poland: | la Pologne |
| Portugal: | le Portugal |
| Spain: | l'Espagne (fem.) |
| Switzerland: | la Suisse |

| African: | africain(e) |
| Algerian: | algérien(ne) |
| American: | américain(e) |
| Australian: | australien(ne) |
| Austrian: | autrichien(ne) |
| Belgian: | belge |
| Canadian: | canadien(ne) |
| Chinese: | chinois(e) |
| French: | français(e) |
| German: | allemand(e) |
| Greek: | grec/grecque |
| Dutch: | néerlandais(e) |
| Indian: | indien(ne) |
| Italian: | italien(ne) |
| Japanese: | japonais(e) |
| Moroccan: | marocain(e) |
| Polish: | polonais(e) |
| Portuguese: | portugais(e) |
| Spanish: | espagnol(e) |
| Swiss: | suisse |

Map labels: L'Écosse, L'Irlande du Nord, La Grande-Bretagne, L'Angleterre, La République d'Irlande, Le pays de Galles, La Hollande, La Pologne, L'Allemagne, La Belgique, La France, La Suisse, L'Autriche, Le Portugal, L'Espagne, L'Italie

| England: | l'Angleterre (f.) |
| Northern Ireland: | l'Irlande du Nord (f.) |
| Scotland: | l'Écosse (f.) |
| Wales: | le pays de Galles |
| Great Britain: | la Grande-Bretagne |
| Republic of Ireland: | la République d'Irlande |

| English: | anglais(e) |
| Irish: | irlandais(e) |
| Scottish: | écossais(e) |
| Welsh: | gallois(e) |
| British: | britannique |

**IMPORTANT:** <u>Don't</u> use a capital letter for all these adjectives.

## Hidden a gender?...

Most of the countries are <u>feminine</u>, but there are a few sneaky exceptions which are <u>masculine</u>. And with the ones where the French word is <u>a bit like the English</u>, check you've got the <u>spelling</u> right. Don't just look at them and <u>assume</u> you know them because they look <u>familiar</u>.

# Catching the Train

Trains, planes and automobiles... Well, just <u>trains</u> for now. This page gives you a few of the <u>basics</u> you might come across in the exam. Examiners like this topic — I think they all have shares in train companies.

## Je veux y aller en train — I want to go there by train

Here's how to buy a <u>ticket</u>. You'd be <u>nuts</u> not to learn this.

*Est-ce qu'il y a un train* pour Paris *?*

= Is there a train <u>to Paris</u>?

*Un* aller simple *pour Paris, en* première classe *.*

*second class:* deuxième classe

= <u>One</u> <u>single</u> to Paris, <u>first class</u>.

*Two:* Deux   *single(s):* aller(s) simple(s)
*Three:* Trois   *return(s):* aller-retour(s)

*Un aller-retour pour Paris, s'il vous plaît.*

= One return ticket to Paris, please.

## Vous voyagez quand? — When are you travelling?

Here are a few more <u>details</u> about rail travel.

*Je voudrais aller à Caen,* samedi *.*

*today:* aujourd'hui
*next Monday:* lundi prochain
*on the tenth of June:* le dix juin

= I would like to travel to Caen <u>on Saturday</u>.

*Quand est-ce que le train* part pour *Caen?*

= When does the train <u>leave for</u> Caen?

*arrive at:* arrive à

\\\\\\\\\\\\\\\\\\\\\
For more info on
times and dates,
see page 2.
/////////////////////

*Le train* part de *quel quai?*

= Which platform does the train <u>leave from</u>?

And this is how to ask <u>where stuff is</u>.

*Où est* le quai *, s'il vous plaît?*

= Where is <u>the platform</u>, please?

*the waiting room:* la salle d'attente

*Où sont* les toilettes *, s'il vous plaît?*

= Where are <u>the toilets</u>, please?

*the left luggage:* la consigne      *the ticket windows:* les guichets (masc.)

*Excusez-moi Monsieur, je cherche* le wagon-restaurant *.*

= Excuse me sir, I'm looking for <u>the restaurant car</u>.

*the sleeping car:* le wagon-lit

## Beds on a train or snakes on a plane...

...not sure which is scarier. Might make a good sequel. (I'll suggest it to Samuel L.) And whilst I'm doing that you can get on and revise <u>train vocabulary</u>, safe in the knowledge that by the time you're done with <u>yucky exams</u>, there'll be a fab new '<u>film d'horreur</u>' on the market. Can't wait.

# Catching the Train

You'll need to know a bit about the <u>French rail network</u> too. You <u>won't believe</u> how exciting it is.

## Si on prenait l'Eurostar? — What about taking Eurostar?

Loads of <u>business people</u> use the Eurostar, as well as tourists. You could get passages like the ones below in the <u>reading</u> or <u>listening</u> parts of the exam.

"J'habite dans le Kent, mais je travaille une journée par semaine en France. Avant je prenais le bateau de Douvres à Calais mais maintenant je préfère prendre l'Eurostar. C'est pratique."

= "I live in Kent, but I work one day a week in France. Before, I used to take the ferry from Dover to Calais but now I prefer to take the Eurostar. It's practical."

"Je suis Parisienne, et je fais souvent des voyages à Nottingham. Je prends l'Eurostar à la gare du Nord et je change à St Pancras. Le trajet dure environ quatre heures et demie."

= "I am a Parisian, and I make a lot of trips to Nottingham. I get the Eurostar at the Gare du Nord and I change at St Pancras. The journey takes about four and a half hours."

## Le chemin de fer — The railway

There are a few different types of trains and stations in France, and you'll need to <u>know</u> them.

| | |
|---|---|
| **La SNCF** | <u>Société Nationale des Chemins de fer Français</u> — wow, no wonder they shortened it. This is the normal French train network. A train station in French is <u>une gare SNCF</u>. |
| **Le TGV** | <u>Train à Grande Vitesse</u> — the pride of the French railway system, these provide high-speed links between big cities. |
| **Le RER** | <u>Réseau Express Régional</u> — express regional network. The type of train that commuters use to get into Paris. |
| **Le Métro** | <u>Métropolitain</u> — the underground. A tube station is <u>une station de métro</u> (<u>not</u> une gare...). |

Not a TGV

## You might have to listen to a Railway Announcement...

Le train à destination de Bordeaux part du quai numéro huit à quinze heures quarante-cinq.

= The train to Bordeaux leaves from platform 8 at 15:45.

And to finish, more <u>vocab</u>... Yes, it's as <u>dull</u> as a big dull thing, but it's also <u>vital</u>.

| | | | | | |
|---|---|---|---|---|---|
| *to depart:* | partir | *to get on:* | monter dans | *timetable:* | l'horaire (masc.) |
| *departure:* | le départ | *to get off:* | descendre de | *reclining seat:* | la couchette |
| *to arrive:* | arriver | *to change (trains):* | changer (de train) | *coming from:* | en provenance de |
| *arrival:* | l'arrivée (fem.) | *compartment:* | le compartiment | *going to:* | à destination de |

## I would catch the train — but it's a bit heavy...*

Lucky you... examiners <u>love</u> to ask about travelling. So you'd better make sure you can answer <u>all</u> the questions they could throw at you about it. The thing is, even if you find this really boring now, when it gets to the exam, you'll be wishing you'd bothered. <u>No doubt</u> about that.

# All Kinds of Transport

Here's what you need to <u>know</u> about other forms of <u>transport</u>. This is another one of those topics that you'll need to know <u>really well</u> — and you need to know loads of <u>vocab</u> for it, too.

## Comment y vas-tu? — How do you get there?

You might need to say <u>how</u> you <u>get about</u>.

> J'y vais à pied.    = I go there on foot.

> D'habitude, je vais  en ville   en bus .

to school: à l'école /
au collège

= I normally go <u>into town</u> <u>by bus</u>.

| | |
|---|---|
| *by bus:* | en bus / en autobus |
| *on the underground:* | en métro |
| *by car:* | en voiture |
| *by coach:* | en car / en autocar |
| *by boat:* | en bateau |
| *by plane:* | en avion |
| *by Eurostar:* | en Eurostar |
| *by bike:* | à vélo |
| *by motorbike:* | à moto |

> J'y vais  par le train .

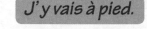

= I go there <u>by train</u>.

## Le départ et l'arrivée — Departure and arrival

These are the kinds of questions which could come up when <u>travelling</u>. Or in your <u>exam</u>, perhaps.

> Est-ce qu'il y a  un bus  pour Toulouse?    = Is there <u>a bus</u> to Toulouse?

*a flight:* un vol     *a coach:* un car     *a train:* un train

> Quand part  le prochain bus  pour Amiens?    = When does <u>the next bus</u> to Amiens leave?

*the (next) coach:* le (prochain) car     *the (next) flight:* le (prochain) vol

> Quand est-ce que  l'avion  arrive à Marseille?    = When does <u>the plane</u> arrive in Marseilles?

## Quel bus...? — Which bus...?

No doubt about it — you need to be able to ask <u>which bus</u> or <u>train</u> goes <u>where</u>. Just learn <u>this</u>.

> Quel bus va  au centre-ville , s'il vous plaît?    = <u>Which bus</u> goes <u>to the town centre</u>, please?

*Which train... :* Quel train...

| | |
|---|---|
| *to the station:* | à la gare |
| *to the airport:* | à l'aéroport (masc.) |
| *to the harbour / port:* | au port |

> C'est bien le bus pour  l'aéroport ?    = Is this the right bus for <u>the airport</u>?

## Buses? I can take them or leave them...

A doddle. Well, it will be if you <u>learn it now</u>. There's a chance it'll come up in your speaking assessments, so <u>practise saying it</u> out loud until there's not a bus driver in France who could catch you out. Shouldn't be too tough, really. "I go..." is "<u>Je vais...</u>" and that's that. Phew.

# Planning Your Holiday

Money transactions, excursions and hiring stuff... all extremely important aspects of effective holiday planning. If you want to get great marks, you'd better get learning these unbelievably useful phrases.

## Le bureau de change — The currency exchange

Well, you won't get far without money — so learn this stuff carefully.

Je voudrais changer **de l'argent** .   = I would like to change some money.

*£50:* cinquante livres sterling     *these traveller's cheques:* ces chèques de voyage

Je voudrais encaisser **ce chèque de voyage** .   = I would like to cash this traveller's cheque.

Voulez-vous voir une pièce d'identité ?   = Do you want to see proof of identity?

## Le syndicat d'initiative — The tourist office

Here's how you find out what a town's got to offer...

Pouvez-vous me donner des renseignements sur **le zoo** , s'il vous plaît?

= Can you give me information about the zoo, please?     *the town:* la ville

## Quelles sont les excursions? — What are the excursions?

Avez-vous des brochures sur **les excursions autour de Lyon** ?     *the museums in Metz:* les musées de Metz

= Do you have any brochures about excursions around Lyons?

Je voudrais **visiter Versailles** .   = I'd like to visit Versailles.

*from the church:* de l'église (fem.)     *to go to a museum:* aller au musée
*from the market:* du marché     *to visit the palace / castle:* visiter le château

Ce car va à Versailles. **Le car** part **de l'hôtel de ville** à **une heure et demie** .

*The train:* Le train     *2 o'clock:* deux heures   *3:15:* trois heures quinze

= This coach goes to Versailles. The coach leaves from the town hall at half past one.

## Je voudrais louer des skis — I'd like to hire some skis

Je voudrais louer **un vélo** pour **deux jours** .   *one week:* une semaine

*sleeping bags:* des sacs de couchage     = I'd like to hire a bike for two days.

Higher...higher...

## Tourists? Initiative? Who are they kidding...

Everyone knows tourists just blindly follow the person at the front holding the umbrella, so why call the tourist office a syndicat d'initiative? I dunno, but I bet it's a word you won't forget now...

# Holiday Accommodation

This page has all the words you need to know about <u>hotels</u>, <u>hostels</u>, <u>camping</u> and <u>foreign exchanges</u>. It's really useful stuff, so you'd better get <u>learning</u>...

## Je cherche un logement — I'm looking for somewhere to stay

Learn these different <u>places to stay</u>...

*hotel:* l'hôtel (masc.)

*campsite:* le camping

*self-catering cottage:* le gîte

*youth hostel:* l'auberge de jeunesse (fem.)

*host family:* la famille d'accueil

## Learn this vocabulary for Hotels and Hostels

**VERBS USED IN HOTELS:**

| | | | |
|---|---|---|---|
| *to recommend:* | recommander | *to stay:* | rester |
| *to reserve:* | réserver | *to leave:* | partir |
| *to confirm:* | confirmer | *to cost:* | coûter |

**THINGS YOU MIGHT WANT TO ASK FOR:**

| | |
|---|---|
| *full board (room + all meals):* | la pension complète |
| *half board (room + some meals):* | la demi-pension |

**PARTS OF A HOTEL OR YOUTH HOSTEL:**

| | |
|---|---|
| *restaurant:* | le restaurant |
| *dining room:* | la salle à manger |
| *dormitory:* | le dortoir |
| *lift:* | l'ascenseur (masc.) |
| *stairs:* | l'escalier (masc.) |
| *car park:* | le parking |

**THINGS ABOUT YOUR ROOM:**

| | |
|---|---|
| *key:* | la clé, la clef |
| *balcony:* | le balcon |
| *bath:* | le bain |
| *shower:* | la douche |
| *washbasin:* | le lavabo |

**PAYING FOR YOUR STAY:**

| | |
|---|---|
| *bill:* | la note |
| *(set) price:* | le prix (fixe) |

## Je fais un échange — I'm going on a school exchange

If you get a question about exchange visits, <u>don't panic</u>. Chances are the <u>vocab</u> will be very <u>similar</u> to the stuff you've learnt for <u>other types</u> of <u>holiday</u>.

Je reste *chez une famille française* .

*with a host family:* en famille d'accueil

= I'm staying <u>with a French family</u>.

J'aurai *ma propre chambre* . = I'll have <u>my own room</u>.

*my own bathroom:* ma propre salle de bains     *a bit of space:* un peu d'espace
*the chance to speak French every day:* l'occasion de parler français tous les jours

**USEFUL EXCHANGE VOCAB:**

| | |
|---|---|
| *to write to:* | correspondre (avec) |
| *to get to know:* | faire la connaissance de |
| *to invite:* | inviter |
| *hospitality:* | l'hospitalité (fem.) |
| *present / gift:* | le cadeau |

## Pension? — but I'm only sixteen...

If anything on <u>logements</u> comes up, you'll be glad I put this page in. It might just look like another load of vocabulary, but it's your <u>ticket to big marks</u>. If you <u>learn it all</u>, you'll <u>sail through</u> this topic.

# Booking a Room / Pitch

It's crucial when you're <u>planning</u> a holiday to be able to talk about your <u>preference</u> for a suite with a gold-plated bath and a view of the Eiffel Tower. <u>Learn</u> this page and you'll be laughing.

## Avez-vous des chambres libres?

## — Do you have any rooms free?

Je voudrais une [chambre] [pour une personne]. = I'd like a <u>single room</u>.

You could be a bit more specific and use these.

room with a bath: chambre avec bain
room with a balcony: chambre avec balcon

double: pour deux personnes

For more numbers, see page 1.

Je voudrais rester ici [deux nuits]. = I'd like to stay here <u>two nights</u>.

for one night: une nuit

If there's more than one person, use deux personne**s**, trois personne**s** etc.

C'est combien par nuit pour [une personne]? = How much is it per night for <u>one person</u>?

Je [la] prends. = I'll take <u>it</u>.

If the 'it' you're talking about is masculine (e.g. l'emplacement') then use 'le'.

it: le / la

Je ne [la] prends pas. = I won't take <u>it</u>.

---

## Est-ce qu'on peut camper ici? — Can I camp here?

Even if you're not the <u>outdoorsy type</u> it's a good idea to get familiar with this camping vocab for your exams.

Je voudrais [un emplacement] pour [une nuit]. = I'd like <u>a pitch</u> for <u>one night</u>.

two weeks: deux semaines

pitch (place for a tent): un emplacement

sleeping bag: un sac de couchage

caravan: une caravane   tent: une tente

You may have to book ahead. See page 11 on writing formal letters.

**YOU MIGHT NEED THESE PHRASES TOO:**

Is there drinking water here?: Est-ce qu'il y a de l'eau potable ici?
Can I light a fire here?: Est-ce que je peux allumer un feu ici?
Where can I find...?: Où est-ce que je peux trouver... ?

---

# Tired arms — Well, you try pitching for a whole night...

Even if you're <u>never</u> going to go on holiday to France, get this page <u>learnt</u>. Make sure you know all the <u>example sentences</u>, and the <u>extra vocab</u> you can stick into each one. It's the <u>only way</u>.

# Where / When is...?

Here's how French people ask __where__ and __when things are__. It's all pretty important stuff for you to know...

## Ask where things are — use 'Où est... ?'

Knowing how the French ask __where__ things are is supremely important — get these __learnt__.

> Où est la salle à manger , s'il vous plaît?

= Where is __the dining room__, please?

the car park: le parking
the games room: la salle de jeu
the telephone: le téléphone

See page 47 for more places you might need to find.

> Où sont les toilettes ?

= Where are __the toilets?__

If the place you're looking for is plural, remember to use 'Où sont...' instead of 'Où est...'

Use 'Elle' for 'la' words, 'Elles' and 'Ils' for plural words and 'Il' for 'le' words.

Use 'au' here because 'étage' is masculine.
Use 'à la' for feminine words, e.g. 'elle est à la piscine'.

> Elle est au troisième étage .

= __It's__ on the __third floor__.

fourth floor: quatrième étage
second floor: deuxième étage
first floor: premier étage
ground floor: rez-de-chaussée

C'est un "stick-up".
Où est le "money"?

For higher floor numbers, see page 1.

**OTHER WORDS YOU MIGHT NEED:**

| | | | |
|---|---|---|---|
| straight on: | tout droit | outside: | à l'extérieur |
| upstairs: | en haut | on the left / right: | à gauche / à droite |
| downstairs: | en bas | at the end of the corridor: | au bout du couloir |

## A quelle heure... ? — When is... ?

When you've understood __where__ everything is, you'll need to know __when__ things happen, too...

> Le petit-déjeuner est servi à quelle heure, s'il vous plaît?

lunch: le déjeuner
evening meal: le dîner

= When is __breakfast__ served, please?

For more times, see page 2.

> Il est servi entre six heures et huit heures.

= It's served between six and eight o'clock.

## Un petit déjeuner énorme, s'il vous plaît...

The French word '__jeûner__' means to '__fast__' (i.e. not to eat anything). When you put '__dé-__' before a verb, it means 'do the opposite' (e.g. 'défaire' means to 'undo'). So 'dé-jeûner' means to 'un-fast', or to __break__ the __fast__... or to __breakfast__. OK, that's enough trivia — make sure you __learn__ this page.

# Problems with Accommodation

Accommodation with problems... cockroaches in the bath, rats in the kitchens — that kind of thing.
Like revision, it's not pleasant, but you know the drill — somebody's got to deal with it...

## Il y a un problème... — There's a problem...

Make sure you can write about at least two problems — safety in numbers.

Il n'y a pas de **serviettes** dans la chambre.

*glasses:* verres (masc.)

= There aren't any **towels** in the room.

*cold:* froid

Il fait trop **chaud** . = It's too **hot**.

L'eau est trop **chaude** . *cold:* froide

= **The water** is too **hot**.

'Eau' is feminine, so remember to add an extra 'e' onto 'chaud(e)' and 'froid(e)'.

La télévision est cassée. = The **TV** is broken.

*The chair:* La chaise

*The phone:* Le téléphone

La douche ne fonctionne pas. = **The shower** doesn't work.

## Pouah, c'est dégoûtant! — Yuck, it's disgusting!

Il y a **de l'eau** partout. = There is **water** everywhere.

*mud:* de la boue

*The bath:* Le bain — La chambre est sale. = **The room** is dirty.

Il y a trop de bruit — je ne peux pas dormir. = There is too much noise — I can't sleep.

## Est-ce que vous pouvez faire quelque chose?

### — Can you do something?

*beds:* des lits (masc.)

Il nous faut **des serviettes** supplémentaires. = We need some extra **towels**.

J'ai besoin des **draps** propres. = I need some clean **sheets**.

*cups:* tasses (fem.)  *towels:* serviettes (fem.)

Je voudrais une autre chambre. = I would like a different room.

## 'There's water everywhere' — 'Well, this is a cruise, Sir...'

Fingers crossed, whether you're in a B&B in Calais or a 5-star hotel in Paris, you'll never need to complain about this stuff when you're on holiday in France. But learn this page just in case.

# At a Restaurant

If you've <u>been</u> to <u>France</u>, a lot of these <u>signs</u> and <u>phrases</u> could be <u>familiar</u> to you. The restaurant theme tends to crop up in the exams year after year, after year, after year, after... — so this is <u>important</u> stuff.

## Au restaurant... — In the restaurant...

Here are some <u>words and phrases</u> you'll find useful when talking about <u>restaurants</u>.

 **Ouvert**

= Open

**Plat du jour
Spécialités**

= **Dish of the day
Specialities**

Attendez ici
s'il vous plaît

= **Wait here, please**

**Heures d'ouverture**

= **Opening hours**

 **Fermé**

= Closed

Service
compris

= **Service included**

*Défense
de fumer*

= **No smoking**

À la carte
À prix fixe

*À la carte:*
= **Individually priced items**
*Menu à prix fixe:*
= **Fixed price menu**

Pourboire

= **Tips**

## Est-ce que vous avez une table libre?

This part's <u>easy</u> —
definitely worth learning.

### — Do you have a table free?

*Je voudrais réserver une table pour* quatre *personnes, s'il vous plaît.*

*two:* deux     *three:* trois

= I would like to reserve a table for <u>four</u>, please.

*Nous sommes* quatre .

= There are <u>four</u> of us.

*Nous voudrions nous asseoir* à l'extérieur .

*on the terrace:* sur la terrasse

= We'd like to sit <u>outside</u>.

*Est-ce que je peux avoir la carte, s'il vous plaît?*

= May I have the menu, please?

*Où* sont les toilettes *, s'il vous plaît?*

*is:* est    *the phone:* le téléphone

See page 49 for help asking where things are.

= Where <u>are</u> <u>the toilets</u>, please?

## I have a dream today, that all tables shall be free...

When a <u>restaurant</u> bit comes up in the exam you'll be kicking yourself if you haven't revised it. And if you're after a <u>top grade</u>, you'll really need to <u>impress</u>. So you have to learn <u>all of it</u>. No missing bits out — if you learn all the stuff on this page (and all the other pages), it'll all be OK.

# At a Restaurant

Now it's time for that all-important part... <u>opinions</u>. You'll need to talk about the <u>foods you prefer</u> and know how to state any <u>problems</u> you have with a meal. Revise this and your <u>French</u> will be complete. Almost.

## Je voudrais... — I would like...

See page 13 for food vocab.

Comme **plat principal** , je voudrais **la pizza au poulet** .

= For <u>main course</u>, <u>I'd like</u> the chicken pizza.

*starter:*     hors d'oeuvre (masc.)
*dessert:*     dessert (masc.)

*the pork with French beans:* le porc aux haricots verts
*the chocolate cake:*        le gâteau au chocolat

## Désolé, il n'y a plus de porc — Sorry, there's no more pork

You may need to understand changes if they <u>haven't got</u> your order or if a <u>mistake</u> is made.

Je prendrai l'agneau à la place du porc.

= I'll have the lamb instead of the pork.

*the lamb:* l'agneau     *the pork:* le porc

Il y a une erreur. Je n'ai pas commandé **ceci** .

= There's been a mistake. I didn't order <u>this</u>.

## Je ne suis pas satisfait(e) — I'm not satisfied

Je voudrais me plaindre.

= I'd like to make a complaint.

*is too hot:*    est trop chaud
*is too cold:*   est trop froid

*The pork:*    Le porc

**Le bœuf** **n'est pas assez cuit** .

= <u>The beef</u> <u>is underdone</u>.

J'ai trouvé **une mouche** dans ma soupe.

= I found <u>a fly</u> in my soup.

*a snail:* un escargot    *a hair:* un cheveu

Le service ici est affreux.

= The service here is awful.

## Est-ce que vous avez fini? — Have you finished?

There's <u>no</u> getting away from having to know <u>this</u>. You can't leave without paying.

Est-ce que je peux payer?

= May I pay?

L'addition, s'il vous plaît.

= The bill, please.

Est-ce que le service est compris?

= Is service included?

## Thanks Mr Federer, the service was ace...

<u>Restaurants</u> — <u>fun</u> to eat at, but a <u>bit of a mouthful</u> when it comes to GCSE French revision. These pages will be <u>really useful</u> in the exam once you've mastered 'em — so go for it...

# Talking About Your Holiday

Everyone wants to bore people by telling them all about their holidays. By the time you've finished this page you'll be able to bore people in French... and get good marks.

## Où es-tu allé(e)? — Where did you go?

This is where you went: ...and this is when you went:

Je suis allé(e) **aux États-Unis** , **il y a deux semaines** .

*Other dates and times: pages 2–3.*
*A bigger list of countries: page 42.*

| | |
|---|---|
| *to Spain:* | en Espagne |
| *to France:* | en France |
| *to Ireland:* | en Irlande |

| | |
|---|---|
| *a week ago:* | il y a une semaine |
| *last month:* | le mois dernier |
| *in July:* | en juillet |
| *in the summer:* | en été |

= I went to the USA, two weeks ago.

## Avec qui étais-tu en vacances?

You'd better answer this question, otherwise there'll be all sorts of gossip.

### — Who were you on holiday with?

J'étais en vacances avec **ma famille** pendant **un mois** .

= I was on holiday with my family for a month.

| | |
|---|---|
| *a fortnight:* | quinze jours |
| *two weeks:* | deux semaines |

*For past tenses, see pages 101-104.*
*For more on family, see page 18.*

| | |
|---|---|
| *my brother:* | mon frère |
| *my friends:* | mes ami(e)s |
| *my classmates:* | mes camarades de classe |

## Qu'est-ce que tu as fait? — What did you do?

You need to be able to say what you did on holiday — learn it well.

Je suis allé(e) **à la plage** .  = I went to the beach.

*For other places, see page 58.*

*to the disco:* en discothèque    *to the museum:* au musée

*For other sports and activities, see page 26.*

This is a reflexive verb — see page 105 for more on these.

Je me suis détendu(e) .  = I relaxed.

| | |
|---|---|
| *I enjoyed myself:* | Je me suis amusé(e) |
| *I played tennis:* | J'ai joué au tennis |

## Comment tu y es allé(e)? — How did you get there?

Remember the little word 'y', which means 'there' — it's a useful one (see page 94 for more on this).

Nous y sommes allé(e)s **en voiture** .  = We went there by car.

| | | | |
|---|---|---|---|
| *by plane:* | en avion | *by train:* | par le train / en train |
| *by boat:* | en bateau | *by bike:* | à vélo |

*For more types of transport, see page 45.*

# So, celeb Z-list — what's the jungle really like...

One final useful tip before you move on — if you're writing about visiting something while on holiday, e.g. a museum, use 'visiter'. If you're writing about visiting a person, it's 'rendre visite à'.

# Talking About Your Holiday

Opinions and tales of woe — the examiners love them. So plough on and learn this stuff as well...

## Comment était le voyage? — How was the trip?

*Comment étaient tes vacances?* = How was your holiday?

*Je les ai aimées.* = I liked it.

*Les vacances étaient formidables.* = The holiday was great.

*Je ne les ai pas aimées.* = I didn't like it.

*Comme ci comme ça.* = So-so.

## Quelle catastrophe — What a disaster

Sometimes things don't quite go to plan when you're on holiday.

*"Nous avons fait du ski. Ma soeur est tombée, et s'est cassé la jambe."* = We went skiing. My sister fell, and broke her leg.

Limb-breakers.

*"Nous sommes allés à une station balnéaire, mais mes parents détestent la plage."* = We went to a seaside resort, but my parents hate the beach.

Not to everyone's taste.

a ski resort:  une station de ski

*"J'ai eu mal de route. Nous avons dû nous arrêter pendant une heure dans une aire de repos."* = I was carsick. We had to stop for an hour at a motorway rest area.

service station: une station-service

> For more on the perfect tense, see pages 101-102.

*"Ma mère a laissé son passeport à l'hôtel. Elle n'a pas pu prendre l'avion."* = My mother left her passport at the hotel. She couldn't take the plane.

*"Mon père s'est fâché parce qu'on nous avait promis une vue de mer, mais notre gîte n'en avait pas."* = My father got annoyed because they'd promised us a sea view, but our gîte didn't have one.

## Il a plu tous les jours — It rained every day

If they ask you to compare different holidays, the weather's a good place to start...

*En Italie, il faisait plus chaud qu'en Écosse.* = In Italy it was hotter than in Scotland.

*En France, il pleuvait moins qu'en Espagne.* = In France, it rained less than in Spain.

This is the comparative. For more examples, see pages 89-90.

*Il faisait aussi froid en Suisse qu'en Autriche.* = It was as cold in Switzerland as in Austria.

For more on weather, see page 56.

## Ça t'a plu? — Non, il a fait très beau...

Watch out with the word 'plu'. It's the past participle of both pleuvoir (to rain) and plaire (to please). 'Ça t'a plu?' means 'Did you like it?', whereas 'A-t-il plu?' means 'Did it rain?'. Tricky.

# Talking About Your Holiday

More on holidays — yay. This time though about where you're <u>planning</u> on going, or where you'd <u>like</u> to go.

## Où iras-tu l'année prochaine? — Where will you go next year?

<u>Tricky</u> stuff now — learn to talk about things you <u>will do</u> in the <u>future</u>...

These are the future tense...

For more info about the future tense, see page 100.

These are the easy future tense...

| | |
|---|---|
| *Where will you go?*<br>*Où est-ce que tu iras?* | *I will go to America in two weeks.*<br>*J'irai en Amérique dans deux semaines.* |
| *How are you going to get there?*<br>*Comment tu vas y aller?* | *I'm going to go there by plane.*<br>*Je vais y aller en avion.* |
| *What are you going to take?*<br>*Qu'est-ce que tu vas prendre?* | *I'm going to take some clothes, my sunglasses and some books.*<br>*Je vais prendre des vêtements, mes lunettes de soleil et des livres.* |

## Mes vacances de rêve — My dream holiday

This bit's all about what you <u>would</u> do if you <u>could</u>. This uses the <u>conditional</u> (see page 107).

*Comment seraient tes vacances de rêve?* = What would your dream holiday be like?

*Mes vacances de rêve seraient de* ...

= My dream holiday would be to...

| | |
|---|---|
| *stay in a five-star hotel:* | rester dans un hôtel cinq étoiles |
| *visit a city like... :* | visiter une grande ville comme... |
| *spend a month in the country:* | passer un mois à la campagne |
| *go away with my friends:* | partir avec mes ami(e)s |
| *go away with my family:* | partir avec ma famille |

You might like to start with a fancy "if" — which examiners <u>love</u>, if you get the tenses right.

*Si j'avais beaucoup d'argent ... / Si j'étais riche ...*     *...je ferais le tour du monde.*

Extra marks for style

= If I had a lot of money ... / If I were rich ...     ...I would take a trip round the world.

## À ton avis, est-ce que les vacances sont importantes? — In your opinion, are holidays important?

If your speaking assessment's on <u>holidays</u>, you might be asked to give your <u>opinions</u> on holidays <u>in general</u>.

*Bien sûr que oui — il faut prendre le temps de se détendre.* = Of course. It's essential to take time to relax.

*Est-ce qu'on prend trop de vacances?* = Do you think we take too many holidays?

*Oui — tous ces* vols *sont mauvais pour l'environnement.* = Yes — all these <u>flights</u> are bad for the environment.

*trips abroad:* voyages à l'étranger

## Holidays — always a tense time...

Like lots of things in GCSE French, talking about holidays comes down to which <u>tense</u> you use.
Think of how to say the activity in the <u>infinitive</u> (e.g. 'partir'), and then put it into the correct tense.

# The Weather

You might have to listen to a <u>weather forecast</u> in your <u>listening</u> exam. But don't panic — learn the weather stuff in the present and future tenses given here and you'll be OK. More than OK — stupendous.

## Quel temps fait-il? — What's the weather like?

These <u>short sentences</u> are the ones you definitely <u>can't do without</u> — and they're <u>easy</u>.

Aujourd'hui, **il pleut** . = <u>It's raining</u> today.

It's snowing: il neige...

*Literally translated, this means 'There is wind.'*

Of course, it doesn't <u>always</u> rain, so here are a few others you could use:

Il fait **froid** . = It's <u>cold</u>.

Il y a **du vent** . = It's <u>windy</u>.

| | |
|---|---|
| *warm:* | chaud |
| *sunny:* | du soleil |
| *hot:* | très chaud |

*You can use any of these words after 'Il fait...'.*

| | |
|---|---|
| *icy:* | de la glace |
| *rainy:* | de la pluie |
| *cloudy:* | des nuages (masc.) |

| | |
|---|---|
| *thundery:* | du tonnerre |
| *stormy:* | des tempêtes (fem.) |
| | / des orages (masc.) |

## Quel temps fera-t-il demain?

### — What will the weather be like tomorrow?

This is quite easy, and it sounds <u>dead impressive</u>:

*It'll snow:* Il neigera / Il va neiger

Il pleuvra / Il va pleuvoir **demain** . = <u>It will rain</u> <u>tomorrow</u>.

*See page 100 for the future tense.*

*the day after tomorrow:* après-demain
*next week:* la semaine prochaine

Il fera **froid** . = It will be <u>cold</u>.

| | |
|---|---|
| *nice:* | beau |
| *bad:* | mauvais |
| *foggy:* | du brouillard |

Il y aura **des vents forts** . = There will be <u>strong winds</u>.

| | |
|---|---|
| *showers:* | des averses (fem.) |
| *sunny intervals:* | des éclaircies (fem.) |
| *lightning:* | des éclairs (masc.) |

## You need to understand a weather forecast

Here's a <u>real</u> weather forecast — time to show what you can do. You <u>won't know all the words</u>, but don't panic. Work through this one — you should be able to get the gist by looking at the words you <u>do know</u>.

*La météo d'aujourd'hui*
Aujourd'hui il fera chaud en France. Demain il y aura du vent dans le sud et des nuages dans le nord. Il va pleuvoir sur la côte.

*Today's Weather Forecast*
Today it will be warm in France. Tomorrow it will be windy in the south and cloudy in the north. It will rain on the coast.

Tomorrow it'll be wet.

*in the east:* dans l'est    *in the west:* dans l'ouest

# France — where time is weather...

'<u>Le temps</u>' can either mean '<u>time</u>' or '<u>weather</u>', but you should always be able to tell from the <u>context</u> which one it is. Weather's a favourite with examiners, so you need to <u>learn</u> the <u>examples</u> on this page and the <u>bits of vocab</u> — then you'll be fine. (Just like the weather, with any luck...)

# Revision Summary

It's that time again folks... another dreaded revision summary. Don't dread it. Work in harmony with it, so that by the time you've answered all of these questions (several times), you'll feel like you're a fully-fledged Frenchified person, and ready to take on that exam. OK, cut the 'yoga speak' — just practise these questions till you can answer them in your sleep.

1) Write down four countries in the UK and five other countries, in French. How would you say that you came from each of these places?

2) Write down the nationality to go with each of the places above (but in French).

3) You're at a French train station. How would you do these in French?
a) Say that you'd like to travel to Marseilles on Sunday. b) Ask if there are any trains there.

4) How do you say these in French?
a) the platform b) the waiting room c) the timetable d) the ticket window e) the departure

5) Ask for three return tickets to Tours, second class. Ask when and what platform the train leaves from and where the left luggage office is.

6) Say that you go to school by car, but your friend walks.

7) You've missed the bus to Pont-Audemer. Ask when the next bus leaves and when it'll arrive.

8) You've arrived in France without any euros. Tell the assistant at the bureau de change that you want to change 100 pounds and cash some traveller's cheques.

9) Imagine that you are a first class impersonator. Impersonate a tourist in France. Ask if the tourist office has any brochures about the Alps. Then ask if you can hire skis for two weeks.

10) What are these in French? a) hotel b) youth hostel c) campsite d) cottage e) host family

11) How do you say these in French? a) key b) bill c) stairs d) tent e) sleeping bag

12) Your friend announces: 'Je reste chez une famille d'accueil et j'aurai ma propre chambre.' What have they just told you about the school exchange they are set to go on?

13) You arrive at a French hotel. Say you want one double room and two single rooms. You want to stay five nights. Say you'll take the rooms and then ask where the restaurant is, in French.

14) Ask when breakfast is served, out loud and in French.

15) You've just arrived at a grotty hotel. The floor in your room is completely flooded and, randomly, there are snails everywhere. How would you complain to the lady at reception?

16) You're in a restaurant. It's all gone wrong — you want to complain. The lamb isn't cooked properly and there's a fly in your soup. How would you say all this in French?

17) How would you ask someone how their holiday was, what they did, how they got there, and how the journey was? Imagine you now have to answer these questions in French.

18) Describe your dream holiday in three French sentences.

19) You've just listened to the forecast. Say that tomorrow it will be hot and the sun will shine.

# Names of Buildings

If you're going to talk about your town, you need to know the names for buildings.
Yes, it's a bit dull, but you absolutely <u>have</u> to learn them.

## Learn all these bâtiments — buildings

These are the basic, bog-standard '<u>learn-them-or-else</u>' buildings.   (Building = le bâtiment.)

**the bank:** la banque

**the butcher's:** la boucherie

**the church:** l'église (fem.)

**the theatre:** le théâtre

**the railway station:** la gare

**the market:** le marché

**the baker's:** la boulangerie

**the cinema:** le cinéma

**the supermarket:** le supermarché

**the castle / palace:** le château

**the post office:** la poste

**the library:** la bibliothèque

## D'autres lieux — Other places

OK, I'll come clean.   There are absolutely <u>loads</u> of buildings you need to <u>know</u>.   Here's the rest:

**See page 34 for more shops.**

**SOME SHOPS**

| | |
|---|---|
| *shop:* | le magasin |
| *bookshop:* | la librairie |
| *newsagent:* | le tabac |
| *chemist's:* | la pharmacie |
| *cake shop:* | la pâtisserie |

**TOURISTY BITS**

| | |
|---|---|
| *hotel:* | l'hôtel (masc.) |
| *youth hostel:* | l'auberge de jeunesse (fem.) |
| *travel agent:* | l'agence de voyages (fem.) |
| *tourist information office:* | le syndicat d'initiative |
| *museum:* | le musée |

**OTHER IMPORTANT PLACES**

| | | | |
|---|---|---|---|
| *cathedral:* | la cathédrale | *bus station:* | la gare routière |
| *park:* | le parc | *town hall:* | l'hôtel de ville (masc.), la mairie |
| *swimming pool:* | la piscine | *sports ground:* | le terrain de sport |
| *airport:* | l'aéroport (masc.) | *recycling centre:* | le centre de recyclage |
| *stadium:* | le stade | *police station:* | le commissariat |
| *town centre:* | le centre-ville | *university:* | l'université (fem.) |
| *hospital:* | l'hôpital (masc.) | *school:* | le collège, l'école (fem.) |

## Take a butcher's... (and a baker's... and a candlesti...)

Learning vocab is just such great fun, don't you think...   OK, so it's pretty dull.   But it <u>will</u> come up in the <u>exams</u>.   The best way to learn it is to <u>turn over</u> the page and try to write all the words down.   Then look back and have another go at the ones you got wrong.   It's <u>boring</u>, but <u>it works</u>.

# Asking Directions

It's pretty likely you'll get at least <u>one</u> question about <u>asking</u> or <u>understanding</u> directions. If you <u>don't</u> learn this stuff, that's one question you <u>won't</u> be able to answer. That's a good enough reason to learn it.

## Où est... ? — Where is... ?

Asking <u>where something is</u> is dead easy — 'Où est...' plus the place name:

Où est **la poste** , s'il vous plaît? = Where is <u>the post office</u>, please?

See page 58 for more buildings.

Est-ce qu'il y a **une bibliothèque** près d'ici? = Is there <u>a library</u> near here?

## Le cinéma est... — The cinema is...

Le cinéma est **entre la banque et le parc** . = The cinema is <u>between the bank and the park</u>.

| | | |
|---|---|---|
| *this way:* par ici | *behind the bank:* derrière la banque | *opposite the bank:* en face de la banque |
| *that way:* par là | *in front of the school:* devant l'école | *below the café:* au-dessous du café |
| *here / there:* ici / là-bas | *on the corner:* au coin | *at the end of the road:* au bout de la rue |
| *next to the park:* à côté du parc | *above the bar:* au-dessus du bar | *at the end of the garden:* au fond du jardin |

## C'est loin d'ici? — Is it far from here?

It's a good idea to check <u>distance</u>, before letting yourself in for a 3-hour trek:

Est-ce que **le cinéma** est loin d'ici? = Is <u>the cinema</u> far from here?

*the post office:* la poste
*the park:* le parc

C'est **à deux kilomètres** d'ici. = It's <u>two kilometres</u> from here.

*several kilometres:* à quelques kilomètres    *not far:* à deux pas    *far:* loin    *near:* près

## Use 'pour aller à...?' to ask the way

You'll probably hear people asking directions in your <u>listening test</u>.

So, tell me again how to get to the library.

*(to a woman):* madame    *to the castle:* au château    *to the hospital:* à l'hôpital

Pardon **monsieur** , pour aller **à la banque** , s'il vous plaît?

Use '<u>au</u>' for 'le' words, '<u>à la</u>' for 'la' words, and '<u>à l'</u>' for words starting with a vowel and most words which start with an 'h'. See page 84.

= Excuse me <u>sir</u>, how do I get <u>to the bank</u>, please?

Look at page 1 for more stuff on 1st, 2nd, etc.

**LEARN THIS IMPORTANT VOCAB FOR DIRECTIONS**

| | | | |
|---|---|---|---|
| *go straight on:* | allez tout droit | *go / turn right at the traffic lights:* | tournez à droite aux feux |
| *go right:* | tournez à droite | *go straight on, past the church:* | allez tout droit, devant l'église |
| *go left:* | tournez à gauche | *take the first road on the left:* | prenez la première rue à gauche |

# How do you get to Wembley — Practise...

Cover it up, scribble it down, check what you got wrong, and try it again. That's the way to learn this stuff. Keep at it until you know it <u>all</u> — then you'll be really ready for the exam. Just reading the page is <u>nowhere near</u> enough — you wouldn't remember it tomorrow, never mind in the exam.

# Where You're From

This page deals with <u>regions</u> and <u>cities</u> that you'll be expected to know the name of in French. Don't just worry about where <u>you</u> come from — you might come across these in <u>any</u> part of the assessments.

## Tu es de quelle région? — Which region are you from?

You'll definitely need to recognise lots of regions of France and French-speaking places:

*Je viens de la Bretagne.*    = I come from Brittany.

Remember that 'de + le = du'.
See page 84.

| | | | |
|---|---|---|---|
| *from the centre of France:* | du Massif central | *from Quebec:* | du Québec |
| *from Corsica:* | de la Corse | *from Normandy:* | de la Normandie |
| *from the south of France:* | du Midi | *from Provence:* | de la Provence |

The counties of Britain have a 'le' or a 'du' in front of them.

*J'habite dans le Surrey.*    *Je viens du Surrey.*

= I live <u>in</u> Surrey.    = I come <u>from</u> Surrey.

## Les grandes villes — Cities

Normally the names of <u>cities</u> are the same in French and English, but there are a few <u>exceptions</u> you're expected to <u>know</u>.

| | | | |
|---|---|---|---|
| *Brussels:* | Bruxelles | *London:* | Londres |
| *Dover:* | Douvres | *Lyons:* | Lyon |
| *Edinburgh:* | Édimbourg | *Marseilles:* | Marseille |

## J'habite au bord de la mer — I live by the sea

There are a few names of <u>seas</u> and <u>mountains</u> you need to know.

| | | | |
|---|---|---|---|
| *the Atlantic:* | l'Atlantique (masc.) | *the mountain(s):* | la montagne |
| *the Mediterranean:* | la Méditerranée | *the Pyrenees:* | les Pyrénées (fem.) |
| *the English Channel:* | la Manche | *the Alps:* | les Alpes (fem.) |

*Mon village se trouve au pied des Pyrénées.*    = My village lies at the foot of the Pyrenees.

You might need to say you live near a <u>river</u>:

*Une rivière*    = A river

*J'habite dans une ville située sur le Severn.*    = I live in a town situated on <u>the Severn</u>.

"Nearly home now, son..."

| | |
|---|---|
| *Thames:* | la Tamise |
| *Seine:* | la Seine |
| *Rhone:* | le Rhône |

# Learn ev'ry mountain, search high and low...

Having said that, there's not an awful lot to learn here, but it is the kind of stuff that can catch you out if you haven't seen it before. Have another quick look at this page before you turn over.

# Talking About Where You Live

You'll have to understand and answer questions about where you **live**.
If you've **learnt** this, you'll be able to understand and answer. Simple as that.

## Où est-ce que tu habites? — Where do you live?

You **won't** get through GCSE French without needing this **vocab** — so make sure you learn it well.

> J'habite à **Barrow** .    = I live in **Barrow**.

> Barrow se trouve dans **le nord-ouest** de l'Angleterre.

*See page 42 for more countries.*

the north: le nord    the west: l'ouest (masc.)
the south: le sud    the east: l'est (masc.)

= Barrow's in **the north-west** of England.

## You have to write about life 'dans ta ville' — 'in your town'

Practise writing a description of **your town**, your favourite **town** or a dream **town** — **know** this **vocab** well...

> Qu'est-ce qu'il y a dans ta ville?

= What is there in your town?

> Il y a **un marché** .    = There's **a market**.

*See page 58 for more buildings and places.*

> Est-ce que tu aimes vivre à Barrow?

= Do you like living in Barrow?

> **J'aime** vivre à Barrow.

*I don't like: Je n'aime pas*

= **I like** living in Barrow.

## Comment est Barrow? — What is Barrow like?

Descriptions of **towns** could come up in any of your **assessments** — it's need-to-know stuff.

> La ville est **très intéressante** .    = The town is **very interesting**.

boring: ennuyeuse
great: chouette
dirty: sale
clean: propre
quiet: tranquille

> Il y a **beaucoup** à faire.    = There's **lots** to do.

*enough: assez    always something: toujours quelque chose*

> Il n'y a rien à faire.    = There's nothing to do.

There's more about where you live on the next page.

*Lie if you need to, but make it believable.*

**Longer descriptions** may seem tough at first — they're simply **all the bits you already know** put together...

> J'aime vivre à **Barrow** , parce qu'il y a toujours quelque chose à faire.

= I like living in **Barrow**, because there's always something to do.

> Je n'aime pas vivre à **Bogville** , parce qu'il n'y a rien à faire.

= I don't like living in **Bogville**, because there's nothing to do.

## Bogville-sur-mer — celebrity playground...

If you come from a really dreary place which has **nothing** going for it, you can **make things up** (within reason) — chances are there'll be **something** to say about a place near you. Start with **where** it is and see how much you can note down about it **without** looking at the page.

# Talking About Where You Live

This page isn't too bad — even the tricky stuff is really just a case of 'learn the sentences and learn what words you can change around in them'. If you spend the time on it, it'll become super easy.

## Add More Detail about where you live

**Le paysage autour de Lancaster est très beau et vert.**

*a town:* une ville    *a village:* un village

= The countryside around Lancaster is very beautiful and green.

**Lancaster est une grande ville avec quarante-six mille habitants et beaucoup d'industrie.**

= Lancaster is a city with 46 000 inhabitants and a lot of industry.

**J'habite au numéro quatre, rue Tub, à Lancaster.**

= I live at 4 Tub Street, Lancaster.

## Tu habites avec qui? — Who do you live with?

**J'habite avec mes grands-parents.**

= I live with my grandparents.

*my parents:* mes parents    *my father:* mon père    *my boyfriend:* mon petit ami
*my friends:* mes ami(e)s    *my mother:* ma mère    *my girlfriend:* ma petite amie

**J'aime habiter en famille parce que ...**

= I like living with family because...

*I don't have to cook:* je ne dois pas cuisiner.
*I can talk about my troubles with someone:*
je peux parler de mes inquiétudes avec quelqu'un.

**Je n'aime pas habiter en famille parce que ...**

= I don't like living with family because...

*my brother annoys me all the time:*
mon frère m'énerve tout le temps.
*I don't have any privacy:* je n'ai pas de vie privée.

## Chez toi — At your home

Being able to write about where you live and understanding others talking about their home is really important too...

*semi-detached house:* maison jumelée    *detached house:* maison individuelle

**J'habite une petite maison moderne.**

= I live in a small, modern house.

*big:* grande    *old:* ancienne
*pretty:* jolie    *green:* verte

In French, you don't need 'dans' when you say where you live. Literally you say, 'I live a house'. It's easiest if you think 'habiter' = 'inhabit'.

**Mon appartement se trouve près du parc.**

*My house:* Ma maison

= My flat is near the park.

*the motorway:* de l'autoroute (fem.)
*the shops:* des magasins (masc.)

*on the ground floor:* au rez-de-chaussée

**Mon appartement est au premier étage.**

= My flat is on the first floor.

## Chez — not just for hairdressers...

You need to be able to say where you live — just say "J'habite au numéro..." and then the number of the house or flat, followed by the street name. Easy really. But only if you bother to learn it.

# Inside Your Home

You've got to be able to <u>describe</u> your home. Luckily, you don't need to say <u>everything</u> that's in it — just some things. And you can always pretend you don't have that indoor swimming pool...

## Comment est ta maison? — What's your house like?

It'll look <u>impressive</u> if you can give more <u>details</u> about your home. <u>Details</u> are the <u>answer</u>...

Comment est | la cuisine | ?  = What's the <u>kitchen</u> like?

Est-ce que | la cuisine | est | grande | ?  = Is the <u>kitchen</u> <u>big</u>?

*the dining room:* la salle à manger

*comfortable:* confortable  *great:* chouette  *ugly:* laid(e) /
*tiny:* tout(e) petit(e)  *beautiful:* beau / belle  moche

La cuisine | est | jolie | .  = <u>The kitchen</u> is <u>nice</u>.

*It's not:* Ce n'est pas  C'est | ma pièce préférée.  = <u>It's</u> my favourite room.

## Est-ce que tu as un jardin? — Have you got a garden?

*My flat:* Mon appartement  Ma maison | a un jardin.  = <u>My house</u> has a garden.

*a tree:* un arbre  *a balcony:* un balcon
*a lawn:* une pelouse  *a swimming pool:* une piscine

Nous avons | des fleurs | dans notre jardin.

= We have <u>flowers</u> in our garden.

## Est-ce que tu as une chambre à toi?
## — Have you got your own room?

You'll pick up more juicy <u>marks</u> with these...

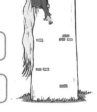

J'ai une chambre à moi. / J'ai ma propre chambre.  = I have my own room.

Je partage une chambre avec | mon frère | .  = I share a room with <u>my brother</u>.

## Décris-moi ta chambre... — Describe your room to me...

<u>Remember</u>, if these aren't in your room, you can be <u>creative</u> (lie) — get the <u>vocab spot on</u>, though.

Il y a quels meubles dans ta chambre?  = What furniture is there in your bedroom?

Dans ma chambre, il y a | ...  = In my bedroom there is / there are...

*a wardrobe:* une armoire  *a mirror:* un miroir  *a bed:* un lit  *some curtains:* des rideaux (masc.)

Le fauteuil est | rouge et | les murs sont | gris.  = <u>The armchair is</u> red and <u>the walls are</u> grey.

'Le fauteuil' is <u>singular</u>, so the verb 'être' is too = <u>est</u>  'Les murs' is <u>plural</u>, so the verb 'être' is too = <u>sont</u>

## For once I wish I lived in a one-room bedsit...

It's all about <u>the little details</u> here. Once you've <u>learnt</u> these <u>phrases</u>, you can go into great detail about your Cliff Richard posters and <u>wow</u> everyone with your <u>descriptive</u> abilities. Super.

# Festivals and Special Occasions

Ahhhh festivals... If you're thinking music and mud, Glastonbury-style, then you may be slightly disappointed by this page — here's all you'll need to know about cultural celebrations...

## Quand est-ce que vous fêtez? — When do you celebrate?

You'll need to be able to understand all the festival lingo — e.g. what is celebrated and when...

On fête le jour de l'An le premier janvier .

Put the time of year here.

= We celebrate New Year's Day on 1st January.

Put a specific date here.

Christmas Eve / Day: la veille / le jour de Noël
New Year's Eve: le réveillon

a bank holiday: un jour férié
Easter: Pâques

Le 14 février , on se joint pour fêter mon anniversaire .

Valentine's day: la Saint-Valentin

= On 14th February, we get together to celebrate my birthday.

For more dates, see page 3.

## Où est-ce que vous fêtez, et avec qui?
## — Where do you celebrate, and who with?

my family: ma famille        my colleagues: mes collègues        everybody: tout le monde

See page 38 for more on parties.

Je vais célébrer avec mes amis .

= I'm going to celebrate with my friends.

On va organiser une fête chez nous .

= We're going to organise a party at home.

at the restaurant: au restaurant        in a hotel: dans un hotel

## Qu'est-ce que vous faites pour célébrer?
## — What do you do to celebrate?

Pour célébrer, on mange de la nourriture de fête .

= To celebrate, we eat festive foods.

we have fun: on s'amuse        we give presents: on offre des cadeaux        we sing together: on chante ensemble
we dance: on danse        we receive presents: on reçoit des cadeaux        we eat as a family: on dîne en famille

Pour Noël ...        Pour la Hanoukka ...

For Christmas ...        For Hanukkah ...

we light 8 candles — one per day, for 8 days:
on allume huit bougies — une par jour, pour huit jours.
we play games and we give presents:
on joue aux jeux et on offre des cadeaux.

we go to midnight mass:
on va à la messe de minuit.
we have a Christmas tree:
on a un sapin de Noël.
we play games as a family:
on joue aux jeux en famille.

For how to say 'I am Christian / Muslim etc.' see page 21.

Pour le Ramadan ...

For Ramadan...

we fast for 30 days:
on jeûne pendant trente jours.
we go to the mosque to pray:
on va prier à la mosquée.

## La fête — not all cream teas and maypole dancing...

Thank your lucky stars you don't have to know about all 5000 of France's annual festivals. It's important that you can give details about some sort of celebration, who you celebrate it with and what you do to celebrate. So. Let the festivities (er... I mean revision) commence...

# The Environment

Things get <u>serious</u> when the environment comes up, and you're supposed to have an opinion. It's a chance for you to write or say what you <u>think</u> about something real and <u>important</u>. Go get 'em...

## Il y a de graves problèmes...

Start with the <u>problems</u>...

### — There are some serious problems...

**Il y a trop de** `pollution` **.**   = There's too much <u>pollution</u>.

| | |
|---|---|
| *deforestation:* | déboisement (masc.) |
| *consumption:* | consommation (fem.) |
| *light:* | lumière (fem.) |
| *noise:* | bruit (masc.) |

**On consomme trop de ressources naturelles et d'énergie.**

= We use too many natural resources and too much energy.

**La pollution de l'air par les** `gaz d'échappement` **est un danger pour l'environnement.**

| | |
|---|---|
| *the hole in the ozone layer :* | le trou dans la couche d'ozone |
| *global warming:* | le réchauffement de la terre |
| *the greenhouse effect:* | l'effet de serre (masc.) |
| *overpopulation:* | la surpopulation |
| *deforestation:* | le déboisement |

= <u>Air pollution from exhaust fumes</u> endangers the environment.

**On ne fait pas assez attention aux espèces en voie de disparition.**

= We don't pay enough attention to endangered species.

## Est-ce que l'environnement est important pour toi?

Then talk about <u>your opinions</u>...

### Is the environment important to you?

`NON!`    `OUI!`

**Non,** `ça ne m'intéresse pas du tout` **.**

= No, <u>I'm not at all interested in it.</u>

*I'm not worried about the environment:*
je ne m'inquiète pas au sujet de l'environnement

**Nous n'avons pas le temps de recycler —** `on travaille tout le temps` **.**

= We don't have time to recycle — <u>we work all the time.</u>

*there are other more important things:*
il y a d'autres choses qui sont plus importantes
*governments should find solutions:*
les gouvernements doivent trouver des solutions

**Oui,** `je m'intéresse beaucoup à l'environnement` **.**

= Yes, <u>I'm very interested in the environment.</u>

*I think the environment is very important:*
je pense que l'environnement est très important

**Il y a de la pollution partout** `parce qu'il y a trop d'embouteillages` **.**

= There is pollution everywhere <u>because there are too many traffic jams.</u>

*we don't recycle as much as we should:*
on ne recycle pas comme il faut
*we use too much packaging:*
on utilise trop d'emballage

## My ideal environment has a TV, a bed and pizza...

There are so many <u>different aspects</u> of the environment you could <u>choose</u> to talk about — or not talk about, if you really couldn't give a monkey's. As always, <u>be wise</u> and learn the <u>basics</u>, eh...

# The Environment

Here's some stuff you can do <u>in the home</u> and in the <u>local area</u> to help the environment.

## À la maison... — In the home...

**On pourrait** ... = We could...

recycle packaging instead of throwing it away:
recycler les emballages au lieu de les jeter
grow vegetables in the garden:
cultiver des légumes dans le jardin

turn off the light / television / heating:
éteindre la lumière / la télévision / le chauffage
use less water / packaging:
utiliser moins d'eau / d'emballage
sort our rubbish:
trier nos déchets

Here are some things you can <u>recycle</u>:

box / tin: la boîte　plastic bag: le sac en plastique　packaging: les emballages (masc.)
cardboard box: le carton　rubbish: les ordures (fem.) / les déchets (masc.)　bottles: les bouteilles (fem.)

## Dans les environs... — In the local area...

**On devrait** ... = We should...

buy products with recyclable packaging:
acheter des produits aux emballages recyclables
find the nearest recycling centre:
trouver le centre de recyclage le plus proche

share the journey to work with friends:
partager le voyage au travail avec des ami(e)s
use public transport to travel to school:
utiliser les transports en commun pour voyager au lycée
create more pedestrian zones:
créer plus de zones piétonnes
build more cycle lanes: construire plus de pistes cyclables

This sentence uses the conditional. See page 107 for more on this.

*Si on conduisait moins, il y aurait moins d'émissions, et moins de pluies acides.*

= If we drove less, there would be fewer emissions and less acid rain.

☆ Extra marks for style

## À l'avenir... — In the future...

Who knows what the <u>future</u> holds...

À l'avenir, *il n'y aura plus de pétrole* . = In the future, <u>there will be no more oil.</u>

we will not have any more natural resources:
on n'aura plus de ressources naturelles
we will use renewable energy sources (wind and solar):
on utilisera des énergies renouvelables (éolienne et solaire)
the world will be even more overpopulated:
le monde sera encore plus surpeuplé
we will have to reduce carbon dioxide emissions:
il faudra réduire les émissions de gaz carbonique

These sentences are written in the future tense. See page 100 for more on this.

*Nous devons protéger l'environnement.
Sinon, nos enfants souffriront terriblement.*

= We must protect the environment. Otherwise, our children will suffer terribly.

☆ Extra marks for style

# Pollution? Load of rubbish...

These pages are <u>hard</u> — there's loads of <u>vocab</u>, and most of it isn't everyday stuff. Still, just think how you'll kick yourself if it comes up in the exam and you haven't learnt it. Shudder.

# *Revision Summary*

Yippee.  I don't really know why I said that.  I think I was trying to put a positive spin on a rather rubbish situation...  It's another revision summary.  You have to do this part to prepare yourself fully for exam time.  Do the questions.  Get 'em right.  Move on with your life.  Or do Section Six — it's all about school and jobs and other extremely uplifting topics.  Yay.

1) You've arrived in Boulogne and are writing to your penfriend Marie-Claire about the sights.  How do you say there's a castle, a swimming pool, a university, a cinema, a cathedral and a theatre?

2) Write down five shops and five other buildings you might find in a town (not the ones above).

3) You need to go to the chemist's.  How do you ask where it is, and if it's far away?

4) What do these directions mean: 'La pharmacie est à un kilomètre d'ici.  Tournez à droite, prenez la première rue à gauche et allez tout droit, devant l'église.  La pharmacie est à droite, entre la banque et le cinéma.'

5) A French tourist has come to see your home town and is looking for the youth hostel.
Tell him to go straight on, turn left at the traffic lights and the youth hostel is on the left.

6) Tell your French penfriend Jean-Jacques where you live, whereabouts it is (which country and whether it's north-east etc.) and what it's like...

7) Say that you like living in your town, there's loads to do and it's quite clean.

8) Say your address and describe the place where you live — is it a town or a village, is the landscape nice, how many people live there, and who do you live with?

9) Your French friend Marie says: 'J'habite avec mes parents et mon frère.  J'aime habiter en famille parce que je peux parler de mes inquiétudes avec quelqu'un.'  What does she mean?

10) Marie-Françoise lives in a big, modern house.  It's near the town centre, shops and a motorway.  How would she say this in French?

11) Write down the names of four rooms in the house and four describing words.  Use these words to create at least 8 sentences to describe the rooms in your house, e.g. La cuisine est jolie.

12) Tom has his own room.  He has red walls and a brown wardrobe in his bedroom.  He has a bed, a mirror, and some curtains.  He doesn't have an armchair.  How will he say all this in French?

13) Quels festivals fêtes-tu?  Quand est-ce que tu les fêtes?  Où est-ce que tu fêtes, et avec qui?  Qu'est-ce que tu fais pour célébrer?

14) Est-ce que l'environnement est important pour toi?  Pourquoi?

15) Sofie's worried about global warming.  Give your views on the problems facing the environment.

16) There's no stopping Sofie — she's just told you she'd like to live in a remote wooden hut and be at one with nature.  Suggest some more realistic options for saving the environment.  You'll need to mention at least six — she's very set on the wooden hut idea.

# School Subjects

There's no way to avoid school and jobs, however much they stress you out. <u>Learn</u> this well — <u>stress</u> less.

## Tu fais quelles matières? — What subjects do you study?

Go over these subjects until you know them <u>all</u> really well...

**SCIENCES**

| | |
|---|---|
| *science:* | les sciences (fem.) |
| *physics:* | la physique |
| *chemistry:* | la chimie |
| *biology:* | la biologie |

**NUMBERS AND STUFF**

| | |
|---|---|
| *maths:* | les mathématiques (fem.), les maths (fem.) |
| *IT:* | l'informatique (fem.) |

**ARTS AND CRAFTS**

| | |
|---|---|
| *art:* | le dessin |
| *music:* | la musique |
| *drama:* | l'art dramatique (masc.) |

**PHYSICAL EDUCATION**

*P.E.:* l'éducation physique (fem.) / le sport / l'EPS (fem.)

**LANGUAGES**

| | |
|---|---|
| *French:* | le français |
| *German:* | l'allemand (masc.) |
| *Spanish:* | l'espagnol (masc.) |
| *Italian:* | l'italien (masc.) |
| *English:* | l'anglais (masc.) |

**HUMANITIES**

| | |
|---|---|
| *history:* | l'histoire (fem.) |
| *geography:* | la géographie |
| *D&T:* | les travaux manuels (masc.) |
| *religious studies:* | l'éducation religieuse (fem.) |
| *PSHE:* | l'instruction civique (fem.) |

*I study:*
J'étudie → **J'apprends** *le français.* = **I'm learning** French.

## Quelle est ta matière préférée?

OK, school stuff may not be exciting, but you <u>definitely</u> need to know it.

## — What's your favourite subject?

*I don't like:* Je n'aime pas
*I hate:* Je déteste → **J'aime** *les maths*. = **I like** <u>maths</u>.

You can put any school subject in the white boxes.

**Je préfère** *la biologie*. = I prefer <u>biology</u>.

**Ma matière préférée est** *le sport*. = <u>PE</u> is my favourite subject.

There's more on how to say what you like and don't like on pages 7–8.

## Depuis quand...? — How long...?

This isn't here because I like it. It's here because it could be in <u>your assessments</u>. So <u>learn it</u>.

**Depuis quand <u>apprends</u>-tu le français?** = How long have you been learning French?

Be careful to use the present tense — you don't say 'I have been' as in English. See pages 98-99.

For more on numbers, see page 1.

**J'<u>apprends</u> le français depuis trois ans.** = I've been learning French for three years.

## Midget "j'aime"s — my favourite sweets...

Play around with this page until you've got it firmly lodged in your brain. Make sure you <u>know</u> all the subjects you do really well, and <u>understand</u> the ones you don't do when you see or hear them.

# The School Routine

Not the most exciting of pages ever, but it's <u>worth</u> all the effort when you get <u>tricky questions</u> on <u>school routine</u>.  Go for <u>short</u> snappy sentences — that way, they're easier to <u>remember</u>.

## Comment vas-tu au collège? — How do you get to school?

This bit's <u>basic</u> — know the basics...

*by bus:* en bus     *by bike:* à vélo

Use 'au lycée' or 'au collège' for 'to school'. For more on forms of transport, see page 45.

Je vais au collège **en voiture** .

= I go to school <u>by car</u>.

Je vais au collège à pied.

= I go to school on foot.

## L'horaire — The timetable

It's important you know how to describe a <u>school day</u> — une <u>journée scolaire</u>.

You're right, this timetable is a bit much.

*finish:* finissent

Les cours **commencent** à neuf heures.

= Lessons <u>begin</u> at 9.00.

For more on times, see page 2.

Nous avons huit cours par jour.

= We have 8 lessons per day.

Chaque cours dure trente minutes.

= Each lesson lasts 30 minutes.

Nous faisons une heure de devoirs par jour.

= We do one hour of homework a day.

*Lunch break:* La pause déjeuner    La récréation est à onze heures.

= <u>Break</u> is at 11.00.

*I talk with friends:*  Je parle avec mes ami(e)s
*I do my homework:*  Je fais mes devoirs
*I play football:*  Je joue au football
*I go in the computer room:*  Je vais dans la salle d'informatique

Je mange un fruit dans la cour pendant la récré.

= <u>I eat a piece of fruit</u> in the playground at break time.

## L'année scolaire — The school year

This is all a bit more <u>tricky</u> but, if you want a top mark, you need to <u>learn it</u>.

Il y a trois trimestres.

= There are three terms.

Slow motion made the school year pass even more slowly...

Nous avons **six semaines** de vacances **en été** .

= We have <u>six weeks</u>' holiday <u>in the summer</u>.

*eight weeks:* huit semaines     *five days:* cinq jours     *at Christmas:* à Noël     *at Easter:* à Pâques

**J'adore** la rentrée parce que **...**

= <u>I love</u> the start of the new school year because...

*I hate:* Je déteste

*I can't wait to see my friends:*          j'ai hâte de voir mes ami(e)s.
*I feel ready to go back to school:*      je me sens prêt(e) à revenir au lycée.
*I have no desire to study again:*        je n'ai aucun désir de recommencer mes études.

## "How did you do that?" — No 'comment'...

Don't forget the phrases for your exciting <u>school routine</u>, and the sentences for saying how you <u>go</u> to school.  Remember the handy phrase '<u>par jour</u>' — you can stick it in loads of sentences.

# More School Stuff

OK, I know this school stuff is a bit close to home and it's a bit boring. (Well, properly boring actually.) But it's revision — it's unlikely to ever get really good. Power through and you'll reap exam rewards galore.

## Portez-vous un uniforme? — Do you wear a uniform?

You may have to understand others talking about the differences between schools in the UK and in France...

*Les élèves anglais portent d'habitude un uniforme à l'école.*

= English students usually wear a uniform to school.

See page 36 for more on clothes and colours.

*Notre uniforme est un pull rouge, un pantalon gris, une chemise blanche et une cravate verte.*

= Our uniform is a red jumper, grey trousers, a white shirt and a green tie.

| | |
|---|---|
| *we go to nursery school from the age of 3 to 6:* | on va à la maternelle de l'âge de trois à six ans |
| *we go to secondary school from the age of 11 to 15:* | on va au collège de l'âge d'onze à quinze ans |
| *we study for the 'baccalauréat' at a 'lycée':* | on étudie pour le bac au lycée |
| *we have to go there on Saturday mornings:* | on doit y aller le samedi matin. |
| *the school day is longer:* | la journée scolaire est plus longue. |

*En France,* on ne va pas au collège le mercredi après-midi.

= In France, we don't go to school on Wednesday afternoons.

For more information on times, see page 2.

## Les règles sont strictes — The rules are strict

*On n'a pas le droit de* parler dans les couloirs.

= We're not allowed to talk in the corridors.

| | | | |
|---|---|---|---|
| *go in the staff room:* | entrer dans la salle des profs | *wear jewellery:* | porter des bijoux |
| *write on the (interactive) whiteboard:* | écrire sur le tableau blanc (intéractif) | *eat in the lab:* | manger au laboratoire |

*En France,* on doit passer un examen à l'âge de quinze ans.   16 : seize ans

*In Great Britain:* En Grande-Bretagne

= In France, we have to take an exam at the age of 15.

*On appelle cet examen* le brevet.   = This exam's called the 'brevet'.

*A-Level equivalent:* le baccalauréat / le bac

French students take the 'brevet' at the age of 15, and the 'baccalauréat' at 18.

## Mes affaires — My stuff

Learn this list of stuff you find in your school bag — and I'm not talking about half-eaten sandwiches, an unwashed P.E. kit, or the crumpled-up newsletter you should have given your mum last week.

| | | | | | |
|---|---|---|---|---|---|
| *biro:* | un bic | *felt-tip pen:* | un feutre | *pen:* | un stylo |
| *pencil:* | un crayon | *scissors:* | des ciseaux (masc.) | *calculator:* | une calculatrice |
| *rubber:* | une gomme | *ruler:* | une règle | *exercise book:* | un cahier |

## School rules — not as far as I'm concerned...

Details, details and more details — they're vital for this section. Close the book and see how many you can remember — the more you can reel off about your school, the better. It's weird, but French 'teens' will love to hear about your uniform, since they don't have them — pretty unfair.

# Classroom Language

We all have our 'off' days, so it's really <u>useful</u> to be able to ask someone to <u>repeat</u> something, or <u>spell out</u> a word you're not sure about.

## Asseyez-vous! — Sit down!

<u>Learn</u> these 6 phrases to avoid teacherly wrath. The '<u>vous</u>' ones are <u>formal</u> and the '<u>tu</u>' ones are <u>informal</u>.

| Levez-vous! | = Stand up! | Asseyez-vous! | = Sit down! | Taisez-vous! | = Be quiet! |
| Lève-toi! | = Stand up! | Assieds-toi! | = Sit down! | Tais-toi! | = Be quiet! |

## Parlez-vous français? — Do you speak French?

We all make <u>mistakes</u> and <u>misunderstand</u> things sometimes, but if you can ask for help you just might never make the same mistake twice. So this stuff can <u>help</u> you <u>understand</u> better — it's really worth <u>learning</u>.

Comment est-ce qu'on prononce ça? = How do you pronounce that?

Comment ça s'écrit? = How do you spell that?

Comment est-ce qu'on dit ça en français? = How do you say that in French?

Pouvez-vous répéter, s'il vous plaît? = Can you repeat that, please?

## If you don't understand, say 'Je ne comprends pas'

These phrases can be <u>vital</u> in your <u>speaking assessments</u>. Even if the worst happens, it's far better to say 'I don't understand' <u>in French</u> than to shrug, give a cheesy smile and mumble something in English.

Je (ne) comprends (pas). = I (don't) understand.

Qu'est-ce que ça veut dire? = What does that mean?

Can you (informal): Peux-tu → Pouvez-vous expliquer ce mot? = <u>Can you</u> explain this word? (formal)

## Est-ce que j'ai fait une erreur? — Did I make a mistake?

| Je ne sais pas. | = I don't know. | Je me suis trompé(e). | = I was wrong. |
| C'est vrai. | = That's right. | C'est faux. | = That's wrong. |
| Tu as raison. | = You're right. | Tu as tort. | = You're wrong. |

## "Comment ça s'écrit?" — "Ç-A"

You can <u>save</u> yourself from an embarrassing silence by asking the person you're talking to if they can repeat or clarify something — there's no shame in it. All you have to do is learn these <u>dead useful</u> phrases. Remember, bouts of forgetfulness happen to everyone — <u>DON'T PANIC</u>.

# Problems at School

If you're anything like me, you'll love to <u>complain</u> about stuff — this is your chance. This page gives you all manner ways to vent school-related <u>stresses</u> and <u>gripes</u>. Go on, folks — indulge...

## J'en ai assez... — I've had enough of it...

Est-ce que tout se passe bien au lycée?

= Is everything going well at school?

Oui, tout va bien.

= Yes, everything's going well.

Non, j'ai beaucoup de problèmes à l'école...

= No, I've got lots of problems at school...

J'ai de bonnes notes mais je ne peux pas sortir avec mes ami(e)s parce que je n'ai jamais le temps.

= I get good marks, but I can't go out with my friends because I never have time.

Au collège, il faut toujours se dépêcher et les explications sont toujours trop rapides pour moi.

*I have difficulties understanding:* j'ai des difficultés à comprendre
*I'm under pressure:* je suis sous pression

= At school, we always have to rush and <u>the explanations are always too quick for me</u>.

*failing:* d'échouer

Je crains de devoir redoubler.

= I fear <u>having to repeat a year</u>.

On doit porter un uniforme démodé et on n'a pas le droit de porter du maquillage.

= We have to wear an old-fashioned uniform and we aren't allowed to wear make-up.

## Je suis stressé(e) — I'm stressed

Je travaille dur mais ce n'est jamais assez pour mes parents.

= I work hard, but it's never enough for my parents.

Mes parents sont stricts. Je dois étudier tout le temps.

= My parents are strict. I have to study all the time.

Les profs ne m'aiment pas et me mettent toujours en retenue.

= The teachers don't like me and always put me in detention.

Il faut toujours porter des vêtements de marque et ça coûte vraiment cher.

= You always have to wear brand-name clothes and it's really expensive.

I have to study all the time for the exams.

## Assez 'stressed', you say 'out' — Stressed, out, stressed, out

Frankly, it would be dull if everyone said everything was great all the time. This stuff's tricky, but really <u>worth learning</u>. Then you can get it <u>all</u> off your chest, just like a proper <u>therapy</u> session.

# Work Experience

These pages make you think even more about your <u>future</u> — it's nearly a public service. If you can't see your future without the aid of a crystal ball, then start exercising your <u>imagination</u>.

## As-tu fait un stage? — Have you done work experience?

Work experience is <u>great</u> — I remember my week spent bored to death in a certain high street bank...

**J'ai fait mon stage en entreprise chez** `Peugeot` **.**

= I did my work experience at <u>Peugeot</u>.

*Put any company name here.*

**J'y ai travaillé pendant une semaine, du deux au sept mars.**

= I worked there for a week, from 2nd to 7th March.

**Je** `n'ai jamais` **fait un stage.**

*haven't yet:* n'ai pas encore

= I <u>have never</u> done work experience.

## Est-ce que tu as aimé le travail? — Did you like the work?

More <u>opinions</u> wanted here...

**Le travail était** `amusant` **.**

= The work was <u>fun</u>.

*stressful:* stressant
*interesting:* intéressant

*were friendly:* étaient sympathiques
*were interesting:* étaient intéressants

*comfortable:* confortable

**Je me suis senti(e)** `seul(e)` **.**

= I felt <u>lonely</u>.

**Mes collègues de travail** `n'étaient pas sympa` **.**

= My colleagues <u>were unfriendly</u>.

## C'est une journée très longue... — It's a very long day...

Imagine that your work experience job is your <u>career</u> for life. Does that change your <u>opinions</u>?

**Les** `conditions` **sont** `terribles` **.**

= The <u>conditions</u> are <u>terrible</u>.

*hours:* horaires (masc.)

*comfortable:* confortables

*fantastic:* fantastiques

*It is:* C'est ▷ **Ce n'est pas** **très bien payé.**

= <u>It's not</u> very well paid.

## J'ai un emploi à mi-temps — I have a part-time job

Make these easier by choosing <u>easy-to-say</u> jobs and <u>simple</u> values — if only the rest of life was like that.

**J'ai** `un travail à mi-temps` **.**

= I've got <u>a part-time job</u>.

*holiday / temporary job:* un emploi temporaire

*£15 per week:* quinze livres par semaine

**Je gagne** `cinq livres par heure` **.**

= I earn <u>£5 per hour</u>.

**Je suis** `boucher/bouchère` **.**

= I am <u>a butcher</u>.

## Are you experienced?...

You <u>might</u> have to comment on your <u>work experience</u> or part-time <u>jobs</u> in the speaking assessment. Talk about anything work-related that you've done in your life, and give your <u>opinions</u> about it too.

# Plans for the Future

If your idea of future plans is what you're doing next weekend, then try thinking a bit further ahead...

## La vie après les examens... — Life after the exams...

There are loads of things to do after GCSEs. Here's the basic vocab.

**Je voudrais** preparer le bac.

= I would like to do A-levels.

*'Bac' is short for 'baccalauréat', the French equivalent of A-levels — except that they do more subjects than we do.*

*to study geography:* étudier la géographie.
*to continue my studies:* continuer mes études.

*I already have some good friends there:*
j'ai déjà de bon(ne)s ami(e)s là.
*I'll be able to concentrate on my favourite subjects:*
je pourrai me concentrer sur mes matières préférées.

**J'ai choisi d'entrer en première au lycée parce que** ...

= I've chosen to go into the Sixth Form because...

**J'ai pris la décision de quitter l'école.**

= I've made the decision to leave school.

**Je voudrais** faire un stage en entreprise.

= I'd like to do a placement at a company.

*to take a year out:* prendre une année sabbatique
*to get married and have children:* me marier et avoir des enfants

**Je vais chercher un emploi.**

= I'm going to look for a job.

If you'd like to do a particular job after school, use some of the vocabulary from page 73.

**Je voyagerai.**

= I will travel.

## Always say Why you want to do something

When you're commenting on your future plans, give a reason for them each time.
For example, 'I want to take a year out so that I can travel'.

**Je voudrais étudier** la musique **, parce que je veux devenir** musicien(ne) **plus tard.**

*accountant:* comptable      *teacher:* prof(esseur)

*Remember to get the gender (le or la) right for the school subjects. Refresh your memory on page 68.*

= I would like to study music, because I want to be a musician afterwards.

**Je voudrais préparer le bac car après je veux étudier la biologie à l'université.**

= I would like to do A-levels because afterwards I want to study biology at university.

## Life after GCSE — hard to imagine....

I know GCSE French seems like a scary mystery, but this sort of stuff comes up year after year...
Learn all this and you'll be laughing. Use words like 'je voudrais' and 'parce que' for extra marks.

# Types of Job

There are more jobs here than you can shake a stick at — and you do need to recognise all of them because any of the little blighters could pop up in your listening and reading exams.

## Female versions of jobs can be tricky

Often, job titles in French are different for men and women. You need to recognise both versions...

### Masculine/Feminine

Watch out for the feminine versions of jobs — although there are lots which just add an 'e' in the feminine, some follow different rules. For example, '-er' often becomes 'ère', '-teur' often becomes '-trice' (but watch out for chanteur/chanteuse), and '-eur' often becomes '-euse'. If you're not sure, check in a dictionary.

| Le musicien (masc.) | La musicienne (fem.) | = Musician |
| Le boucher (masc.) | La bouchère (fem.) | = Butcher |
| L'acteur (masc.) | L'actrice (fem.) | = Actor / actress |
| Le coiffeur (masc.) | La coiffeuse (fem.) | = Hairdresser |

## The gender of a job depends on who is doing it

To be on the safe side, best learn to recognise these too...

The gender of the job is masculine (le) for a man and feminine (la) for a woman — except for 'médecin', 'docteur', 'plombier', 'pompier', 'ingénieur' and 'mannequin', which are always masculine.

### GREY-SUIT-TYPE JOBS

| accountant: | le/la comptable |
| secretary: | le/la secrétaire |
| architect: | l'architecte (masc./fem.) |
| lawyer/solicitor: | l'avocat(e) |
| manager: | le/la gérant(e) |

I've been soliciting for 20 years now, and it hasn't got me anywhere.

### A LOAD MORE JOBS

| salesperson: | le vendeur, la vendeuse |
| waiter/waitress: | le serveur, la serveuse |
| journalist: | le/la journaliste |
| head teacher: | le directeur, la directrice |
| policeman/woman: | le/la gendarme / le policier, la policière |
| fireman/woman: | le pompier |
| soldier: | le soldat, la soldate |
| postman/woman: | le facteur, la factrice |
| primary teacher: | l'instituteur, l'institutrice |
| air hostess/ | l'hôtesse de l'air (fem.), |
| air steward: | le steward de l'air |
| receptionist: | l'hôte d'accueil (masc.), l'hôtesse d'accueil (fem.) |
| computer scientist: | l'informaticien(ne) |
| cashier: | le caissier, la caissière |
| model: | le mannequin |

### GET-YOUR-HANDS-DIRTY JOBS

| mechanic: | le mécanicien, la mécanicienne |
| electrician: | l'électricien, l'électricienne |
| plumber: | le plombier |
| chef: | le cuisinier, la cuisinière |
| baker: | le boulanger, la boulangère |
| farmer: | le fermier, la fermière |
| gardener: | le jardinier, la jardinière |
| labourer: | l'ouvrier, l'ouvrière |
| engineer: | l'ingénieur |

### MEDICAL JOBS

| dentist: | le/la dentiste |
| chemist: | le pharmacien, la pharmacienne |
| nurse: | l'infirmier, l'infirmière |
| doctor: | le médecin |
| vet: | le/la vétérinaire |

### OTHER JOB SITUATIONS

| student: | l'étudiant(e) |
| part-time worker: | l'employé(e) à mi-temps |
| unemployed person: | le chômeur / la chômeuse |
| apprentice: | l'apprenti(e) |

### ARTY JOBS

| writer: | l'écrivain, l'écrivaine |
| designer: | le dessinateur, la dessinatrice |

## Good job you've learnt all this...

Not nice. But start with the jobs you find easiest — then learn the rest. All the female versions too — ooh, I don't envy you. But think how knowledgeable you'll be at the end of it all.

# Jobs: Advantages and Disadvantages

What a page title... It pretty much sums up what's _important_ here, I think.

## Say what job you'd like to do and why

**Use 'devenir' (to become) to say what job you'd like to do.**

State the job you'd like to do with a _short_ and _simple_ reason why — easy.

_I hope:_ J'espère → **Je voudrais devenir médecin, ...** | = _I would like_ to become a doctor, ...

**IMPORTANT:** In French you DON'T use 'un'/'une' when you're talking about a job you have or want to have.

**... parce que le travail serait intéressant .** | See page 75 for more jobs.

_varied:_ varié    _fun:_ amusant    _easy:_ facile

= ... because the work would be _interesting_.

**Dans mon travail, je voudrais résoudre des problèmes .** | = In my job, I'd like _to solve problems_.

_work with people/numbers:_ travailler avec les gens/les chiffres

## Je n'aimerais pas être... — I wouldn't like to be...

**Je n'aimerais pas être avocat(e) .** | = I wouldn't like to be a _lawyer_.

**Je serais toujours fatigué(e) .** | You can put any job from page 75 here.

= I'd always be _tired_. | _unhappy:_ malheureux(euse)   _stressed:_ stressé(e)   _under pressure:_ surchargé(e)

**Le travail serait trop difficile.** | = The work would be too difficult.

**Les heures au bureau seraient trop longues.** | = The hours _in the office_ would be too long.

_at work:_ au travail   _in the classroom:_ dans la salle de classe   _in the operating theatre:_ dans la salle d'opération

## Je préférerais travailler comme... — I'd prefer to work as...

**Je préférerais devenir écrivain(e) .** | = I would prefer to become a _writer_.

For comparisons with 'more' or 'less', see page 89. | You can put any job from page 75 here.

**Ce serait plus intéressant et moins stressant.** | = It'd be more interesting and less stressful.

See pages 85-87 for more adjectives.

**J'aurais l'occasion de voyager .** | = I'd have the chance _to travel_.

_to be creative:_ d'être créatif / créative   _to work with animals:_ de travailler avec des animaux
_to be myself:_ d'être moi-même   _to work in a hospital:_ de travailler dans un hôpital

## I'll take the pros and leave the cons...

Valuable stuff. Saying _what job_ you want to do and _why_ is pretty _essential_. If the truth's too hard to say, e.g. you want a job in inverse-polarity-dynamo maintenance, then say something _simpler_. Don't forget these little bits and pieces for the assessments — they could be useful...

# Working Abroad

Fed up of working in the same old country?  Why not try another...

## Tu voudrais travailler à l'étranger? — Would you like to work abroad?

The world's your oyster...

**J'aimerais faire un stage en entreprise [en France].**

= I would like to do a work placement <u>in France</u>.

**Je vais travailler chez un fleuriste à Aix-en-Provence. Ce métier m'intéresse beaucoup.**

= I'm going to work at a florist's in Aix-en-Provence.  I'm really interested in this kind of work.

See page 42 for a list of countries.  Remember 'au' for masculine countries ('en' if starting with a vowel), and 'aux' when it's plural.

## Je voudrais prendre une année sabbatique en France — I'd like to take a gap year in France

...or should I say your huître...

**Après le bac, je veux aller en France pour [ ... ] .**

= After A-levels, I want to go to France to ...

**Je voudrais voir le monde avant de continuer mes études.**

= I would like to see the world before continuing my education.

| | |
|---|---|
| étudier à l'université: | *study at university* |
| faire une formation professionnelle: | *do some professional training* |
| travailler dans un bar: | *work in a bar* |
| travailler dans une station de ski: | *work in a ski resort* |
| être au pair: | *be an au pair* |
| voir le pays et rencontrer des gens: | *see the country and meet people* |

## J'ai passé une année magnifique — I had a brilliant year

People talking about a gap year — this could <u>easily</u> come up in the exam.

**Je n'avais pas de salaire, donc je n'avais pas d'argent pour [m'amuser] .**

= I didn't get paid, so I didn't have any money to <u>enjoy myself</u>.

| | |
|---|---|
| *travel around:* | voyager |
| *go out in the evening:* | sortir le soir |
| *buy a car:* | acheter une voiture |

**C'était une très belle expérience.  Et ce sera une bonne chose pour ma carrière, je pense.**

= It was a really good experience.  And it will be a good thing for my career, I think.

**Le boulot ne m'a pas beaucoup plu, mais mes collègues étaient formidables.**

= I didn't like the work much, but my colleagues were great.

## Never have a gap year in a leap year...

A gap year may not be for you, but have a think about it and make sure you have an <u>opinion</u> one way or the other.  Also, it might come up in the <u>listening</u> or <u>reading</u> exams, so you can't ignore it.

# Getting a Job

Hate to break it to you, but stuff on getting a job could come up <u>anywhere</u> in the exam/assessments.

## Je cherche un emploi... — I'm looking for a job...

Je cherche un emploi dans un hôtel .

= I'm looking for a job in <u>a hotel</u>.

See page 1 for more numbers.

| a restaurant: | un restaurant | an office: | un bureau |
| a leisure centre: | un centre de loisirs | a shop: | un magasin |

J'ai déjà deux ans d'expérience.

= I already have <u>two</u> years' experience.

Je serais idéal(e) pour ce poste parce que je suis bilingue .

= I'd be ideal for this job because <u>I'm bilingual</u>.

I speak English / French / Italian / Spanish:
je parle anglais / français / italien / espagnol.
I like working with children / animals / the public:
j'aime travailler avec les enfants / les animaux / les gens.
I have lots of experience: j'ai beaucoup d'expérience.

I am practical:          je suis pratique
I am hard-working:       je suis travailleur / travailleuse
I am always bubbly:      je suis toujours plein(e) de vie
I am never impolite:     je ne suis jamais impoli(e)

## On cherche... — We are looking for...

See page 19 for more character traits.

Offre d'emploi:
On cherche un serveur / une serveuse.
Lundi et vendredi soir.
19 - 21:00

Vous aimez travailler avec les animaux?
On cherche un(e) assistant(e).
20 heures par semaine.
Appelez Jean au
033 12-24-38-42

On cherche quelqu'un pratique, travailleur(euse), honnête et aimable pour vendre et organiser.
Entrez pour plus d'infos.

= Wanted:
We're looking for a waiter/waitress.
Monday and Friday evening.
7 - 9pm.

= Do you like working with animals?
We're looking for an assistant.
20 hours per week.
Call Jean on 033 12-24-38-42

= We're looking for someone practical, hard-working, honest and nice to sell products and organise.
Come in for more info.

## J'aimerais poser ma candidature — I'd like to apply

So, you've <u>applied</u>. Hopefully they'll <u>call back</u> and say something like this:

Est-ce que vous pouvez venir pour un entretien ...

= Can you come <u>for an interview</u>...

the boss: le / la patron(ne)

and meet us: nous rencontrer

... lundi, le 14 février à 10h?

... avec Monsieur LeBrun ...

= ... on Monday, 14th February at 10am?

= with <u>Mr LeBrun</u>

Apportez une copie de votre CV , s'il vous plaît.

| a photo: | une photo |
| your passport: | votre passeport (masc.) |
| your driving licence: | votre permis de conduire (masc.) |

= Please bring <u>a copy of your CV</u>.

# I'm perfect because I'm blingin' — oops, bilingue

It's useful stuff this — <u>rip</u> this <u>page</u> out, tuck it in your rucksack and you could go and get a <u>summer job</u> in Paris. No ripping 'til you've <u>learnt</u> it, though — you've got exams to pass first...

# Getting a Job

Good <u>covering letter</u>, dazzling <u>CV</u>, nice <u>tie</u>, job's <u>yours</u>.

## J'ai lu votre annonce — I read your advertisement

Every job application needs a good letter...

Rachael Johnson
46 Loxley Road,
Ambridge,
Borsetshire.  BO12 2AM

Madame de Villiers
Commerce Tapisserie,
19 rue du Conquérant,
14066 Bayeux

Madame,                              Bayeux, le 8 février 2009

J'ai lu votre annonce dans *Le Monde* hier, et je voudrais poser ma candidature pour le poste de Chef de Projet.

Vous verrez dans mon CV ci-joint que ma carrière a été variée, puisque j'ai travaillé dans les secteurs privé et publique.  Je pense que j'ai l'expérience nécessaire pour ce rôle.

Ce poste m'intéresse beaucoup, et je suis disponible pour un entretien dès que vous le souhaiterez.

Je vous prie d'agréer, Madame, l'expression de mes sentiments distingués.

Rachael Johnson

See p.11 for more on writing formal letters.

I read your advertisement in *Le Monde* yesterday, and I would like to apply for the position of Project Manager.

You will see in my attached CV that my career has been varied, as I have worked in the private and public sectors.  I think that I have the necessary experience for this role.

I am very interested in this position, and I am available for an interview as soon as you wish.

## Vous verrez dans mon CV ci-joint...

And every applicant needs a good CV...

## — You will see in my CV attached...

### CURRICULUM VITAE

Rachael Johnson
46 Loxley Road, Ambridge, Borsetshire.  BO12 2AM
Téléphone 02 40 54 10 66
Nationalité anglaise

ÉDUCATION
1998:   Licence d'Histoire (première classe)
1995:   A-levels (équivalence Baccalauréat):
          Histoire (B), Anglais (B), Mathématiques (C)

EXPÉRIENCE PROFESSIONNELLE
Depuis 2005:  Gérante de ventes chez 'Sales Albion', Loxley.
1998-2005:    Fonctionnaire

AUTRES RENSEIGNEMENTS
Programme de formation d'informatique (mars 2007)
Permis de conduire
Je parle couramment anglais, français et gallois.

EDUCATION
1998: History degree (first class)
1995: A-levels (equivalent to Bac)
        History (B), English (B), Maths (C)

PROFESSIONAL EXPERIENCE
Since 2005: Sales manager at 'Sales Albion', Loxley.
1998-2005: Civil servant

OTHER INFORMATION
Training course in IT (March 2007)
Driving licence
I speak fluent English, French and Welsh.

## Et une belle cravate...

Work — a necessary part of life, alas, and a necessary part of GCSE French.  Work/job-related tasks could crop up <u>anywhere</u>, so it's a good idea to get all this stuff well and truly <u>off pat</u>.

# Telephones

You have to know French phone vocab and understand messages and stuff — it's simple. No. Really it is.

## Je dois faire un appel — I have to make a phone call

This is easy marks — learn it...

Use 'ton' for someone you know well.
If you need to be more formal, use 'votre'.

See page 1 for all the numbers.

Quel est **ton** numéro de téléphone?  = What is your telephone number?

Mon numéro de téléphone est le **vingt-huit, dix-neuf, cinquante-six** . = My telephone number is **28 19 56**.

Phone numbers are always given in 2-digit numbers, e.g. twenty-eight rather than two-eight. And don't ask me why they stick a 'le' in front of it — they just do.

the right area code: le bon indicatif

Vous n'avez pas **le bon numéro** . = You don't have the right number.

## When you make a call, say 'ici Bob' — 'It's Bob here'

You need to be able to understand the general phone vocab used in France...

You might hear this when someone answers the phone:

Allô! C'est **Philippe** à l'appareil. = Hello! **Philippe** speaking.

These questions are common phone enquiries:

Est-ce que **Bob** est là? = Is **Bob** there?

Est-ce que je peux parler à **Joanie** ? = Can I speak to **Joanie**?

These are common phone responses:

to her: la

Je vous **le** passe. = I'll put you through to him.

Je vous écoute. = I'm listening.

Allô?

Allô?

These are common conversation closers:

À bientôt. = See you soon.   À plus tard. = See you later.   Appelle-moi. = Call me.

## Je voudrais laisser un message — I'd like to leave a message

You have to be able to understand phone messages. This is a typical run-of-the-mill one:

Hello, this is Nicole Smith.

The caller's name should go here.

I have a message for Jean-Claude.

This is who needs to call back.

Allô, ici **Nicole Smith** . J'ai un message pour **Jean-Claude** .
Est-ce qu'il peut me rappeler vers **dix-neuf heures** ce soir?
Mon numéro de téléphone est le **cinquante-neuf,**
**dix-huit, quarante-sept** . Merci beaucoup. Au revoir.

My phone number is 59 18 47.

Can he call me back at around 7pm tonight?

This is the phone number he should return the call to.

Thank you. Goodbye.

This is what time he should call back.

## Le téléphone — sounds phoney to me...

I wouldn't rate your chances with French GCSE if you don't learn this stuff — phones come up pretty frequently. But, with this lot under your belt, you'll have more than a fighting chance.

# The World of Business

Examiners quite like listening and reading scenarios in which people discuss <u>goods</u> and <u>services</u> they need, or are providing. Don't ask me why — just <u>read on</u> and <u>learn</u> the examples.

## Je vais me renseigner — I'll make some enquiries

Knowing how to <u>ask for information</u> is really important. As is <u>understanding the answer</u>.

*Est-ce que vous savez où je peux trouver* *un plombier* *?*

= Do you know where I can find <u>a plumber</u>?

| a dentist | un dentiste |
| a doctor | un médecin |
| a hairdresser | un coiffeur |

*Je vous conseille de chercher* *dans l'annuaire*.

= I advise you to look <u>in the phone book</u>.

| in the yellow pages: | dans les pages jaunes |
| in the post office: | à la poste |
| on the internet: | sur internet |
| at the tourist information office: | à l'office de tourisme |

To 'advise someone to do something' is 'conseiller quelqu'un de faire quelque chose'. See page 99 for more verbs that work in this way.

## Il y a un problème avec ma commande
## — There's a problem with my order

Here's a phone conversation between a <u>customer</u> and a <u>supplier</u>.

### Le vendeur:

"Ordi-vendeur, bonjour."
*Hello, this is Ordi-vendeur.*

Remember: <u>nom</u> = surname, <u>prénom</u> = first name.

"Alors, est-ce que je peux prendre votre nom, s'il vous plaît?"
*Right, can I take your name please?*

"Merci. J'ai trouvé votre commande. Quel est le problème, monsieur?"
*Thank you. I've found your order. What is the problem, sir?*

"Je suis désolé, monsieur. On a eu des problèmes avec notre fournisseur. On peut vous l'envoyer demain après-midi."
*I'm sorry, sir. We've been having some problems with our supplier. We can send it to you tomorrow afternoon.*

"Merci monsieur. Bonne journée."
*Thank you sir. Have a good day.*

### Le client:

"Bonjour monsieur. J'ai commandé un ordinateur la semaine dernière, mais il y a un problème avec la commande."
*Hello sir. I ordered a computer last week, but there's a problem with the order.*

"Oui, c'est Césaire, Henri Césaire."
*Yes, it's Césaire, Henri Césaire.*

See page 32 for more <u>technical vocab</u>.

"Vous m'avez envoyé l'ordinateur, l'écran et la souris, mais je n'ai pas encore reçu le clavier."
*You've sent me the computer, the screen and the mouse, but I haven't yet received the keyboard.*

"Donc je l'aurai après-demain... D'accord, ça ira."
*So I'll have it the day after tomorrow... OK, that'll be all right.*

For more on the <u>future tense</u>, see page 100.

"Merci monsieur. Au revoir."
*Thank you sir. Goodbye.*

## Order? Chaos, more like...

In the exams you're likely to come across vocab and phrases that you've seen before in a <u>completely different context</u>. The important thing is <u>not</u> to let the different scenarios <u>throw</u> you.

# Revision Summary

This is an <u>extremely important</u> page. You should <u>stop</u> and spend some minutes here and only trek on when you know all of this stuff effortlessly. OK, rant over. Now just learn this stuff, then go and have a nice cold drink and play on one of those new-fangled games consoles...

1) Say what all your GCSE subjects are in French. I guess one of them will be 'le français'...

2) What's your favourite subject? What subject(s) don't you like? Answer in French.

3) Depuis quand apprends-tu le français? Translate the question. And then answer it in French.

4) How would you say that your lunch break begins at 12.30pm and that you eat salad and then play volleyball?

5) How would you say that you have six lessons every day and each lesson lasts 50 minutes?

6) Pete is describing his school to his French penfriend Christophe. How would he say that there are three terms, that he wears a school uniform and that the rules are very strict?

7) Au collège, on n'a pas le droit de porter un pull à capuche et on ne peut pas parler dans les couloirs. Your French friend has just told you this in her latest email. What does she say?

8) Décris-moi ton uniforme.

9) Your teacher has just said a very long sentence in French and you don't understand. What three questions could you ask to help clarify the situation?

10) Stéphanie says, 'J'ai des difficultés à comprendre au collège — les explications sont toujours trop rapides pour moi et je crains de devoir redoubler.' What does she mean?

11) Write a full French sentence explaining where you did your work experience. If you didn't do work experience anywhere then write that down. Also answer: 'As-tu un emploi à mi-temps?'

12) Qu'est-ce que tu voudrais faire après les examens?

13) Tell a French passer-by what you look for in a job, what job you'd most like to do and why.

14) Write down in French that you would like to have a gap year in France in order to see the country and meet people.

15) Complete this tiebreaker question (in no more than 30 French words): Je serais idéal(e) pour ce poste parce que...

16) Translate into French: "He's looking for a job in a restaurant. He has two years' experience."

17) Quel est ton numéro de téléphone? *(No cheating and writing it in numerals — do it in French. And say it out loud.)*

18) What would you say in French when:
   a) you answer the phone in French?          b) you want to put someone through?
   c) you tell someone you'll see them later?   d) you have a message for Daniel Craig?

19) Impress your French teacher by telling them in French that they should look online for a dentist.

## Words for People and Objects

NOUNS

Stop — before you panic, this stuff is a lot less scary than it looks. It's all <u>pretty</u> <u>simple</u> stuff about words for <u>people</u> and <u>objects</u> — nouns. This is <u>really important</u>.

## Every French noun is masculine or feminine

Whether a word is <u>masculine</u>, <u>feminine</u>, <u>singular</u> or <u>plural</u> affects a heck of a lot of things. All '<u>the</u>' and '<u>a</u>' words change and, if that wasn't enough, the adjectives (like 'new', 'shiny') change to fit the word.

**EXAMPLES:** an interesting book: <u>un</u> livre intéressant  (masculine)
an interesting programme: <u>une</u> émission intéressant<u>e</u>  (feminine)

For details on changing stuff like this, see pages 84 and 85.

It's no good just knowing the French words for things — you have to know whether each one's <u>masculine</u> or <u>feminine</u> too...

| THE GOLDEN RULE |
Each time you <u>learn</u> a <u>word</u>, remember a <u>le</u> or <u>la</u> to go with it — don't think 'dog = chien', think 'dog = <u>le</u> chien'.

| LE AND LA |
LE in front of a noun means it's <u>masculine</u>. LA in front = <u>feminine</u>.

## These rules help you guess what gender a word is

If you have to guess whether a word is <u>masculine</u> or <u>feminine</u>, these are good rules of thumb.

**RULES OF THUMB FOR MASCULINE AND FEMININE NOUNS**

**MASCULINE NOUNS:**
most nouns that end:
-age  -er  -eau  -ing  -ment  -ou
-ail  -ier  -et  -isme  -oir  -eil
also: male people, languages, days, months, seasons

**FEMININE NOUNS:**
most nouns that end:
-aine  -ée  -ense  -ie  -ise  -tion
-ance  -elle  -esse  -ière  -sion  -tude
-anse  -ence  -ette  -ine  -té  -ure
also: female people

## Making Nouns Plural

1) Nouns in French are usually made plural by adding an '<u>s</u>' — just like English, really.

e.g.: une orange → des oranges
an orange → oranges

2) But there are always <u>exceptions</u> to the rule in French. Nouns with the endings in the table below have a <u>different</u> plural form — and this lot are just the beginning.

| Noun ending | Irregular plural ending | Example |
|---|---|---|
| -ail | -aux | travail → **travaux** |
| -al | -aux | journal → **journaux** |
| -eau | -eaux | bureau → **bureaux** |
| -eu | -eux | jeu → **jeux** |
| -ou | -oux | chou → **choux** |

| TOP TIP FOR PLURALS |
Each time you <u>learn</u> a new word, make sure you know <u>how</u> to make it into a plural too.

3) Some nouns have completely irregular plurals, e.g.: œil → yeux (eye → eyes). You'll have to learn these nouns by practising them over and over.

4) Some nouns <u>don't change</u> in the plural. These are usually nouns that end in <u>-s</u>, <u>-x</u> or <u>-z</u>.

5) When you make a noun plural, instead of 'le' or 'la' to say '<u>the</u>', you have to use '<u>les</u>' — see page 84.

*un nez → des nez*
*a nose → noses*
*un os → des os*
*a bone → bones*

un œil   trois yeux

## Gender reassignment — don't try it in the exam...

The bottom line is — <u>every time</u> you learn a word in French, you <u>have</u> to learn whether it's <u>le</u> or <u>la</u>, and how to make it <u>plural</u>. If you get it wrong, you'll <u>lose marks</u> for accuracy — and then I'll cry.

## ARTICLES — 'The' and 'A'

'<u>The</u>' and '<u>a</u>' — you use these words more than a mobile phone. They're tricky. <u>Revise</u> 'em well.

### 'A' — un, une

*Grammar Fans: these are called '<u>Indefinite Articles</u>'.*

1) In English we don't have <u>genders</u> for nouns — simple.
2) In French, you need to know whether a word is <u>masculine</u> or <u>feminine</u>.

| masculine | feminine |
|-----------|----------|
| un | une |

**EXAMPLES:**

Masculine — *J'ai un frère.* = I have a brother.

Feminine — *J'ai une sœur.* = I have a sister.

### 'The' — le, la, l', les

*Grammar Fans: these are called '<u>Definite Articles</u>'.*

1) Like the French for 'a', the word for 'the' is different for <u>masculine</u> and <u>feminine</u>. This one has a <u>plural</u> form as well, though.
2) For words starting with a <u>vowel</u> (a, e, i, o, u) the '<u>le</u>' or '<u>la</u>' are shortened to '<u>l</u>'', e.g. l'orange.
3) Some words starting with an '<u>h</u>', also take '<u>l</u>'' instead of 'le' or 'la'. Sadly there's no rule for this — you just have to learn which ones take 'l'' and which ones take 'le' or 'la'.

*That's an affirmative*
*Absolutely! No doubt at all.*
*100% positive. Couldn't be surer.*

| masculine singular | feminine singular | in front of a vowel /some words beginning with 'h' | masculine or feminine plural |
|--------------------|-------------------|----------------------------------------------------|------------------------------|
| le | la | l' | les |

**EXAMPLES:**

*Le garçon.* = <u>The</u> boy.

*La fille.* = <u>The</u> girl.

*L'homme.* = <u>The</u> man.

*Les hommes.* = <u>The</u> men.

*Le hamster.* = <u>The</u> hamster.

*Les hamsters.* = <u>The</u> hamsters

### 'De' and 'à' change before 'le' and 'les'

1) Weird stuff happens with '<u>à</u>' (to) and '<u>de</u>' (of).
2) You <u>can't</u> say 'à le', 'à les', 'de le' or 'de les'.
3) '<u>À</u>' and '<u>de</u>' combine with '<u>le</u>' and '<u>les</u>' to make new words — '<u>au</u>', '<u>aux</u>', '<u>du</u>' and '<u>des</u>'.

|       | le | la | l' | les |
|-------|----|----|----|-----|
| à +   | au | à la | à l' | aux |
| de +  | du | de la | de l' | des |

**EXAMPLES :**

*Je vais à* + *le café* = *Je vais au café.* = I go to the café.

*Je viens de* + *le Canada* = *Je viens du Canada.* = I come from Canada.

### 'Some' or 'any' — du, de la, de l', des

*Grammar Fans: these are called '<u>Partitive Articles</u>'.*

These don't just mean '<u>of the</u>' — they can also mean '<u>some</u>' or '<u>any</u>'.

**EXAMPLES:**

*Avez-vous <u>du</u> pain?* = Have you got <u>any</u> bread?

*J'ai <u>des</u> pommes.* = I have <u>some</u> apples.

| masculine singular | feminine singular | in front of a vowel / 'h' which takes 'l' | masculine or feminine plural |
|--------------------|-------------------|-------------------------------------------|------------------------------|
| du | de la | de l' | des |

**NB** In <u>negative</u> sentences, like 'I don't have any apples', you just use '<u>de</u>' — 'Je n'ai pas <u>de</u> pommes'.

## A page on 'the' — not the most fun...

Phew, am I glad I speak English — just one word for '<u>the</u>' and no genders (in grammar anyway). But there's no getting around it — you <u>need</u> this stuff to get your <u>French right</u> in the <u>assessments</u>. <u>Cover up</u> the page and write out <u>all four tables</u> — keep on scribbling till you can do it in your sleep.

# Words to Describe Things

Gain <u>more marks</u> and show what an interesting person you are by using some <u>juicy describing</u> words.

## Adjectives must 'agree' with the thing they're describing

1) In <u>English</u>, the describing word (adjective) stays the <u>same</u> — like <u>big</u> bus, <u>big</u> bananas...
2) In <u>French</u>, the describing word has to <u>change</u> to <u>match</u> whether what it's describing is <u>masculine</u> or <u>feminine</u> and <u>singular</u> or <u>plural</u>. Look at these examples where 'intéressant' has to change:

| *Masculine Singular* | *Masculine Plural* | *Feminine Singular* | *Feminine Plural* |
|---|---|---|---|
| le garçon intéressant | les garçons intéressants | la fille intéressante | les filles intéressantes |
| (the <u>interesting</u> boy) | (the <u>interesting</u> boys) | (the <u>interesting</u> girl) | (the <u>interesting</u> girls) |

The Rules Are:

① Add an '<u>-e</u>' to the describing word if the word being described is <u>feminine</u> (see page 83).

Only if the describing word doesn't already end in 'e'.

② Add an '<u>-s</u>' to the describing word if the word being described is <u>plural</u> (see page 83).

(Of course, that means if it's <u>feminine plural</u>, then you have to add '<u>-es</u>'.)

"You stink!"    "I agree"

IMPORTANT NOTE: When you look an adjective up in the <u>dictionary</u> it gives the <u>masculine singular</u> form. Don't ask me why — it must have been a load of single blokes who wrote the dictionary.

## Learn the describing words which don't follow the rules

1) Adjectives which end in <u>-x</u>, <u>-f</u>, <u>-er</u>, <u>-on</u>, <u>-en</u>, <u>-el</u>, <u>-il</u> and <u>-c</u> follow different rules:

Adjectives ending in these letters <u>double</u> their <u>last letter</u> before adding 'e' in the feminine.

| Group of words ending: | Most important ones in the group | masculine singular | feminine singular | masculine plural | feminine plural |
|---|---|---|---|---|---|
| -x | sérieux (serious), ennuyeux (boring), délicieux (delicious), dangereux (dangerous), merveilleux (marvellous) & heureux ➡ | heureux (happy) | heureuse | heureux | heureuses |
| -f | actif (active), négatif (negative), sportif (sporty), vif (lively) & neuf ➡ | neuf (new) | neuve | neufs | neuves |
| -er | dernier (last), fier (proud), cher (dear), étranger (foreign) & premier ➡ | premier (first) | première | premiers | premières |
| -on, -en, -el, -il | mignon (sweet), ancien (old/former), cruel (cruel), gentil (kind) & bon ➡ | bon (good) | bonne | bons | bonnes |
| -c | sec (dry), franc (frank) & blanc ➡ | blanc (white) | blanche | blancs | blanches |

'<u>Sèche</u>' (f.sing.) and '<u>sèches</u>' (f.pl.) add an accent.

| masculine singular | before a m. sing. noun beginning with a vowel or 'h' which takes 'l' | feminine singular | masculine plural | feminine plural |
|---|---|---|---|---|
| vieux (old) | vieil | vieille | vieux | vieilles |
| beau (fine/pretty) | bel | belle | beaux | belles |
| nouveau (new) | nouvel | nouvelle | nouveaux | nouvelles |
| fou (mad) | fol | folle | fous | folles |
| long (long) | long | longue | longs | longues |
| tout (all) | tout | toute | tous | toutes |

2) There are also some adjectives which are <u>completely irregular</u> — you'll have to learn these ones off by heart.

## Quelque and chaque — rule-breakers...

'Quelque' only changes from singular to plural, by adding an 's'. There is no difference for masc. and fem.

'Chaque' always stays the same.

Grammar Fans: '<u>Indefinite Adjectives</u>'.

*I bought some sweets:*
J'ai acheté quelques bonbons.

*Every person here likes chocolate:*
Chaque personne ici aime le chocolat.

## Even 'désagréable(s)' agrees...

Aaaargh — more tables to learn, but then that's the nature of French grammar. For these endings to be of any <u>use</u> to you, you need to learn the <u>genders</u> of the nouns in the first place — you have to know <u>what</u> your adjective needs to <u>agree</u> with. To get it right, <u>get learning</u>.

## ADJECTIVES

# Words to Describe Things

Details and descriptions are key to doing well in the exam — so, words to <u>describe</u> things are quite <u>important</u>.

## Top 21 Describing Words

Here are 21 <u>describing words</u> — they're the ones you really <u>have</u> to know.

*Grammar Fans:*
*These are '<u>Adjectives</u>'.*

| | | | | | |
|---|---|---|---|---|---|
| *good:* | bon(ne) | *normal:* | normal(e) | *young:* | jeune |
| *bad:* | mauvais(e) | *interesting:* | intéressant(e) | *new:* | nouveau / nouvelle |
| *beautiful:* | beau / belle | *boring:* | ennuyeux / ennuyeuse | *brand new:* | neuf / neuve |
| *happy:* | heureux / heureuse | *terrible:* | affreux / affreuse | *fast:* | rapide |
| *sad:* | triste | *long:* | long(ue) | *slow:* | lent(e) |
| *easy:* | facile | *small/short:* | petit(e) | *practical:* | pratique |
| *difficult:* | difficile | *old:* | vieux / vieille | *strange:* | étrange |

## Most describing words go after the word they describe

It's the opposite of English — in French <u>most</u> describing words (adjectives) <u>go after</u> the word they're describing (the noun).

**EXAMPLES:**

*J'ai une voiture <u>rapide</u>.*  = I have a <u>fast</u> car.

*J'ai lu un livre <u>intéressant</u>.*  = I read an <u>interesting</u> book.

**noun** (dress)

*la robe rouge*

**adjective** (red)

You can also use describing words in sentences with verbs like '<u>être</u>' (to be) and '<u>devenir</u>' (to become). The adjective still needs to <u>agree</u> with the noun though.

**EXAMPLES:**

*Ils sont <u>prêts</u>.*  = They are <u>ready</u>.

*Elle est devenue <u>belle</u>.*  = She has become <u>beautiful</u>.

Adjectives are always <u>masculine</u> <u>singular</u> after '<u>ce</u>'. E.g. 'C'est nouveau' (It's new), 'Ce sera cher' (It will be expensive), etc.

## There are some odd ones out that go in front

These describing words almost always go <u>before</u> the noun — a real pain:

| | | | | | |
|---|---|---|---|---|---|
| *good:* | bon(ne) | *young:* | jeune | *bad:* | mauvais(e) |
| *fine / pretty:* | beau / belle | *old:* | vieux / vieil(le) | *high:* | haut(e) |
| *better / best:* | meilleur(e) | *nice / pretty:* | joli(e) | *nasty:* | vilain(e) |
| *new:* | nouveau / nouvel(le) | *small:* | petit(e) | *first:* | premier / première |

**EXAMPLES:** *J'ai un <u>nouveau</u> chat.*  = I have a <u>new</u> cat.

*J'ai une <u>petite</u> maison, avec un <u>joli</u> jardin et une <u>belle</u> vue.*

= I have a <u>small</u> house, with a <u>pretty</u> garden and a <u>beautiful</u> view.

Adjectives still have to agree, regardless of whether they come before or after the noun.

# Good, bad... indifferent?

By now you're probably thinking you could get through life without adjectives and you could well be right — as long as you never want to tell anyone how <u>interesting</u>, <u>beautiful</u> and <u>happy</u> you are. Start by learning those <u>21 key words</u> at the top of the page — they'll <u>spice</u> your writing up no end.

# Words to Describe Things

More <u>really</u> important stuff on describing words, including words that show <u>who something belongs to</u>...

## Some mean different things before and after the noun

Some adjectives <u>change their meaning</u> according to whether they are <u>before</u> or <u>after</u> the noun.
Here are some important ones — learn them <u>carefully</u>.

| adjective | meaning if <u>before</u> | meaning if <u>after</u> |
|---|---|---|
| ancien | former    un <u>ancien</u> soldat (a <u>former</u> soldier) | old/ancient    un homme <u>ancien</u> (an <u>old</u> man) |
| cher | dear    mon <u>cher</u> ami (my <u>dear</u> friend) | expensive    une voiture <u>chère</u> (an <u>expensive</u> car) |
| propre | own    ma <u>propre</u> chambre (my <u>own</u> room) | clean    ma chambre <u>propre</u> (my <u>clean</u> room) |
| grand | great    un <u>grand</u> homme (a <u>great</u> man) | grand    un homme <u>grand</u> (a <u>big</u> man) |

**EXAMPLES:**    *J'ai ma <u>propre</u> voiture.*    = I have my <u>own</u> car.

*J'ai une voiture <u>propre</u>.*    = I have a <u>clean</u> car.

## My, your, our — words for who it belongs to

You have to be able to <u>use</u> and <u>understand</u> these words
to say that something <u>belongs</u> to someone:

Like in English, these go <u>before the noun</u>.
E.g. '<u>mon ami</u>', '<u>notre cousin</u>', etc.

Grammar Fans: These are
'<u>Possessive Adjectives</u>'.

| | masculine singular | feminine singular | plural |
|---|---|---|---|
| my | mon | ma | mes |
| your (informal, sing.) | ton | ta | tes |
| his/her/its | son | sa | ses |
| our | notre | notre | nos |
| your (formal/pl.) | votre | votre | vos |
| their | leur | leur | leurs |

You have to choose the <u>gender</u> (masculine, feminine or plural) to match the thing it's <u>describing</u>, and **NOT**
the person it <u>belongs</u> to. So in the example below, it's always 'mon père' even if it's a girl talking.

*<u>Mon</u> père est petit, <u>ma</u> mère est grande.*    = <u>My</u> father is short, <u>my</u> mother is tall.

This means that <u>son</u>/<u>sa</u>/<u>ses</u> could mean either '<u>his</u>' or '<u>her</u>'. You can usually tell which one it
is by the <u>context</u>.

*J'ai vu Pierre avec <u>sa</u> sœur.*    = I saw <u>Pierre</u> with <u>his sister</u>.

*<u>Marie</u> et <u>sa</u> sœur sont inséparables.*    = <u>Marie</u> and <u>her sister</u> are inseparable.

## 'Ma amie' becomes 'mon amie'

Before a noun beginning with a <u>vowel</u> or words beginning with '<u>h</u>',
always use the masculine form. You do this because it's easier to <u>say</u>.

*Écoutez <u>son histoire</u>.*

*<u>Mon amie</u> s'appelle Helen.*    = <u>My friend</u>'s called Helen.

Listen to <u>his / her story</u>.

## My, oh my...

...what fun we're having. It's so important, all this — especially that the possessive adjectives
change according to the thing <u>being described</u>, **NOT** the <u>owner</u>. And when you see words like
'<u>cher</u>', it should set a little bell ringing in your mind that it could have one of <u>two meanings</u>.

| **ADVERBS** | # Words to Describe Actions |

The three previous pages describe <u>objects</u>, e.g. the bus is <u>red</u>. This page is about describing things you <u>do</u>, e.g. 'I speak French <u>perfectly</u>', and about adding <u>more info</u> — 'I speak French <u>almost</u> perfectly'.

## Make your sentences better by saying how you do things

1) In <u>English</u>, you don't say 'I talk slow' — you have to <u>add</u> a '<u>ly</u>' on the end to say 'I talk slow<u>ly</u>'.
2) In <u>French</u>, you have to <u>add</u> a '<u>ment</u>' on the end, but first you have to make sure the describing word is in the <u>feminine</u> form (see page 85).

*Grammar Fans:*
*These are '<u>Adverbs</u>'.*

**EXAMPLES:**   *Il parle* lentement .   = He speaks <u>slowly</u>.

*normally:* normalement
*strangely:* étrangement

The French word for 'slow' is '<u>lent</u>', but the feminine form is '<u>lente</u>'. Add '<u>ment</u>' and you get '<u>lentement</u>' = slowly.

3) <u>Unlike adjectives</u> (page 85) you <u>don't</u> ever have to <u>change</u> these words — they're describing the <u>action</u>, not the person doing it:   Always the same.

Feminine   *Elle parle* lentement .   Plural   *Nous parlons* lentement .

## Learn these odd ones out off by heart

Just like in English there are <u>odd ones out</u> — for example, you <u>don't</u> say 'I sing <u>goodly</u>'. The adjective 'good' changes to 'well' when it becomes an adverb. Have a look at the other odd ones out in the table:

| ENGLISH | FRENCH |
|---------|--------|
| good → well | bon(ne) → bien |
| bad → badly | mauvais(e) → mal |
| fast → fast | rapide → vite |

*Je chante.*
*I sing.*

*Je chante <u>bien</u>.*   *Je chante <u>mal</u>.*
*I sing <u>well</u>.*   *I sing <u>badly</u>.*

## Use one of these fine words to give even more detail

Add any one of these simple <u>words</u> or <u>phrases</u> to make that impressive sentence even more so... You can use them for sentences saying <u>how something is done</u>:

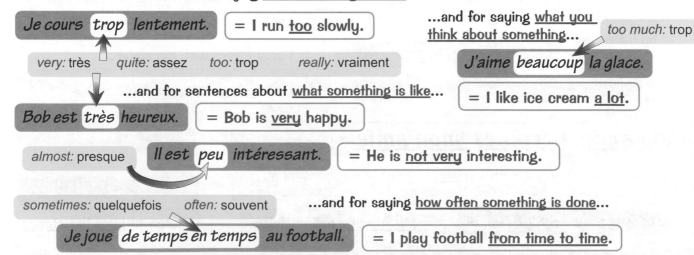

*Je cours* trop *lentement.*   = I run <u>too</u> slowly.

...and for saying <u>what you think about something</u>...

*very:* très   *quite:* assez   *too:* trop   *really:* vraiment

*too much:* trop

*J'aime* beaucoup *la glace.*

...and for sentences about <u>what something is like</u>...

= I like ice cream <u>a lot</u>.

*Bob est* très *heureux.*   = Bob is <u>very</u> happy.

*almost:* presque   *Il est* peu *intéressant.*   = He is <u>not very</u> interesting.

*sometimes:* quelquefois   *often:* souvent   ...and for saying <u>how often something is done</u>...

*Je joue* de temps en temps *au football.*   = I play football <u>from time to time</u>.

# I eat too quickly and run too slowly...

Alrighty — this is <u>a bit like</u> English — you have a set ending (-ment) to learn and stick on, and it's not too tricky either. Make sure you <u>really know</u> the standard <u>rule</u> and all the <u>exceptions</u>. <u>Practise</u> taking a few French sentences and <u>adding</u> detail... then use them when you're doing your <u>assessments</u>.

# Comparing Things

Often you don't just want to say that something is <u>tasty</u>, <u>juicy</u> or whatever — you want to say that it's the <u>tastiest</u>, or (to create a nice amount of jealousy) that it's <u>juicier than</u> someone else's...

## How to say more strange, most strange

In French you can't say '<u>stranger</u>' or '<u>strangest</u>' — you have to say '<u>more strange</u>' or '<u>the most strange</u>':

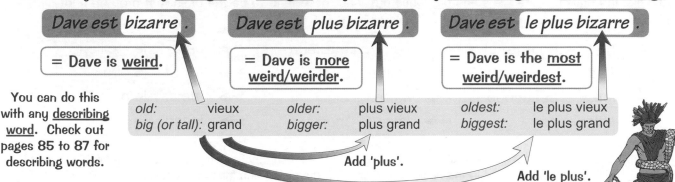

| *Dave est* | bizarre | . | | *Dave est* | plus bizarre | . | | *Dave est* | le plus bizarre | . |

= Dave is <u>weird</u>.

= Dave is <u>more weird/weirder</u>.

= Dave is the <u>most weird/weirdest</u>.

You can do this with any <u>describing word</u>. Check out pages 85 to 87 for describing words.

| *old:* | vieux | *older:* | plus vieux | *oldest:* | le plus vieux |
| *big (or tall):* | grand | *bigger:* | plus grand | *biggest:* | le plus grand |

Add 'plus'.

Add 'le plus'.

## Don't forget agreement

///// See page 85 for more on how adjectives <u>agree</u>. /////

The adjectives still need to <u>agree</u> as normal:

*less pretty:* moins jolie

| *Cette robe est* | plus jolie | . | = This dress is <u>prettier</u>.

*less strong:* moins forts

| *Ils sont* | plus forts | . | = They're <u>stronger</u>.

When you're saying 'the most ...', you need to say '<u>le</u> plus', '<u>la</u> plus' or '<u>les</u> plus' to match the word you're describing (see page 84).

*the least funny:* la moins amusante

| *Liz est* | la plus amusante | . |

= Liz is <u>the funniest</u>.

*the least strong:* les moins forts

| *Ed et Jo sont* | les plus amusants | . |

= Ed and Jo are <u>the funniest</u>.

## The three ways of comparing things — More, Less and As

If you want to say '<u>less ...</u>' or '<u>as ... as</u>', you just use the words '<u>moins</u>' and '<u>aussi</u>' instead of '<u>plus</u>'. And the word for '<u>than</u>' is '<u>que</u>'.

| *Ed est <u>plus</u> grand <u>que</u> Tom.* | = Ed is tall<u>er</u> <u>than</u> Tom. |

| *Ed est <u>moins</u> grand <u>que</u> Tom.* | = Ed is <u>less</u> tall <u>than</u> Tom. |

| *Ed est <u>aussi</u> grand <u>que</u> Tom.* | = Ed is <u>as</u> tall <u>as</u> Tom. |

| *Ed est le moins grand.* |

= Ed is <u>the least</u> tall.

To say '<u>the least ...</u>', you just say '<u>le/la/les moins ...</u>':

## Mirror, mirror on the wall...

Yup, the comparative is a favourite of wicked stepmothers and it's a favourite with French teachers too — they simply adore it when you get it <u>right</u>. To learn this kind of thing you just need to <u>repeat some examples</u> to yourself about 30 times in a kind of <u>weird chant</u> until it <u>sticks</u>.

# Comparing Things

Right, just a bit more on comparisons. A few common exceptions, and also how to compare the way people do things. Chomping at the bit? Trois, deux, un... go.

## Pour le meilleur et pour le pire... — For better or worse...

Just like in English, there are some odd ones out, and these tend to be the ones that crop up a lot. With these ones, you don't say 'plus ...' or 'moins ...'.

| | | | | | | |
|---|---|---|---|---|---|---|
| *good:* | bon(ne)(s) | ➡ *better:* | meilleur(e)(s) | ➡ *best:* | le meilleur |
| *bad:* | mauvais(e)(s) | ➡ *worse:* | pire(s) | ➡ *worst:* | le pire |
| *lots:* | beaucoup | ➡ *more:* | plus | ➡ *most:* | le plus |
| *little:* | peu | ➡ *less:* | moins | ➡ *least:* | le moins |

With these four, the 'le' can be replaced with 'la' or 'les' if the thing that's being described is feminine or plural. 'Meilleur' still takes an 'e' in the feminine and an 's' in the plural, and 'pire' still takes an 's' in the plural.

**EXAMPLES:**

*Ce livre est meilleur que le dernier.*   = This book is <u>better</u> than the last (one).

*Le vélo bleu est le pire.*   = The blue bike is <u>the worst</u>.

## More or most strangely is pretty much the same...

When you're comparing how people do things, it works pretty much how you'd expect.

*Dave parle* bizarrement.   = Dave talks <u>weirdly</u>.

*Dave parle* plus bizarrement.   = Dave talks <u>more weirdly</u>.

*Dave parle* le plus bizarrement.   = Dave talks <u>the most weirdly</u>.

Words like 'bizarrement' (adverbs) <u>don't agree</u>, and you always use '<u>le</u>'.

'Bizarrement' is an <u>adverb</u>. See page 88 for more on this.

*Jessica court* le plus vite.   = Jessica runs <u>the fastest</u>.

DON'T fall into the trap of saying 'vitement' for fast. The <u>adverb</u> is always '<u>vite</u>' and the <u>adjective</u> is '<u>rapide</u>'.

## Je chante mieux que toi — I sing better than you

There are some <u>odd ones out</u> you need to know with <u>comparative adverbs</u>:

| | | | | | | |
|---|---|---|---|---|---|---|
| *well:* | bien | ➡ *better:* | mieux | ➡ *best:* | le mieux |
| *badly:* | mal | ➡ *worse:* | pire | ➡ *worst:* | le pire |

In English we might say "I'm a better singer than you" and "You're a good player, but Henri's the best."

*Tu joues <u>bien</u>, mais c'est Henri qui joue <u>le mieux</u>.*   = You play <u>well</u>, but Henri plays <u>the best</u>.

## And that's more or less it...

This'll help you sound much more <u>sophisticated</u> when you talk French. Instead of saying "It's a <u>good</u> film", you can say "It's a <u>better</u> film than...", or "It's the <u>best</u> film of this year". '<u>Mieux</u>' comes up all the time, like when people say, '<u>Ça va mieux</u>' meaning 'I'm feeling better'.

# *Sneaky Wee Words*

It all <u>looks terrifying</u>. But you've got to <u>learn</u> it if you want tip-top marks. It's really only a <u>few words</u>.

## *TO — à or en*

Where we use '<u>to</u>', the French usually use '<u>à</u>':  | *Il va <u>à</u> Paris.* |  = He's going <u>to</u> Paris.

But for feminine countries and ones beginning with a vowel, it's usually '<u>en</u>':

| *Il va <u>en</u> France.* |  = He's going <u>to</u> France.

> For 'the train <u>to</u> Calais' see 'the train <u>for</u> Calais' on page 92. For times, like '10 to 4', see page 2.

For things like <u>to go</u>, <u>to do</u>, just use the <u>infinitive</u> (see page 97); you <u>don't</u> need an extra word for '<u>to</u>'. E.g. aller = <u>to go</u>, faire = <u>to make</u>.

## *ON — sur or à*

For '<u>on top</u>' of something, it's '<u>sur</u>':

| *Sur la table.* |  = <u>On</u> the table.

For days of the week, it's <u>left out</u>:

| *Je pars lundi.* |  = I'm leaving <u>on</u> Monday.

When it's <u>not</u> 'on top', it's usually '<u>à</u>':

| *Je l'ai vu <u>à</u> la télé.* |  = I saw it <u>on</u> TV.

| *J'irai <u>à</u> pied.* |  = I'll go <u>on</u> foot.

## *IN — dans, à or en*

If it's actually <u>inside</u> something, then it's usually '<u>dans</u>':  | *C'est <u>dans</u> la boîte.* |  = It's <u>in</u> the box.

If it's <u>in</u> a town, it's '<u>à</u>':  | *J'habite <u>à</u> Marseille.* |  = I live <u>in</u> Marseilles.

If you want to say <u>in</u> a feminine country, or one beginning with a vowel, then it's usually '<u>en</u>':  | *J'habite <u>en</u> France.* |  = I live <u>in</u> France.

## *FROM — de or à partir de*

Where we use '<u>from</u>', they usually use '<u>de</u>':

| *De Londres à Paris.* |  = <u>From</u> London to Paris.

| *Je viens <u>de</u> Cardiff.* |  = I come <u>from</u> Cardiff.

For dates, it's '<u>à partir de</u>':

| *À partir du 4 juin.* |

= <u>From</u> the 4th of June.

## *OF — de or en*

Where we use '<u>of</u>', they usually use '<u>de</u>':  | *Une bouteille <u>de</u> lait.* |  = A bottle <u>of</u> milk.

> <u>Watch out</u>: sometimes it's hard to spot the '<u>de</u>' in a sentence, because '<u>de</u>' + '<u>le</u>' = <u>du</u>, and '<u>de</u>' + '<u>les</u>' = '<u>des</u>' — see page <u>84</u>.

> You don't say 'of' with <u>dates</u> (see page 3):

'<u>Made of</u>' is '<u>en</u>':  | *C'est <u>en</u> cuir.* |  = It's made <u>of</u> leather.

| *Le 2 juin.* |  = The 2nd <u>of</u> June.

## *Tiny but deadly...*

There's <u>so</u> much on this page that catches people out. Before carrying on, go back over this page and cover up all the <u>boxes</u> with <u>French</u> in them, and translate back all the <u>English</u> sentences.

# Sneaky Wee Words

A couple more sneaky words, and then the dreaded <u>qui</u> and <u>que</u>...

## FOR — pour or depuis

Where we use '<u>for</u>', they usually use '<u>pour</u>':

| Un cadeau _pour_ moi. | = A present <u>for</u> me. |

For 'the train for...', it's '<u>pour</u>':

| Le train _pour_ Calais. | = The train <u>for</u> Calais. |

To say how long you're going to do something for in the future, use '<u>pour</u>':

| Je vais aller en France _pour_ le week-end. | = I'm going to go to France <u>for</u> the weekend. |

To say things like 'I've studied French for 5 years', use the <u>present tense</u> and '<u>depuis</u>':

| J'apprends le français _depuis_ cinq ans. | = I've studied French <u>for</u> 5 years. |

## AT — à

| À six heures. | = <u>At</u> six o'clock. |

| Elle est _à_ l'école. | = She is <u>at</u> school. |

<u>Watch out</u>: It can be hard to spot the 'à' in a sentence, because 'à' + 'le' = 'au' and 'à' + 'les' = 'aux' — see page 84.

## Qui and que — Which / who / that...

Grammar Fans:
'Relative Pronouns'.

These are probably the <u>trickiest</u> of the <u>tricky</u> French words. Practise them lots...

1) If the person/thing you are talking about is the <u>subject</u> of the verb, i.e. the person/thing that <u>does the verb</u>, then you use '<u>qui</u>'.

| Un professeur _qui_ aime bien sa classe. | = A teacher <u>who</u> likes his class. |

subject    verb

It's the teacher that's <u>doing the liking</u>, so it's <u>QUI</u>.

2) If the person/thing you are talking about is the <u>object</u> of the verb, i.e. the person/thing that <u>has something done to it</u>, then you use '<u>que</u>'.

| Un professeur _que_ sa classe aime bien. | = A teacher <u>that</u> his class likes. |

object    subject    verb

It's the teacher that is <u>being liked</u> (NOT doing the liking), so it's <u>QUE</u>.

EXAMPLES:

| Où est le bâtiment qu'on a vu? | = Where is the building we saw? |

The building is not doing the seeing — so QUE.

| Où est le chien qui courait? | = Where is the dog that was running? |

The dog was doing the running — so QUI.

## Des mots que je déteste...

Not the easiest stuff in the world, but after a while you should get a <u>feel</u> for <u>qui</u> and <u>que</u>. <u>Definitely</u> worth learning these examples by heart, and then making up <u>a few of your own</u>.

# I, You, Him, Them...

Pronouns are words that replace nouns — things like 'you', 'she' or 'them'.

## je, tu, il, elle — I, you, he, she

You need 'I', 'you', 'he' and 'she' most often — for the subject (main person/thing) in a sentence...

> Paul finally has a new job. (He) shaves poodles at the poodle parlour.

> 'He' is a pronoun. It means you don't have to say 'Paul' again.

### THE SUBJECT PRONOUNS

| | | | |
|---|---|---|---|
| *I* | je | nous | *we* |
| *you* (informal singular) | tu | vous | *you* (informal plural or formal) |
| *he/it* | il | ils | *they* (masc. or masc. & fem.) |
| *she/it* | elle | elles | *they* (all fem.) |
| *one/we* | on | | |

> Le chien mange la brosse.

= The dog eats the brush.

> (Il) mange la brosse.

= <u>He</u> eats the brush.

The French often use 'on' when they're talking about 'we'. E.g. 'On mange' = 'We eat', 'On va aller au cinéma' = 'We are going to go to the cinema.' It's a very useful pronoun.

## me, te, le, la — me, you, him, her

These are for the person/thing in a sentence that's having the action done to it (the direct object)

> Dave lave le chien.

= Dave washes the dog.

> Dave (le) lave.

= Dave washes <u>it</u>.

### THE DIRECT OBJECT PRONOUNS

| | | | |
|---|---|---|---|
| *me* | me | nous | *us* |
| *you* (inf. sing.) | te | vous | *you* (informal plural or formal) |
| *him/it* | le | les | *them* |
| *her/it* | la | | |

## C'est le mien / la mienne... — It's mine...

You'll only need to <u>recognise</u> these — you won't have to use them.

### POSSESSIVE PRONOUNS

| | Singular Masc. | Fem. | Plural Masc. | Fem. |
|---|---|---|---|---|
| *mine:* | le mien | la mienne | les miens | les miennes |
| *yours* (informal sing.): | le tien | la tienne | les tiens | les tiennes |
| *his / hers:* | le sien | la sienne | les siens | les siennes |
| *ours:* | le nôtre | la nôtre | les nôtres | les nôtres |
| *yours* (plural or formal): | le vôtre | la vôtre | les vôtres | les vôtres |
| *theirs:* | le leur | la leur | les leurs | les leurs |

> Donne-moi <u>la</u> brosse, c'est <u>la</u> mienne.

= Give me the brush, it's mine.

> Donne-lui <u>le</u> ballon, c'est <u>le</u> sien.

= Give him the ball, it's his.

For more info on 'moi' and 'lui' see age 94.

## There are special words for to me, to her, to them

For things that need 'to', 'for' or 'by' — like writing <u>to someone</u> — use the <u>indirect object</u> pronouns.

### THE INDIRECT OBJECT PRONOUNS

| | | | |
|---|---|---|---|
| *to me* | me | nous | *to us* |
| *to you* (inf. sing.) | te | vous | *to you* (informal plural or formal) |
| *to him/her/it* | lui | leur | *to them* |

> Le chien donne la brosse à Dave.

= The dog gives the brush to Dave.

> Le chien (lui) donne la brosse.

= The dog gives the brush <u>to him</u>.

# Paul and Dave — loving your work...

You're not going to get very far in the exams if you can't understand things like <u>I</u>, <u>you</u>, <u>he</u>, <u>she</u> and <u>we</u>. The good news is that it's pretty darn <u>easy</u>. You don't even have to learn any sentences on this page — just a few <u>words</u> you probably already know. You've got <u>no excuse</u> whatsoever. Hm.

**PRONOUNS**

# Me, You, Him, Them, and En & Y

You'll need to learn the pronouns here too. Yuck...

## Special words for me, you, him, her...

In some sentences, you need to <u>emphasise</u> exactly who is being talked about. For example, you can say 'he's taller', but you can make the sentence clearer using an <u>emphatic pronoun</u>, e.g. 'he's taller than <u>you</u>'. There are <u>four occasions</u> when you need to use emphatic pronouns in French:

### EMPHATIC PRONOUNS

| | | | |
|---|---|---|---|
| *me* | moi | *us* | nous |
| *you* (informal sing.) | toi | *you* (informal plural or formal) | vous |
| *him/it* | lui | *they* (masc. or masc. & fem.) | eux |
| *her/it* | elle | *they* (all fem.) | elles |
| *one* | soi | | |

| | | |
|---|---|---|
| 1) Telling people what to do. | *Écoutez-moi!* | = Listen to <u>me</u>! |
| 2) Comparing things. | *Il est plus grand que toi.* | = He is taller than <u>you</u>. |
| 3) After words like 'with', 'for', 'from'... (prepositions). | *Nous allons avec eux.* | = We're going with <u>them</u>. |
| 4) Where the words are on their own, or after 'c'est'. | *Qui parle? Moi! C'est moi!* | = Who's speaking? Me! It's me! |

*For more on this, see page 108.*

*For more on comparing, see page 89.*

*For more on prepositions, see pages 91-92.*

When French people want to be <u>even clearer</u> about who's being talked about, e.g. 'I made this cake <u>myself</u>,' they use one of these words instead of a normal emphatic pronoun. They all mean '...-<u>self</u>' (myself, yourself, himself etc.).

moi-même, toi-même, lui-même, elle-même, soi-même, nous-mêmes, vous-mêmes, eux-mêmes, elles-mêmes

## Two Top Words — 'En' & 'Y'

### EN — MEANING 'OF IT'

<u>EN</u> — this pronoun usually translates as '<u>of it</u>', '<u>of them</u>', '<u>some</u>' or '<u>any</u>'.

If a verb needs <u>de</u> after it, like 'avoir besoin de' you translate '<u>it</u>' or '<u>them</u>' as '<u>en</u>':

e.g.: J'ai besoin de la banane.   J'<u>en</u> ai besoin.

I need the banana.  ⟹  I need <u>it</u>.

### Y — MEANING 'THERE'

e.g.: J'y vais.          I'm going there.

It's also used to mean '<u>it</u>' or '<u>them</u>' after verbs followed by <u>à</u>, e.g.: penser à — to think about.

e.g.: Je n'<u>y</u> pense plus.

I don't think about it any more.

It's also used in several common expressions.

Il <u>y</u> a...      There is/There are...

Ça <u>y</u> est!      That's it! — as in 'I've finished!'

## Stick all Object Pronouns Before the Verb

These pronouns always go <u>before</u> the verb. If you're using <u>two</u> object pronouns in the same sentence, they <u>both</u> go before the verb, but they go in a <u>special order</u>. This is a bit tricky, so get it learnt:

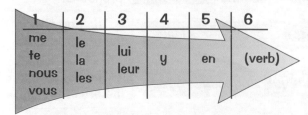

| 1 | 2 | 3 | 4 | 5 | 6 |
|---|---|---|---|---|---|
| me te nous vous | le la les | lui leur | y | en | (verb) |

Examples:  Il <u>me les</u> donne.      He gives <u>them to me</u>.
Je <u>le lui</u> ai donné.      I gave <u>it to him</u>.

If you're using a <u>negative</u>, the '<u>ne</u>' goes <u>before</u> the object pronoun, and the '<u>pas</u>' after the verb.

Example:  Je ne <u>les</u> mange pas.   I don't eat <u>them</u>.

## Special words for me — you don't deserve them...

This stuff is pretty <u>grisly</u>, I'll admit. You have to understand these when you see or hear them, and if you can <u>use</u> them, your teacher will be really impressed. Which means you'll pick up more marks in the assessments. Which is the whole point. You know the drill by now — <u>cover</u> and <u>scribble</u>.

# This & That and Which

**DEMONSTRATIVES & RELATIVE PRONOUNS**

Pointing things out in shops, and generally making it clear <u>which</u> thing you're on about, is <u>important</u>.

## How to say this thing or these things

Use 'ce', 'cet'... in front of another word for saying things like '<u>this man</u>', '<u>these apples</u>' — i.e. when you're using '<u>this</u>' as a <u>describing word</u>.

*Grammar Fans: 'Demonstrative Adjectives'.*

| masculine singular | masculine singular before vowel or 'h' which takes 'l' | feminine singular | plural |
|---|---|---|---|
| ce | cet | cette | ces |

**EXAMPLES:**

ce stylo: *this pen*    cet oiseau: *this bird*
cette maison: *this house*    ces pommes: *these apples*

## Je veux celui-là — I want that one

When you say 'this is mine', you're using 'this' as a <u>noun</u>.

*Grammar Fans: These are the 'Demonstrative Pronouns'.*

| masculine singular | masculine plural | feminine singular | feminine plural |
|---|---|---|---|
| celui | ceux | celle | celles |

1) You often use these words with '<u>-ci</u>' or '<u>-là</u>' on the end.
2) Adding '<u>-ci</u>' makes it mean '<u>this one</u>' or '<u>this one here</u>', and '<u>-là</u>' makes it mean '<u>that one</u>' or '<u>that one there</u>'.

If you're <u>not</u> pointing something out, you can use these ones:
ceci = this    cela = that    ça = that

**EXAMPLES:**
<u>Cela</u> n'est pas vrai. — <u>That</u> isn't true.
Lisez <u>ceci</u>. — Read <u>this</u>.

*J'ai deux chiens. <u>Celui-ci</u> est mignon, mais <u>celui-là</u> est méchant.*
= I have two dogs. <u>This one here</u>'s nice, but <u>that one there</u>'s nasty.

3) On their own, these words can mean '<u>the one(s)</u>'.

*J'aime bien cette chanson, mais je préfère <u>celle</u> qu'on a écoutée hier soir.*
= I like this song, but I prefer <u>the one</u> we listened to yesterday evening.

## Dont — which...

*Grammar Fans: This is a 'Relative Pronoun'.*

1) '<u>Dont</u>' can be translated as '<u>of which</u>' or '<u>about which</u>'.
2) This is difficult. But don't panic — you only need to <u>recognise it</u>.
3) <u>Dont</u> is used if the verb in the sentence is followed by '<u>de</u>' e.g. '<u>avoir peur de</u>', '<u>avoir besoin de</u>'.

*Le monstre* dont *j'ai peur est là.*
= The monster <u>which</u> I'm scared <u>of</u> is there.

*Le livre* dont *j'ai besoin est fantastique.*
= The book <u>which</u> I need is fantastic.

4) You also see it where we would say 'whose'.

*Le garçon* dont *le père est médecin.*
= The boy <u>whose</u> father is a doctor.
(Literally 'The boy <u>of whom</u> the father is a doctor.')

## So, what are you studying — oh, this and that...

OK, so the bits about '<u>which</u>' get pretty tricky. What am I saying... very tricky. But the stuff about '<u>this</u>' and '<u>that</u>' is pretty <u>straightforward</u>, so it's not as bad as it seems at first. Keep at it — practice might not make perfect, but it does make it a lot better, and that's the point.

## CONJUNCTIONS — Joining Words — Longer Sentences

Everyone knows long sentences are clever — and clever people are popular when it's assessment-marking time. So learn these joining words to help you make longer sentences, and get more marks for being smart.

### Et = And

| J'aime jouer au football. | AND | J'aime jouer au rugby. | = | J'aime jouer au football et au rugby. | = I like playing football and rugby. |

= I like playing football.    = I like playing rugby.

**ANOTHER EXAMPLE:** J'ai un frère et une sœur.    = I have a brother and a sister.

### Ou = Or

This is different from 'où' (with an accent), which means 'where' — see page 4.

| Il joue au football tous les jours. | OR | Il joue au rugby tous les jours. | = | Il joue au football ou au rugby tous les jours. |

= He plays football every day.    = He plays rugby every day.    = He plays football or rugby every day.

**ANOTHER EXAMPLE:** Je voudrais être médecin ou ingénieur.    = I would like to be a doctor or an engineer.

For 'nor' see page 106.

### Mais = But

| J'aime jouer au football. | BUT | Je n'aime pas jouer au rugby. | = | J'aime jouer au football mais je n'aime pas jouer au rugby. |

= I like playing football.    = I don't like playing rugby.    = I like playing football but I don't like playing rugby.

**ANOTHER EXAMPLE:** Je veux jouer au tennis, mais il pleut.    = I want to play tennis, but it's raining.

### Parce que = Because

This is a really important one you need to use to explain yourself. There's loads more about it on page 8.

J'aime le tennis parce que c'est amusant.    = I like tennis because it's fun.

### Other wee joining words to understand

You don't have to use all of these, but you should understand them all...
**EXAMPLES:**

Tu peux sortir si tu veux.    = You can go out if you want.

J'ai faim, donc je vais manger.    = I'm hungry, so I'm going to eat.

Il est comme son frère.    = He's like his brother.

Elle joue au hockey pendant qu'il pleut.    = She plays hockey while it's raining.

See page 8 for more on 'car'.

| because: | car |
| if: | si |
| with: | avec |
| as, like: | comme |
| so, therefore: | donc |
| while, during: | pendant (que) |

## But me no buts....

You use 'and', 'or' and 'but' all the time when you're speaking English — and if you don't use the equivalent words when you speak French, you'll sound a bit weird. But don't confuse 'ou' and 'où'. Try to recognise all the extra words in the last bit too, and, better still, use them.

# The Lowdown on Verbs

You have to know about <u>verbs</u> — you just can't get away from them.
Learn the stuff on this page to make the whole of GCSE French <u>easier</u>.

## Verbs are action words — they tell you what's going on

These are <u>verbs</u>.

Ethel **plays** football every Saturday.

And so is this.

Alex **wished** his grandma **preferred** knitting.

There's a load of stuff you need to know about verbs, but it all boils down to these <u>two things</u>...

## 1) You have different words for different times

You say things <u>differently</u> if they happened last week, or aren't going to happen till tomorrow.

| HAS ALREADY HAPPENED | HAPPENING NOW | HASN'T HAPPENED YET |
|---|---|---|
| I went to Tibet last year.<br>I have been to Tibet.<br>I had been to Tibet. | I am going to Tibet.<br>**PRESENT** | I go to Tibet on Monday.<br>I will go to Tibet.<br>I will be going to Tibet. |
| **PAST** | | **FUTURE** |

These are all different <u>tenses</u>, in case you're interested.

## 2) You have different words for different people

You say 'he plays', but you <u>don't</u> say '<u>I plays</u>' — it'd be daft.  You change the verb to fit the person.

| <u>ME DOING IT</u> | <u>YOU DOING IT</u> | <u>HIM DOING IT</u> |
|---|---|---|
| I <u>am</u> eating parsnips. | You <u>are</u> eating parsnips. | He <u>is</u> eating parsnips. |

OK, you get the picture — verbs are <u>dead important</u>.  You use them all the time, so you
need to learn all this stuff.  That's why I've gone on about them so much on pages 98-112.

## The word you look up in the dictionary means 'to...'

When you want to say 'I dance' in French, you start by looking up 'dance' in the dictionary.
But you can't just use the first word you find — there's more to it than that...

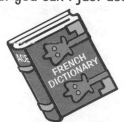

When you look up a verb <u>in the dictionary</u>, this is what you get:

For grammar fans, this is called the <u>infinitive</u>.

*to give:* donner
*to go:* aller

Most of the time you won't want to use the verb in its <u>raw state</u> — you'll
have to <u>change</u> it so it's right for the <u>person</u> and <u>time</u> you're talking about.

There's loads about this on pages 98-112 — learn it all now, and you'll get it right in the assessments.

## Ah, verbs — what would we do without them...

I'm not kidding — this is <u>mega-important</u> stuff.  Over the next few pages I'll give you <u>loads of stuff</u>
on verbs because there's loads you <u>need to know</u>.  Some of it's easy, some of it's tricky — but
if you <u>don't understand</u> the things on <u>this page</u> before you start, you'll have <u>no chance</u>.

# Verbs in the Present Tense

The present tense mostly describes things that are <u>happening now</u>. You'll probably need it more than any other form of the verb, so it's <u>really important</u>.

## The Present tense describes What's Happening Now

Present tense verbs describe either something that's happening <u>now</u>, e.g. 'I am brushing my teeth' or something which happens <u>repeatedly</u>, e.g. 'I brush my teeth every day'. There are <u>3 easy steps</u> to put a verb into the present tense:

| Examples of Present Tense Stems | | | |
|---|---|---|---|
| Infinitive | regarder | finir | vendre |
| Stem | regard | fin | vend |

1)  Get the <u>infinitive</u> of the verb you want, e.g. '<u>regarder</u>'

2)  Knock off the <u>last two letters</u>: regard~~er~~ This gives you the <u>stem</u>.

3)  Add the new <u>ending</u>. This depends on the kind of verb and the person doing the verb (see below).

   E.g. Il regard**e**, vous regard**ez**, ils regard**ent**.

## Endings for -er verbs

To form the present tense of <u>regular</u> '-er' verbs, add the endings shown to the verb's stem — e.g.:

The first bit ('regard')
doesn't change.

<u>regarder = to watch</u>

*See page 5 for when to use '<u>tu</u>' and when to use '<u>vous</u>'.*

| | | | | | |
|---|---|---|---|---|---|
| I watch = | je | regard **e** | nous | regard **ons** = | *we watch* |
| you *(informal singular)* watch = | tu | regard **es** | vous | regard **ez** = | *you (formal & plural)* watch |
| he/it watches = | il | regard **e** | ils | regard **ent** = | *they (masc. or mixed masc. and fem.)* watch |
| she/it watches = | elle | regard **e** | elles | regard **ent** = | *they (fem.)* watch |
| one watches = | on | regard **e** | | | |

**IMPORTANT:** 'il', 'elle' and 'on' <u>always</u> have the same ending, and so do 'ils' & 'elles'.

## Endings for -ir verbs

To form the present tense of <u>regular</u> '-ir' verbs, add the endings shown to the verb's stem — e.g.:

The first bit ('fin')
doesn't change.

<u>finir = to finish</u>

| | | | | | |
|---|---|---|---|---|---|
| I finis = | je | fin **is** | nous | fin **issons** = | *we finish* |
| you *(inf. sing.)* finish = | tu | fin **is** | vous | fin **issez** = | *you (formal & plural)* finish |
| he/she/it/one finishes = | il/elle/on | fin **it** | ils/elles | fin **issent** = | *they finish* |

## Endings for -re verbs

To form the present tense of <u>regular</u> '-re' verbs, add the endings shown to the verb's stem — e.g.:

The first bit ('vend')
doesn't change.

<u>vendre = to sell</u>

| | | | | | |
|---|---|---|---|---|---|
| I sell = | je | vend **s** | nous | vend **ons** = | *we sell* |
| you *(inf. sing.)* sell = | tu | vend **s** | vous | vend **ez** = | *you (formal & plural)* sell |
| he/she/it/one sells = | il/elle/on | vend | ils/elles | vend **ent** = | *they sell* |

<u>NOTE:</u> For <u>il/elle/on</u> there's <u>no</u> ending for '-re' verbs.

## The present tense — not just for Christmas...

You use the present tense for both '<u>I do</u> something' and '<u>I am doing</u> something'. Make sure you avoid disasters like 'Je suis... jouer... le tennis' for 'I am playing tennis'. Ouch. Roger Federer wouldn't say that, French-speaking Swiss pro that he is. He'd say '<u>Je joue au tennis</u>'.

# Verbs in the Present Tense

Verbs that <u>don't</u> follow the <u>same pattern</u> as regular verbs are called '<u>irregular verbs</u>' (crazy, I know).
Most of the <u>really useful verbs</u> are irregular — d'oh.  Anyway, here are <u>a few</u> you'll need most...

## Some of the most useful verbs are irregular

These are some of the <u>most important</u> verbs in the world, so you <u>really must</u> learn <u>all</u> the bits of them.

**① _être_** = to be

I am = *je* suis
*you* (informal singular) are = *tu* es
he/she/it/one is = *il/elle/on* est
we are = *nous* sommes
*you* (formal & plural) are = *vous* êtes
they are = *ils/elles* sont

**② _avoir_** = to have

I have = *j'*ai
*you* (informal singular) have = *tu* as
he/she/it/one has = *il/elle/on* a
we have = *nous* avons
*you* (formal & plural) have = *vous* avez
they have = *ils/elles* ont

**③ _faire_** = to make / to do

I make = *je* fais
*you* (informal singular) make = *tu* fais
he/she/it/one makes = *il/elle/on* fait
we make = *nous* faisons
*you* (formal & plural) make = *vous* faites
they make = *ils/elles* font

**④ _aller_** = to go

I go = *je* vais
*you* (informal singular) go = *tu* vas
he/she/it/one goes = *il/elle/on* va
we go = *nous* allons
*you* (formal & plural) go = *vous* allez
they go = *ils/elles* vont

**⑤ _pouvoir_** = to be able to / can

I can = *je* peux ← '<u>Puis-je</u>' in questions
*you* (informal singular) can = *tu* peux
he/she/it/one can = *il/elle/on* peut
we can = *nous* pouvons
*you* (formal & plural) can = *vous* pouvez
they can = *ils/elles* peuvent

**⑥ _vouloir_** = to want

I want = *je* veux
*you* (informal singular) want = *tu* veux
he/she/it/one wants = *il/elle/on* veut
we want = *nous* voulons
*you* (formal & plural) want = *vous* voulez
they want = *ils/elles* veulent

**⑦ _devoir_** = must / to have to

I must = *je* dois
*you* (informal singular) must = *tu* dois
he/she/it/one must = *il/elle/on* doit
we must = *nous* devons
*you* (formal & plural) must = *vous* devez
they must = *ils/elles* doivent

**⑧ _savoir_** = to know

I know = *je* sais
*you* (informal singular) know = *tu* sais
he/she/it/one knows = *il/elle/on* sait
we know = *nous* savons
*you* (formal & plural) know = *vous* savez
they know = *ils/elles* savent

## To say 'we like eating', use 'we like to eat'

swimming: nager
fishing:   pêcher
singing:   chanter

To say 'we <u>like</u> <u>eating</u>' you need <u>two</u> verbs.  The
<u>first verb</u> ('like') needs to be in the <u>right form</u> for the
person.  The <u>second</u> ('eat'), is just the <u>infinitive</u>.

*nous aimons* **manger** = we like <u>eating</u>

Sometimes the first verb has a <u>preposition</u> — a small but important word that comes <u>before the second verb</u>:

*il <u>arrête de</u> fumer* = he is stopping smoking     *je <u>commence à</u> parler* = I start speaking

In the infinitive, you say: '<u>arrêter de faire quelque chose</u>', '<u>commencer à faire quelque chose</u>', etc.

You can use part of '<u>venir</u>' followed
by '<u>de</u>' and the <u>infinitive</u> to mean
'<u>to have just</u> done something':

*I have just*: je viens de   *you (pl.) have just*: vous venez de    <u>Prepositions
are on pages
91-92.</u>

*il **vient de** parler* = he <u>has just</u> spoken

## Irregular verbs — they should eat more fibre...

Don't worry, all these verb forms will become second nature eventually.  The thing is that the
irregular verbs tend to be the ones that are <u>most used</u> in French, so you <u>can't</u> just ignore them.

# Talking About the Future

You'll need to talk about things that are <u>going to happen</u> at some point in the <u>future</u>. There are <u>two ways</u> you can do it — and the first one's a <u>piece of cake</u>, so I'd learn that first if I were you.

## 1) You can use 'I'm going to' to talk about the Future

This is pretty easy, so there's no excuse for not learning it.

| *je vais* | = I am going |

This is the present tense of '<u>aller</u>' (see page 99). It changes depending on whether it's "<u>I</u> am going", "<u>you</u> are going"...

**+**

Another Verb (infinitive — see p. 97)

| *danser* |
| = to dance |

**=**

Easy sentence about the future:

| *Je vais danser.* |
| = I am going to dance. |

| *Elle <u>va jouer</u> au tennis <u>ce soir</u>.* |

Put in days, dates or times to say when you're going to do it (see pages 2-3).

= She <u>is going to play</u> tennis <u>this evening</u>.

| *Samedi, on va aller en France.* |

= <u>On Saturday</u>, we <u>are going to go</u> to France.
Remember — 'on' is often used as 'we'.

## 2) "I will" — the proper Future Tense

The <u>proper future</u> tense in French is the equivalent of '<u>will</u>' in English. It's another one of those tenses where it's all about sticking endings onto something (the '<u>stem</u>').

**FUTURE TENSE ENDINGS**

| | | | | | |
|---|---|---|---|---|---|
| I: *je* | **-ai** | *nous* | **-ons** | = *we* |
| you (informal singular): *tu* | **-as** | *vous* | **-ez** | = *you* (plural & formal) |
| he/she/it/one: *il/elle/on* | **-a** | *ils/elles* | **-ont** | = *they* |

<u>NOTE:</u> The <u>conditional</u> uses the same 'stems', but different endings. See page 107.

Luckily, the '<u>stems</u>' that you stick the endings onto are pretty <u>easy</u>:

1) For -er and -ir verbs, you just stick the ending onto the <u>infinitive</u> (see page 97).

   **EXAMPLES:** | *Je <u>jouerai</u> au tennis.* | = I <u>will play</u> tennis. | *Tu <u>dormiras</u>.* | = You <u>will sleep</u>.

2) For <u>-re verbs</u>, you take the 'e' off the end of the infinitive first, then stick on the ending.

   **EXAMPLES:** | *Il <u>prendra</u> le bus cet après-midi.* | *Nous <u>vendrons</u> le chien la semaine prochaine.*

   = He <u>will take</u> the bus this afternoon. | = We <u>will sell</u> the dog next week.

3) The verbs below <u>don't</u> follow the pattern. You have to <u>learn them by heart</u>.

These are the most important ones:

| VERB | STEM | VERB | STEM |
|---|---|---|---|
| *aller* | ir- | *pouvoir* | pourr- |
| *être* | ser- | *devoir* | devr- |
| *avoir* | aur- | *venir* | viendr- |
| *faire* | fer- | *vouloir* | voudr- |

Learn these ones too:

| VERB | STEM | VERB | STEM |
|---|---|---|---|
| *voir* | verr- | *falloir* | faudr- |
| *envoyer* | enverr- | *mourir* | mourr- |
| *recevoir* | recevr- | *tenir* | tiendr- |
| *savoir* | saur- | | |

# Feeling brave — use the proper future tense...

'Aller + infinitive' is all very well, but you'll get higher marks in the speaking and writing assessments if you can use the <u>proper future tense</u>. Notice how the future tense <u>endings</u> are just the same as the present tense of the verb '<u>avoir</u>' (except <u>nous</u> and <u>vous</u>, which have <u>-ons</u> and <u>-ez</u>, like in the present).

# Past Participles

The <u>perfect tense</u> is used for things that happened in the <u>past</u>. It's a bit tricky so we've given you two pages on it. Like most grammar stuff, it's just a question of a few <u>rules</u> to follow, and a few bits and pieces to <u>learn</u>. Nothing you can't handle, I'm sure.

## Qu'est-ce que tu as fait? — What have you done?

You have to be able to make and <u>understand</u> sentences like this:

There are two important bits:  **J'ai  joué  au tennis.**  = <u>I (have)</u> <u>played</u> tennis.

1) You always need a bit to mean '<u>I have</u>' (more on the next page). In <u>English</u>, you don't always need the 'have', like in 'last week, I played tennis'. BUT in <u>French</u> you <u>have</u> to have the 'have'.

2) This bit means '<u>played</u>'. It's a <u>special</u> <u>version</u> of 'jouer' (to play). In English, most of these words end in '-ed'. See below.

## Joué = played;  these are Past Participles

Learn the <u>patterns</u> for making the special past tense words like 'joué' (played).

### -ER VERBS

**FORMULA**

> **Remove '-er', then add 'é'**

*EXAMPLES*

| | |
|---|---|
| jouer — | joué |
| to play | played |
| aller — | allé |
| to go | gone |

### -IR VERBS

**FORMULA**

> **Remove '-r'**

*EXAMPLES*

| | |
|---|---|
| partir — | parti |
| to leave | left |
| choisir — | choisi |
| to choose | chosen |

### -RE VERBS

**FORMULA**

> **Remove '-re', then add 'u'**

*EXAMPLES*

| | |
|---|---|
| vendre — | vendu |
| to sell | sold |
| attendre — | attendu |
| to wait | waited |

**Some verbs <u>don't</u> follow the patterns. It's dead annoying, because a lot of the <u>most useful</u> verbs are <u>irregular</u> — you just have to learn them <u>by heart</u>:**

| Verb | Past Participle | Translation |
|---|---|---|
| avoir: | eu | *had* |
| boire: | bu | *drank / drunk* |
| conduire: | conduit | *drove / driven* |
| connaître: | connu | *knew / known* |
| courir: | couru | *ran / run* |
| craindre: | craint | *feared* |
| devenir: | devenu | *became / become* |
| devoir: | dû | *had to* |
| dire: | dit | *said* |
| écrire: | écrit | *wrote / written* |
| être: | été | *was / been* |
| faire: | fait | *did / done* |

| Verb | Past Participle | Translation |
|---|---|---|
| lire: | lu | *read* |
| mettre: | mis | *put* |
| mourir: | mort | *died* |
| naître: | né | *was born / been born* |
| ouvrir: | ouvert | *opened* |
| pouvoir: | pu | *was able / been able* |
| prendre: | pris | *took / taken* |
| rire: | ri | *laughed* |
| savoir: | su | *knew / known* |
| venir: | venu | *came / come* |
| voir: | vu | *saw / seen* |
| vouloir: | voulu | *wanted* |

## That's all perfectly clear...

Loads to learn, but it's all really important. You'll definitely need to <u>talk or write</u> about something that's <u>happened in the past</u> for your GCSE. In a way it's easier than English though, because '<u>j'ai fait</u>' can mean either '<u>I have done</u>', or '<u>I did</u>'. So no excuses — get these past participles <u>learnt</u>.

# How to Form the Perfect Tense

Okay, you're halfway there... The last page was about <u>past participles</u>: 'played', 'done' etc.
Now you have to put it together with the '<u>have</u>' part to make the whole sentence.

## I have played: for 'have' use 'avoir' or 'être'

For the '<u>have</u>' bit of these past tense phrases, you use the present tense (see page 99) of '<u>avoir</u>'.

**EXAMPLES**

| | |
|---|---|
| *Tu as joué au tennis.* | = <u>You have</u> played tennis. |
| *Elle a joué au tennis.* | = <u>She has</u> played tennis. |
| *Nous avons joué au tennis.* | = <u>We have</u> played tennis. |

**AVOIR = TO HAVE**

| | |
|---|---|
| *I have* = | j'ai |
| *you (informal singular) have* = | tu as |
| *he/she/it/one has* = | il/elle/on a |
| *we have* = | nous avons |
| *you (formal & plural) have* = | vous avez |
| *they have* = | ils/elles ont |

## There are always exceptions (15 to be precise)

| Verb | Past Participle | Translation |
|---|---|---|
| aller: | allé | went / gone |
| rester: | resté | stayed |
| venir: | venu | came / come |
| devenir: | devenu | became / become |
| arriver: | arrivé | arrived |
| partir: | parti | left |
| sortir: | sorti | went out / gone out |
| entrer: | entré | entered |
| monter: | monté | went up / gone up |
| descendre: | descendu | went down / gone down |
| rentrer: | rentré | went back / gone back |
| retourner: | retourné | returned |
| tomber: | tombé | fell / fallen |
| naître: | né | was born / been born |
| mourir: | mort | died |

Yep, there are some <u>odd ones out</u>, just to make it more fun... <u>Instead</u> of 'avoir', you have to use '<u>être</u>' for these 15 verbs in the past tense.

> The être verbs are mostly about <u>movement</u>, <u>being born</u> or <u>dying</u>. You also have to use être with <u>reflexive verbs</u> — see page 105.

**ÊTRE = TO BE**

| | |
|---|---|
| *I am* = | je suis |
| *you (informal singular) are* = | tu es |
| *he/she/it/one is* = | il/elle/on est |
| *we are* = | nous sommes |
| *you (formal & plural) are* = | vous êtes |
| *they are* = | ils/elles sont |

See below for why this 'e' is there.

**EXAMPLES:**

| | |
|---|---|
| *Je suis allé(e) au cinéma.* | = <u>I have gone</u> to the cinema. |
| *Il est arrivé.* | = <u>He has arrived</u>. |
| *Tu es devenu(e) très laid(e).* | = <u>You have become</u> very ugly. |

## With Être as the Auxiliary Verb, the Past Participle must Agree:

When you use <u>être</u> to form the perfect tense, the past participle has to <u>agree</u> with the subject of the verb, just like an adjective.

| L'été dernier... | Last summer... |
|---|---|
| ...<u>il</u> est allé en France. | = ...he went to France. |
| ...<u>elle</u> est allé<u>e</u> en France. | = ...she went to France. |
| ...<u>ils</u> sont allé<u>s</u> en France. | = ...they (m. pl.) went to France. |
| ...<u>elles</u> sont allé<u>es</u> en France. | = ...they (f. pl.) went to France. |

Add <u>e</u> if the subject is <u>feminine singular</u>
Add <u>s</u> if the subject is <u>masculine plural</u>
Add <u>es</u> if the subject is <u>feminine plural</u>

## Bit of 'avoir' or bit of 'être' plus the past participle...

...and you're done. Whenever you've used <u>être</u> though, you need to be doubly <u>on your guard</u>.
Loads of people miss out the <u>agreements</u>, and lose <u>marks</u>. <u>Please</u> don't be one of those losers.

# 'Was Doing' or 'Used to Do'

Another past tense for you. The difference here is that this one's <u>not</u> for actions that were <u>completed</u> in the past, it's for actions that were <u>ongoing</u>. More on that later — here's how you <u>form</u> it.

## The stem comes from the nous form

There are 3 easy steps to make this past tense:

**1) Get the present tense 'nous' form of the verb (see p.98-99).**

**2) Knock the '-ons' off the end.**

The only verb that doesn't make its stem in this way is <u>être</u> (see below).

**3) Add on the correct ending:**

I used to have a life

### IMPERFECT TENSE ENDINGS

| | | | | | |
|---|---|---|---|---|---|
| *I:* | *je* | **-ais** | *we:* | *nous* | **-ions** |
| *you (informal sing.):* | *tu* | **-ais** | *you (plural & formal):* | *vous* | **-iez** |
| *he/she/it/one:* | *il/elle/on* | **-ait** | *they:* | *ils/elles* | **-aient** |

This bit depends on whether you're saying '<u>I</u>', '<u>you</u>', '<u>he</u>', etc.

### EXAMPLES

| <u>In English</u> | <u>Present of 'nous' form</u> | <u>Minus the '-ons'</u> | <u>Add on ending</u> | <u>Ta-da</u> |
|---|---|---|---|---|
| I was waiting | attendons | attend- | attend-**ais** | J'**attendais** |
| He was speaking | parlons | parl- | parl-**ait** | Il **parlait** |
| We were going | allons | all- | all-**ions** | Nous **allions** |

## Être, Avoir and Faire crop up a lot

You're more likely to come up against some verbs than others, so it's a good idea to become <u>really familiar</u> with them.

I'm afraid '<u>être</u>' is a bit different from the others (wouldn't it just be). The <u>endings</u> are the <u>same</u> though — it's just that the <u>stem</u> is '<u>ét-</u>'.

### EXAMPLES

*Ce roman <u>était</u> magnifique.*   = This novel <u>was</u> great.

*Vous <u>étiez</u> très petit à l'époque.*   = You <u>were</u> very small at the time.

And of course...

*C'était...*  = It was...  *On est allé au Canada — <u>c'était</u> formidable.*   = We went to Canada — <u>it was</u> great.

| ÊTRE = TO BE | |
|---|---|
| *j' étais:* | *I was* |
| *tu étais:* | *you (informal sing.)* were |
| *il/elle/on était:* | he/she/it/one was |
| *nous étions:* | we were |
| *vous étiez:* | you (formal & pl.) were |
| *ils/elles étaient:* | they were |

<u>All</u> the other verbs make their imperfect in the <u>normal way</u>.

'<u>Avoir</u>' is definitely one you'll need, especially because...

*Il y avait...*  = <u>There was / There were...</u>

E.g.   Il y <u>avait</u> deux stylos sur la table.
= There were two pens on the table

And you'll need '<u>faire</u>' in the imperfect tense too, especially to describe the <u>weather</u>.

E.g.   Il <u>faisait</u> beaucoup trop froid pour faire une promenade.
= It was far too cold to go for a walk.

# Another tense, another stem, more endings...

French verbs really are quite hard, and it's really easy to get confused between all the <u>stems</u> and <u>endings</u>. But remember that French teachers get <u>embarrassingly excited</u> when you get them <u>right</u>.

| IMPERFECT TENSE | ## *'Was Doing' or 'Used to Do'* |

Big question — how do you know when to use the perfect tense (see p.101-102), and when to use the imperfect tense? Well there's no simple answer actually, but here are a few useful pointers.

# Use the imperfect for Describing the past

Basically, you use the imperfect to describe what was going on, or to set the scene:

Il était six heures du matin. Il faisait très froid. J'attendais le train.
= It was six o'clock in the morning. It was very cold. I was waiting for the train.

Description in the imperfect tense

And then, suddenly, something happens. This goes in the perfect tense:

Tout à coup j'ai vu mon frère sur l'autre quai.
= All of a sudden I saw my brother on the other platform.

Event in the perfect tense

The French offer presents rather than give them.

### MORE EXAMPLES

**IMPERFECT**

Quand j'avais dix ans, je voulais une console de jeux.
Ma mère n'était pas d'accord, donc...

= When I was ten, I wanted a games console.
My mother didn't agree, so...

**PERFECT**

...on m'a offert une bicyclette.

= ...they gave me a bike.

We'd probably say, "I was given a bike". That would be a passive sentence (see page 111). The French often change passive into active sentences by using 'on'.

Sometimes the event comes first, and then the description:

**PERFECT**

J'ai rencontré une femme...

= I met a woman...

**IMPERFECT**

...qui était très amusante.

= ...who was very amusing.

So remember — the imperfect is for description, and the perfect is for events.

# Use the imperfect for what Used To happen

The imperfect is used for talking about what you used to do. That could be something you did regularly:

J'allais au cinéma tous les jeudis.   = I used to go to the cinema every Thursday.

Or something that was just the general state of affairs:   Je jouais du violon.   = I used to play the violin.

# Depuis + imperfect — had been

'Depuis' is always a tricky one. You know how if you want to say "I have been learning French for three years", you have to use the present tense: "J'apprends le français depuis trois ans"? (If not, refresh your memory on page 68.) Well, when it's "...had been...", you have to use the imperfect tense.

Il pleuvait depuis deux heures quand...   = It had been raining for two hours when...

J'attendais depuis deux minutes quand il est arrivé.   = I had been waiting for two minutes when he arrived.

# *Once upon a time, there was a lovely tense...*

If you want to say 'was doing', or 'used to do', it's a pretty safe bet that you need the imperfect in French. The best way to get a feel for where to use the imperfect is to learn some examples.

# Myself, Yourself, etc.

REFLEXIVE VERBS

Sometimes you have to talk about things you do to <u>yourself</u> — like washing yourself or getting yourself up in the morning.

## Talking about yourself — me, te, se...

*Grammar fans: these are <u>reflexive pronouns</u>.*

Here are all the different ways to say '<u>self</u>':

*You can tell <u>which</u> verbs need 'self' by checking in the <u>dictionary</u>. If you look up 'to <u>get up</u>', it'll say '<u>se lever</u>'.*

| | | | |
|---|---|---|---|
| *myself:* | me | | |
| *yourself (informal):* | te | *ourselves:* | nous |
| *himself:* | se | *yourself (formal), yourselves:* | vous |
| *herself:* | se | *themselves, each other:* | se |
| *oneself:* | se | | |

## Je me lave — I wash myself

You need to be able to talk about your '<u>daily morning routine</u>' (what you do when you get up), and other things which are about what you do to yourself.

*Grammar fans call these <u>reflexive verbs</u>.*

### SE LAVER = TO WASH ONESELF

| | | | |
|---|---|---|---|
| *I wash myself:* | je me lave | *one washes oneself:* | on se lave |
| *you wash yourself (informal):* | tu te laves | *we wash ourselves:* | nous nous lavons |
| *he washes himself:* | il se lave | *you wash yourself (formal) / yourselves:* | vous vous lavez |
| *she washes herself:* | elle se lave | *they wash themselves:* | ils/elles se lavent |

There are lots of these verbs, but here are the ones you should know for the exams. Learn these:

### THE 10 IMPORTANT REFLEXIVE VERBS

| | | | |
|---|---|---|---|
| *to enjoy oneself:* | s'amuser | Il s'amuse: | *He's enjoying himself.* |
| *to go to bed:* | se coucher | Je me couche à onze heures: | *I go to bed at 11 o'clock.* |
| *to get up:* | se lever | Je me lève à huit heures: | *I get up at 8 o'clock.* |
| *to feel:* | se sentir | Tu te sens mal?: | *Do you feel ill?* |
| *to be called (literally = to call oneself):* | s'appeler | Je m'appelle Bob: | *I'm called Bob.* |
| *to excuse oneself / to be sorry / to apologise:* | s'excuser | Je m'excuse...: | *(literally = I call myself Bob)* *I'm sorry / I apologise.* |
| *to be (literally = to find oneself):* | se trouver | Où se trouve la banque?: | *Where is the bank?* |
| | | | *(literally = Where does the bank find itself?)* |
| *to be spelt:* | s'écrire | Comment ça s'écrit?: | *How is that spelt?* |
| *to be interested in:* | s'intéresser à | Je m'intéresse au tennis: | *I'm interested in tennis.* |
| *to happen:* | se passer | Qu'est-ce qui se passe?: | *What's happening?* |

## Je me suis lavé(e) — I have washed myself

1) The <u>perfect tense</u> of these verbs is pretty much the same as normal (see p.101-102) except they <u>all go with 'être'</u>, not 'avoir'. The only tricky bit is working out where to put the '<u>me</u>' or '<u>te</u>' or '<u>se</u>' or whatever — and it goes right after the '<u>je</u>', '<u>tu</u>' or '<u>il</u>' etc. (In other words, it's <u>before</u> the bit of 'être'.)

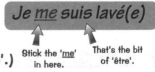

*Je <u>me</u> suis lavé(e)*

Stick the '<u>me</u>' in here. That's the bit of 'être'.

2) Like other verbs which use '<u>être</u>' for the <u>perfect tense</u>, you might have to add on an '<u>e</u>' and/or an '<u>s</u>', to <u>match who's</u> doing it. If you're <u>female</u>, make sure you add an '<u>e</u>' when you're talking about <u>yourself</u>.

EXAMPLES:

| *Je me suis lav<u>ée</u>.* | *Elle s'est lav<u>ée</u>.* | *Ils se sont lav<u>és</u>.* | *Elles se sont lav<u>ées</u>.* |
|---|---|---|---|
| = I (fem.) washed myself. | = She washed herself. | = They (masc. or mixed gender) washed themselves. | = They (fem.) washed themselves. |

## Reflexive verbs are really common in French...

...even when it's not obvious that someone's doing something to themselves. Try writing down a few sentences with reflexive verbs — some in the <u>present</u> and some in the <u>perfect</u> tense. Do it <u>NOW</u>.

## NEGATIVES — How to Say 'Not', 'Never' and 'Nothing'

This stuff's easy enough. Well, most of it is...

## Use 'ne ... pas' to say not

1) In English you change a sentence to mean the opposite by adding 'not'.

2) In French, you have to add two little words, 'ne' and 'pas'. They go either side of the verb (see p.97).

Je suis Bob. [ = I am Bob. ] ➡ Je ne suis pas Bob. [ = I am not Bob. ]

This is the verb. The 'ne' goes in front, and the 'pas' goes after.

3) For verbs in the perfect tense (see p.101-102), you stick the 'ne' and 'pas' around the bit of avoir or être.

Je n'ai pas vu ça. [ = I have not seen that. ]   Elle n'est pas arrivée. [ = She has not arrived. ]

## For an infinitive, the ne and pas go together

The 'ne' and 'pas' usually go either side of the action word (the verb).
BUT if the action word is an infinitive (see page 97) then the 'ne' and the 'pas' both go in front of it.

Je préfère voir un film.  ➡  Je préfère ne pas voir un film.

[ = I prefer to see a film. ]   [ = I prefer not to see a film. ]

## ne ... jamais — never   ne ... rien — nothing

There are more negatives you need to understand, and for top marks you should use them too.

Je ne vais plus à York.   Je ne vais jamais à York.   Je ne vais ni à York ni à Belfast.

= I don't go to York any more. (I no longer go to York.)   = I never go to York. (I don't ever go to York.)   = I neither go to York nor to Belfast.

*not any more (no longer):* ne ... plus   *not ever (never):* ne ... jamais   *neither ... nor:* ne ... ni ... ni

*not anybody (nobody):* ne ... personne   *not anything (nothing):* ne ... rien   *not any / not one:* ne ... aucun(e) *(not a single...)*

= There isn't anybody here. (There is nobody here.)   = There isn't anything here. (There is nothing here.)   = There aren't any bananas. (There is not a single banana.)

Il n'y a personne ici.   Il n'y a rien ici.   Il n'y a aucune banane.

'Y' and 'en' go between the 'ne' and the verb.

## Je n'ai pas de... — I don't have any...

After a negative, articles such as 'un/une', 'du', 'de la' or 'des' are always replaced by just 'de'.

Je n'ai pas d'argent. [ = I haven't got any money. ]

Elle n'a plus de chocolat. [ = She hasn't got any more chocolate. ]

The 'de' is only shortened if the next word begins with a vowel or an 'h' which takes 'l'. E.g. 'd'argent', 'd'animaux'.

## Just say no — & nobody & nothing & never & not...

OK, just one more thing, then I'll be quiet. When you want 'nobody' or 'nothing' to be the subject of the sentence, you have to say "Personne ne..." or "Rien ne...". E.g. "Personne ne nous a vus" = "Nobody saw us", and "Rien ne s'est passé" = "Nothing happened" (se passer = to happen).

# *Would, Could & Should*

OK, I'll admit it. This <u>is</u> tricky. But it is <u>important</u>, so <u>learn</u> it.

## *Je voudrais et j'aimerais... — I would like...*

These two verbs are really useful in the <u>conditional</u> — you can use them lots in your speaking assessment.

① **VOULOIR = TO WANT**

| | |
|---|---|
| *I would like:* | je voudrais |
| *you (informal singular) would like:* | tu voudrais |
| *he/she/it/one would like:* | il/elle/on voudrait |
| *we would like:* | nous voudrions |
| *you (formal & plural) would like:* | vous voudriez |
| *they would like:* | ils/elles voudraient |

② **AIMER = TO LIKE**

| | |
|---|---|
| *I would like:* | j'aimerais |
| *you (informal singular) would like:* | tu aimerais |
| *he/she/it/one would like:* | il/elle/on aimerait |
| *we would like:* | nous aimerions |
| *you (formal & plural) would like:* | vous aimeriez |
| *they would like:* | ils/elles aimeraient |

*Je voudrais aller à l'hôpital.* = <u>I would like</u> to go to hospital.

*J'aimerais du lait.* = <u>I would like</u> some milk.

## *The conditional = future stem + imperfect endings*

The <u>conditional</u> (for saying '<u>would</u>', '<u>could</u>', '<u>should</u>') is simple to form, but you have to be on the ball to spot it if it comes up in the reading or listening exams — it's easy to <u>mistake</u> it for the <u>imperfect</u> tense (because the endings are the same) or the <u>future</u> tense (because the stem is the same). This is how you form it:

**1) Take the stems from the future tense (see page 100).**

**2) Add the endings from the imperfect tense (see page 103).**

**FUTURE**

*Vous pourrez chanter.* = <u>You will be able to</u> sing.

*Tu devras m'écrire.* = <u>You will have to</u> write to me.

*Elle ira en France.* = <u>She will go</u> to France.

*Je mangerai du pain.* = <u>I will eat</u> some bread.

**IMPERFECT**

*Vous pouviez chanter.* = <u>You were able to</u> sing.

*Tu devais m'écrire.* = <u>You had to</u> write to me.

*Elle allait en France.* = <u>She was going</u> to France.

*Je mangeais du pain.* = <u>I was eating</u> some bread.

**CONDITIONAL**

*Vous pourriez chanter.* = <u>You would be able to</u> / <u>could</u> sing.

*Tu devrais m'écrire.* = <u>You should</u> write to me.

*Elle irait en France.* = <u>She would go</u> to France.

*Je mangerais du pain.* = <u>I would eat</u> some bread.

The '<u>je</u>' one ('-ais') can be <u>hard to spot</u> when you're <u>listening</u>, because it sounds very <u>similar</u> to the <u>future</u> ending ('-ai'). You have to <u>think</u> about what the <u>rest</u> of the sentence means and <u>work out</u> whether the person's saying what they <u>would</u> do, or what they <u>will</u> do.

## *If I were a tense, I'd be the conditional...*

You often use the conditional when you have '<u>if</u>' followed by the <u>imperfect tense</u>. For example, '<u>If I had</u> a lot of money, <u>I would buy</u> seven horses' = '<u>Si j'avais</u> beaucoup d'argent, <u>j'achèterais</u> sept chevaux'. A really useful tense, but rather tricky to form. Still, nobody said it was easy...

| IMPERATIVE | # Ordering People Around |
|---|---|

Ordering people around — the <u>quicker</u> you <u>learn</u> it, the <u>quicker</u> you can get on with your life...

## You need this for bossing people about

*Grammar Fans: This is called the <u>Imperative</u>.*

It looks like the present tense (see p.98) but <u>without</u> the 'tu', 'vous' or 'nous' bits.

*For when to choose 'tu' or 'vous' see page 5.*

*You need this one for <u>suggesting</u> doing something — like 'Let's go' or 'Let's dance'.*

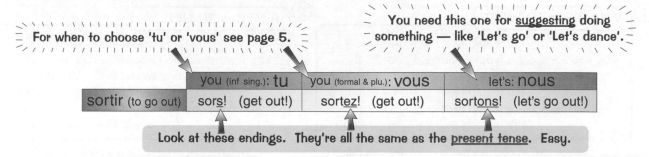

| | you (inf. sing.): tu | you (formal & plu.): vous | let's: nous |
|---|---|---|---|
| sortir (to go out) | sor**s**! (get out!) | sort**ez**! (get out!) | sort**ons**! (let's go out!) |

Look at these endings. They're all the same as the <u>present tense</u>. Easy.

**EXAMPLES**

*Vendons la voiture!*
= Let's sell the car!

*Écoute ceci!*
= Listen to this!

*Finissez vos devoirs!*
= Finish your homework!

## Whip off the 's' from the 'tu' form of '-er' verbs

The odd one out is any '<u>tu</u>' form that ends in '<u>es</u>'. That means you have to be careful with <u>regular -er verbs</u>. You just have to lose the final '<u>-s</u>':

*Regarde Jean-Paul!*
= Look at Jean-Paul!

*Arrête de m'énerver!*
= Stop annoying me!

The ones below are <u>irregular</u>. They're nothing like the present tense, so you have to learn them by heart.

| | you (inf. sing.): tu | you (formal & plu.): vous | let's: nous |
|---|---|---|---|
| to be: être | sois (be) | soyez (be) | soyons (let's be) |
| to have: avoir | aie (have) | ayez (have) | ayons (let's have) |
| to know: savoir | sache (know) | sachez (know) | sachons (let's know) |

## Negatives work normally, except for reflexives

Put '<u>ne</u>' in front of the verb and '<u>pas</u>' after, like normal (see page 106). Add the noun at the end.

**EXAMPLES:** *N'écoute pas!* = Don't listen!   *Ne vendez pas la voiture!* = Don't sell the car!

In sentences with a <u>reflexive</u> verb (see p.105) you have to use an emphatic pronoun (p.94), and fiddle the word order...

**E.g.** *Tu <u>te</u> lèves.* = You get up. ➡ *Lève-<u>toi</u>!* = Get up!

**WATCH OUT** though — in negative sentences, you use normal pronouns and normal word order.

**E.g.** *Tu ne te lèves pas.* = You don't get up. ➡ *Ne te lève pas!* = Don't get up!

## If it's imperative, it must be important...

Hopefully you haven't found this too horrendous. But <u>do</u> be careful about dropping the '<u>s</u>' from the '<u>tu</u>' form of '<u>-er</u>' verbs — that catches out many a weary traveller. Oh, and <u>negatives</u> aren't obvious, so take another look at those before you whizz on blithely to the next page.

# Know and Can

<u>Sooo</u> many people get these verbs confused — so learn them right now.

## *'To know information' is 'Savoir'*

1) <u>Savoir</u> means '<u>to know</u>' in the sense of knowing <u>information</u> (e.g. knowing what time the bus leaves).

**DIFFERENT FORMS OF SAVOIR**

| | |
|---|---|
| *I know* | je sais |
| *you (informal singular) know* | tu sais |
| *he/she/it/one knows* | il/elle/on sait |
| *we know* | nous savons |
| *you (formal and plural) know* | vous savez |
| *they know* | ils/elles savent |

*Elle <u>sait</u> la réponse.* = She knows the answer.

*Je ne <u>sais</u> pas si nous avons des bananes.*

= I don't know if we have any bananas.

2) <u>Savoir</u> followed by an <u>infinitive</u> means '<u>to know how to do something</u>', in the sense of a skill...

EXAMPLES: *Je <u>sais</u> conduire.* = I can drive. *Elle ne <u>sait</u> pas lire.* = She can't read.

## *'To be familiar with' is 'Connaître'*

Connaître means to know a person or place — to '<u>be familiar with</u>'.
If someone asks you whether you know their mate Bob, this is the one to use.

Je connais la lune.

**DIFFERENT FORMS OF CONNAÎTRE**

| | |
|---|---|
| *I know* | je connais |
| *you (informal singular) know* | tu connais |
| *he/she/it/one knows* | il/elle/on connaît |
| *we know* | nous connaissons |
| *you (formal and plural) know* | vous connaissez |
| *they know* | ils/elles connaissent |

*Connais-tu mon ami?* = Do you know my friend?

*Je <u>connais</u> bien Paris.* = I know Paris well.

## *'Pouvoir' — to be able to*

Pouvoir (to be able to/can) has three very important meanings:

1) Being <u>able</u> to do something (<u>not</u> knowing <u>how</u>, but just being able — like 'Yes, I can come tomorrow').

*Je <u>peux</u> porter les bagages, si tu veux.* = I can carry the luggage, if you like.

*Elle ne <u>peut</u> pas venir ce matin.* = She cannot come this morning.

2) <u>Permission</u> to do something. *On <u>peut</u> prendre des photos ici.* = You can take photos here.

*Tu ne <u>peux</u> pas rester demain.* = You can't stay tomorrow.

3) <u>Possibility</u> — something <u>could</u> or <u>might</u> be the case.

*Cela <u>peut</u> arriver.* = That can happen.

**DIFFERENT FORMS OF POUVOIR**

| | |
|---|---|
| *I can* | je peux |
| *you (informal singular) can* | tu peux |
| *he/she/it/one can* | il/elle/on peut |
| *we can* | nous pouvons |
| *you (formal and plural) can* | vous pouvez |
| *they can* | ils/elles peuvent |

# When the can-can's a know-know...

If you learn how to use these three <u>key words</u> correctly, you'll be well on your way to a top mark.

# Had Done and '-ing'

Three more bits to learn — keep at it, the grammar section's nearly over...

## J'avais fait — I had done

Grammar fans: this is the **Pluperfect Tense**.

1)  The pluperfect is <u>like</u> the perfect tense (see p.101-102) — that's for saying what you <u>have</u> done, but this is for what you <u>had</u> done.

2)  It's still made up of a bit of <u>avoir</u> or <u>être</u> + a <u>past participle</u> (see p.102), but the bit of avoir or être is in the <u>imperfect tense</u>.

For stuff on the imperfect tense, see p.103-104.

**FORMING THE PLUPERFECT**

**IMPERFECT TENSE OF AVOIR / ÊTRE + PAST PARTICIPLE**

*J'<u>avais écrit</u> une lettre à mon père.* | = I <u>had written</u> a letter to my father.

*Nous <u>étions allés</u> voir un film au cinéma.* | = We <u>had gone</u> to see a film at the cinema.

*Betty et Sarah <u>étaient arrivées</u>.* | = Betty and Sarah <u>had arrived</u>.

## Doing, saying, thinking are present participles

<u>En</u> + the <u>present participle</u> means 'while doing something':

*Il lit le journal <u>en déjeunant</u>.* | = He reads the paper <u>while having lunch</u>.

This is how you form the present participle:

**FORMING THE PRESENT PARTICIPLE**

**IMPERFECT STEM + '-ANT'**

Remember — the imperfect stem is made from the 'nous' form of the present minus the '-ons'. See p.103.

**EXAMPLES**

PLAYING: *jou<s>ons</s>* + *ant* = *jouant*     SAYING: *dis<s>ons</s>* + *ant* = *disant*     BLUSHING: *rougiss<s>ons</s>* + *ant* = *rougissant*

<u>CAREFUL THOUGH</u> — you translate things like 'I am doing' with <u>normal tenses</u>, e.g. "je fais" and things like 'I like doing' with the present tense followed by the infinitive (see page 99).

## Après avoir mangé... — After having eaten...

This could easily crop up in the exam/assessments. '<u>Après avoir + past participle</u>' means '<u>after having done something</u>'. The verbs which go with <u>être</u> in the perfect tense (p.102) take <u>être</u> here too.

*Après avoir joué au foot, j'ai mangé.* | = After having played football, I ate.

*Après être arrivé(e), j'ai...* | = After having arrived, I...

Extra marks for style

## Better than perfect...

In French the pluperfect's called the '<u>plus-que-parfait</u>'. Makes sense in a way, as it describes a <u>further step</u> back into the past from the perfect tense. Useful stuff on this page — get it <u>learnt</u>.

# The Passive

The stuff on this page all sounds quite <u>grammary</u>, but in fact the passive in French is not very different from how we form it in English. <u>And</u> you only really need to <u>recognise</u> this stuff, not <u>use</u> it.

## La tasse est cassée — The cup is broken

1) In most sentences, there's a person or thing <u>doing</u> the action that's described by the verb. In a <u>passive</u> sentence, the person or thing is having <u>something done to it</u>.

2) The passive in French is made up of a <u>person</u> or <u>thing</u> + <u>être</u> + <u>past participle</u>.

3) The <u>past participle</u> has to <u>agree</u> with the <u>person</u> or <u>thing</u> that is having the <u>action done to it</u>.

| Elle <u>est renversée</u> par la voiture. | = She <u>is run over</u> by the car. |

See p.101-102 for more past participles.

'est' is a present tense form of the verb 'être' — to see the rest of it in the present, go to page 99.

## In the Past and Future, only the 'être' bit Changes...

1) You also need to <u>recognise</u> the passive when it's describing what happened in the <u>past</u> or what will happen in the <u>future</u>.

2) Don't worry though — the passive in the different tenses is formed in basically the same way as in the <u>present</u>. The only thing that changes is the <u>tense</u> of 'être'.

The **IMPERFECT PASSIVE** describes what happened to someone in the past. It's formed using the <u>imperfect</u> tense of <u>être</u> and a <u>past participle</u>:

| L'homme <u>était blessé</u>. | = The man <u>was injured</u>. | Ils <u>étaient tués</u>. | = They <u>were killed</u>. |

The **PERFECT PASSIVE** tells you about an event in the past that lasted for a fixed amount of time. It's formed using the <u>perfect tense</u> of <u>être</u> and a <u>past participle</u>:

| Un homme <u>a été renversé</u> par un camion. | = A man <u>has been run over</u> by a lorry. |

| Les chiens <u>ont été volés</u> par le voisin. | = The dogs <u>have been stolen</u> by the neighbour. |

The future passive is made up of part of the <u>future tense</u> of <u>être</u> + <u>past participle</u>:

| Elles <u>seront tuées</u>. | = They <u>will be killed</u>. |

| Tu seras puni(e). | = You <u>will be punished</u>. |

Don't forget that with all tenses of the passive, if it's talking about something feminine or plural the past participle has to agree.

One last thing — there's a <u>reason</u> why you'll need to <u>recognise</u> this but not <u>use</u> it. French doesn't use the passive as much as it's used in English. In French, they often use an <u>active</u> sentence with '<u>on</u>' instead.

| I wasn't seen. | = On ne m'a pas vu(e). |

## 'Injured', 'killed', 'punished', 'run over' — what a day...

The thing to understand about the passive is that it looks much more complicated than it actually is — all you need to remember to do is make sure that absolutely <u>everything</u> (e.g. bit of être, past participle) <u>agrees</u> with the person who's having something done to them. Or just use '<u>on</u>' instead...

# Impersonal Verbs & the Subjunctive

Some pretty <u>meaty stuff</u> on this page. But don't despair — one <u>final push</u> and you'll have finished the grammar section.

## Impersonal verbs only work with 'il'

Impersonal verbs always have '<u>il</u>' as the subject. For example:

**_Il faut aller au collège tous les jours._**   = <u>It is necessary to</u> go to school every day.

You also use impersonal verbs to talk about the <u>weather</u>:

**_Il a plu hier, et aujourd'hui il neige._**   = <u>It rained</u> yesterday, and today <u>it's snowing</u>.

Some impersonal verbs <u>combine</u> with other verbs in the <u>infinitive</u>:

**_Il est nécessaire de courir._**   = <u>It is necessary to</u> run.

For more on infinitives, see page 97 and the bottom of page 99.

**_Il me semble raisonnable d'arrêter._**   = <u>It seems</u> reasonable <u>to me</u> to stop.

See p.93 for indirect object pronouns.

**_Il s'agit d'argent._**   = <u>It's a question of</u> money.

## You may see the subjunctive instead of the infinitive

Not all <u>impersonal verbs</u> are followed by the infinitive — some are followed by the <u>subjunctive</u> instead. You just need to understand what <u>common verbs</u> look and sound like in the subjunctive in case they come up in your <u>listening</u> or <u>reading</u> exam. The <u>expressions</u> that use the subjunctive that you're most likely to see are:

**_il faut qu'il parte demain_**   = <u>It is necessary</u> for him to leave tomorrow.

**_il semble qu' il ne vienne pas_**   = <u>It seems</u> that he's not coming.

**_bien qu'elle ait deux enfants_**   = <u>Although</u> she has two children.

**_pour qu'il fasse ses devoirs_**   = <u>So that</u> he does his homework.

**_avant que vous partiez_**   = <u>Before</u> you leave.

And these are the <u>verbs</u> you really need to <u>recognise</u> in the subjunctive:

'<u>Avoir</u>' and '<u>être</u>' in the subjunctive are the same as the imperative (those command words you met on p.108).

### SUBJUNCTIVE FORMS

| | | | | | | |
|---|---|---|---|---|---|---|
| _Avoir_ | j'aie | tu aies | il/elle/on ait | nous ayons | vous ayez | ils/elles aient |
| _Être_ | je sois | tu sois | il/elle/on soit | nous soyons | vous soyez | ils/elles soient |
| _Faire_ | je fasse | tu fasses | il/elle/on fasse | nous fassions | vous fassiez | ils/elles fassent |
| _Pouvoir_ | je puisse | tu puisses | il/elle/on puisse | nous puissions | vous puissiez | ils/elles puissent |

## It's nothing personal...

Basically, if you see a <u>funny-looking</u> verb after the word '<u>que</u>', it's probably the <u>subjunctive</u>. You won't be expected to use it, but don't let it throw you if it comes up in the exam. Usually it'll be <u>obvious</u> what verb it's from, but there are a few banana skins, like '<u>être</u>'. Best get them <u>learnt</u>.

# Revision Summary

<u>Boogie on</u>... It's the last time you'll see the shocking words above — words that spread fear and loathing across the nation. That's right, this is the final French 'Revision Summary'. Whoop whoop.

1) What are the words for both '<u>the</u>' and '<u>a</u>' (where appropriate) which have to accompany these:
a) maison  b) chien   c) chaussure  d) soleil   e) travail   f) jeu  g) jeux  h) journaux

2) Je vais à la maison...  Change this sentence to tell people you're going to:
a) le cinéma     b) l'église    c) la banque    d) le stade    e) les magasins      f) les Alpes

3) What is the French word for:  a) my horse     b) our house       c) his clothes      d) her house

4) "Janie is cool.  Janie is cooler than Jimmy.  She is the coolest."  Translate these three sentences into French, then swap "cool" for each of the following words and write them out all over again:
a) formidable      b) intelligent(e)      c) célèbre     d) pratique     e) bavard(e)

5) Write a French sentence for each of the following French words.  Then put them all together... et voilà... you have your very own (probably weird) French poem.  You truly are the next Prévert...
a) à    b) en    c) dans    d) pour    e) depuis    f) de

6) Place the missing <u>qui</u>'s and <u>que</u>'s in the following text and then translate it, please...
J'ai rencontré un homme __ adorait les sports.  Cet homme __ j'ai rencontré, __ adorait les sports, n'aimait pas les escargots __ je lui avais achetés, surtout ceux __ venaient de la France.

7) Replace the underlined parts of these sentences with either 'y' or 'en':
a) J'ai besoin <u>du chocolat</u>.  b) Je vais aller <u>au cinéma</u>.  c) Je prends six kilos <u>de bonbons</u>, s.v.p.

8) What are the French words for:
a) and        b) or        c) but        d) because      e) with      f) while      g) therefore

9) How do you say the following in French:
a) I have   b) she has   c) we have   d) they have   e) I am   f) he is   g) we are   h) they are

10) What does each of these French phrases mean in English:  a) Je mange un gâteau
b) J'ai mangé un gâteau        c) Je mangeais un gâteau     d) J'avais mangé un gâteau
e) Je vais manger un gâteau   f) Je mangerai un gâteau      g) Je mangerais un gâteau

11) Sadly, growing up means learning to do things for yourself.  Use reflexive verbs to say:
a) We wash ourselves.   b) She went to bed.   c) They had fun.   d) I'm interested in French.

12) Ah, negativity.  We'll have none of that here.  Well, apart from these phrases.  How do you say these in French:   a) I don't go out.      b) I never go out.      c) I don't go out any more.

13) Going commando.  Turn these sentences from the present tense to the imperative:
a) Tu arrêtes de faire ça. b) Vous êtes tranquille.      c) Nous allons au Portugal.
d) Tu te lèves.      e) Vous ne vous inquiétez pas.      f) Nous ne regardons pas le film.

14) Translate:   a) He reads the paper while taking a shower.   b) I talk after having eaten.
c) They play Scrabble while walking the dog.   d) We work after having listened to the radio.

15) Final question.  What does 'Il faut que tu apprennes toutes les choses dans ce livre avant de le jeter' mean?

# Do Well in Your Exam

Here are some little gems of advice, whichever exam board you're studying for.

## Read the Questions carefully

Don't go losing easy marks — it'll break my heart.
Make sure you definitely do the things on this list:

> 1) Read all the instructions properly.
> 2) Read the question properly.
> 3) Answer the question — don't waffle.

## Don't give up if you don't Understand

If you don't understand, don't panic. The key thing to remember is that you
can still do well in the exam, even if you don't understand every French word
that comes up. Just use one of the two methods below:

### If you're reading or listening — look for lookalikes

1) Some words look or sound the same in French and English — they're called cognates.

2) These words are great because you'll recognise them when you see them in a text.

3) Be careful though — there are some exceptions you need to watch out for.
   Some words look like an English word but have a totally different meaning:

| | | | | | |
|---|---|---|---|---|---|
| sensible: | *sensitive* | la journée: | *day* | le car: | *coach* |
| grand(e): | *big* | la pièce: | *room, coin or play* | le crayon: | *pencil* |
| large: | *wide* | la cave: | *cellar* | les affaires: | *business* |
| mince: | *slim* | la veste: | *jacket* | le pain: | *bread* |
| joli(e): | *pretty* | le médecin: | *doctor* | les baskets: | *trainers* |

Words like these are called 'faux amis' — false friends.

## Make use of the Context

You'll likely come across the odd word that you don't know, especially in the reading exam.
Often you'll be able to find some clues telling you what the text is all about.

> 1) The type of text, e.g. newspaper article, advertisement, website
> 2) The title of the text
> 3) Any pictures
> 4) The verbal context

Say you see the following in the reading exam, and don't know what any of these words mean:

"...des vêtements en polyester, en soie, en laine et en coton."

1) Well, the fact that this is a list of things all starting with 'en ...' coming after the French word for
   'clothes' suggests they're all things that clothes can be made out of.

2) You can guess that 'polyester' means 'polyester', and 'coton' means 'cotton'.

3) So it's a pretty good guess that the two words you don't know are different types of fabric.
   (In fact, 'soie' means 'silk' and 'laine' means 'wool'.)

4) Often the questions won't depend on you understanding these more difficult words. It's important
   to be able to understand the gist though, and not let these words throw you.

## Friend or faux?

Don't get caught out by words that look like English words, but in fact mean something different.
Generally speaking, if a word doesn't seem to fit into the context of the question, have a re-think.

# Do Well in Your Exam

These pages could <u>improve</u> your grade — they're all about exam technique.

## Look at how a word is made up

You may read or hear a sentence and not understand <u>how the sentence works</u>.  You need to remember all the <u>grammar bits</u> in Section 7 to give you a good chance at <u>piecing it all together</u>.

1) A word that ends in '<u>-é</u>', '<u>-u</u>' or '<u>-i</u>' may well be a <u>past participle</u>.  Look for a bit of '<u>avoir</u>' or a bit of '<u>être</u>' nearby to work out who's done what.

2) A word that ends in '<u>r</u>' or '<u>er</u>' might be an <u>infinitive</u>.  If you take off the 'er', it might look like an English word which may tell you what the verb means.

> E.g. 'confirmer' = to <u>confirm</u>

3) If you see '<u>-ment</u>' at the end of a word, it could well be an <u>adverb</u> (see page 88).  Try replacing the '-ment' with '<u>-ly</u>' and see if it makes sense.

> E.g. 'généralement' ➡ 'généralely' = <u>generally</u>

4) '<u>Dé-</u>' at the beginning of a word is often '<u>dis-</u>' in the equivalent word in English.

> E.g. 'décourager' = to <u>discourage</u>

5) Sometimes <u>letters with accents</u> show that there may have been an '<u>s</u>' at some point in the past.  This may help you find the corresponding English word.

> E.g. 'tempête' = <u>tempest</u>    'mât' = <u>mast</u>    'forêt' = <u>forest</u>

6) A word beginning with '<u>in-</u>' might be a <u>negative prefix</u>.

> E.g. 'inconnu' = '<u>in</u>+<u>connu</u> = <u>unknown</u>

A prefix is a part of a word that comes before the main bit of the word.

## Take notes in the listening exam

1) You'll have <u>5 minutes</u> at the start of the listening exam to have a <u>quick look</u> through the paper.  This'll give you a chance to see <u>how many questions</u> there are, and you might get a few clues from the questions about what <u>topics</u> they're on, so it won't be a horrible surprise when the recording starts.

2) You'll hear each extract <u>twice</u>.  Different people have different strategies, but it's a good idea to jot down a few details that you think might come up in the questions, especially things like:

Dates
Numbers
Names

3) But... don't forget to <u>keep listening</u> to the gist of the recording while you're making notes.

4) You won't have a <u>dictionary</u> — but you probably wouldn't have time to use it anyway.

## And don't forget to keep your ears clean...

The examiners aren't above sticking a few tricky bits and pieces into the exam to see how you <u>cope</u> with them.  Using all your expert knowledge, you should stand a pretty good chance of working it out.  And if you can't make an <u>educated</u> guess, make an <u>uneducated</u> guess... but try <u>something</u>.

# How to Use Dictionaries

Don't go mad on dictionaries — it's the path to <u>ruin</u>. However, you're allowed to use one in the writing task, so it's good to know how to make the <u>most</u> of it.

## Don't translate Word for Word — it DOESN'T work

If you turn each word of this phrase into English, you get <u>rubbish</u>.

*Il y a une pomme.*  *It there has an apple.*

**NO!**

It's the <u>same</u> the other way round — turn English into French word by word, and you get <u>balderdash</u> — <u>don't do it</u>.

*I am reading.*  *Je suis lisant.*

## If it Doesn't make Sense, you've got it Wrong

Some words have several meanings — don't just pick the first one you see.
Look at the <u>meanings</u> listed and <u>suss out</u> which one is what you're looking for.

If you read this... *J'ai mal à l'oeil droit.*

...you might look up '<u>droit</u>' and find this:

So the sentence could mean:

*My straight eye hurts.* ✗

*My right eye hurts.* ✔

*My law eye hurts.* ✗

This is the only one that sounds sensible.

**droit, e**
<u>adj</u> upright; straight;
// right, right-hand
// <u>adv</u> straight
  <u>tiens-toi droit</u>: stand up straight
// <u>nm</u> law; justice
// droits; rights; taxes, duties
  <u>droits d'auteur</u>: royalties

## Verbs change according to the person

When you look up a <u>verb</u> in the dictionary, you'll find the <u>infinitive</u> (the 'to' form, like '<u>to</u> run', '<u>to</u> sing' etc.). But you may need to say '<u>I</u> run', or '<u>we</u> sing' — so you need to change the verb <u>ending</u>.

Say you need to say '<u>I work</u>'.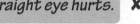

For the low-down on verbs and all their different endings, see the grammar section.

1) If you looked up '<u>work</u>', you'd find the word '<u>travailler</u>', meaning 'to work'.
2) But '<u>travailler</u>' is the <u>infinitive</u> — you can't put 'je travailler'.
3) You need the '<u>I</u>' (je) form of the verb — 'je <u>travaille</u>'.
4) Check the <u>tense</u> — e.g. you might want the future: 'je travaillerai'.

If you're looking up a <u>French</u> verb, look for its <u>infinitive</u> (it'll probably end in 'er', 'ir' or 're'). If you want to know what 'nous poussons' means, you'll find '<u>pousser</u>' (to push, or to grow) in the dictionary. So 'nous poussons' must mean '<u>we push</u>' or '<u>we grow</u>'.

## Dictionaries — useful for holding doors open...*

Don't get put off dictionaries by this page. They're lovely really. Just make sure your technique isn't to look up every single word and then bung them down in order. Cos it'll be rubbish.

# Hints for Writing

Here are a few general hints about how you should approach the writing tasks.

## Write about what you know

1) You won't be asked to write about 19th century French novelists — it'll be easier than that.

2) You will need to cover certain specific things that the question asks you to, but there'll be plenty of scope to be imaginative.

3) Usually the writing tasks will give you some flexibility so you can base your answer on something you know about.

Que sais-je?

## You get marks for saying When and Why...

1) Saying when and how often you did things gets you big bonus marks. Learn times, dates and numbers carefully (pages 1-3).

2) Make sure you talk about what you've done in the past (see pages 101-104) or what you will do in the future (page 100).

3) Give descriptions where possible, but keep things accurate — a short description in perfect French is better than a longer paragraph of nonsense.

4) Opinions (pages 7-8) also score highly. Try to vary them as much as possible.

So, if I add one more drop we'll go back in time two hours...

...two hours later...

## ...and Where and Who With...

Most teachers are really quite nosy, and love as many details as you can give. It's a good idea to ask yourself all these 'wh-' questions, and write the bits that show your French off in the best light. Also, it doesn't matter if what you're writing isn't strictly true — as long as it's believable.

## Use your dictionary, but sparingly

1) The time to use the dictionary is NOT to learn a completely new, fancy way of saying something.

2) Use it to look up a particular word that you've forgotten — a word that, when you see it, you'll know it's the right word.

3) Use it to check genders of nouns — that's whether words are masculine (le/un) or feminine (la/une).

4) Check any spellings you're unsure of.

> Most importantly, don't use the dictionary to delve into the unknown.
> If you don't know what you've written is right, it's probably wrong.

## Take your time

1) Don't hurtle into writing about something and then realise halfway through that you don't actually know the French for it.

2) Plan how you can cover all the things that the task mentions, and then think about the extra things you can slip in to show off your French.

Take me.

## And lastly, don't forget your pen...

I suppose the key is variety — lots of different tenses, plenty of meaty vocabulary and loads of details. This is your only chance to show what you can do, so don't waste all your hard work.

# Hints for Writing

Accuracy is really important in the writing assessment. Without it, your work will look like sloppy custard.

## Start with the Verb

1) Verbs really are the cornerstone of every French sentence.
If you get the verb right, the rest of the sentence should fall into place.

*Verbs are doing words.*
*See page 97.*

2) Be careful that you get the whole expression that uses the verb, not just the verb itself.

EXAMPLE: Say you want to write the following sentence in French:

*On Sundays, we go for a walk, if the weather is nice.*

Don't see 'go' and jump in with 'aller'.
The expression for 'go for a walk' is 'faire une promenade'.

You know that 'the weather is nice' is 'il fait beau'.

Make sure your tenses and the endings of the verbs are right, then piece it all together:

*Le dimanche, nous faisons une promenade, s'il fait beau.*

## Check and re-check

No matter how careful you think you're being, mistakes can easily creep into your work.

Go through the checklist below for every sentence straight after you've written it.

1) Are the verbs in the right TENSE?

Demain, je travaillais dans le jardin. ✘          Demain, je travaillerai dans le jardin. ✔

2) Are the ENDINGS of the verbs right?

Tu n'aime pas les carottes? ✘          Tu n'aimes pas les carottes? ✔

3) Do your adjectives AGREE as they should?

Elle est grand. ✘          Elle est grande. ✔

4) Do your past participles AGREE?

Ils sont parti. ✘          Ils sont partis. ✔

5) Do your adjectives come in the RIGHT PLACE?

Une rose chemise ✘          Une chemise rose ✔

6) Have you used TU / VOUS correctly?

Monsieur, peux-tu m'aider, s'il vous plaît? ✘          Monsieur, pouvez-vous m'aider, s'il vous plaît? ✔

Then when you've finished the whole piece of work, have another read through with fresh eyes.
You're bound to pick up one or two more mistakes.

## Do nothing without a verb...

I know there's loads to remember, and French verbs are a pain, but checking over your work is a real must. Reread your work assuming there are errors in it, rather than assuming it's fine as it is.

# Hints for Speaking

The speaking assessment fills many a student with <u>dread</u>. Remember though — it's your chance to show what you can <u>do</u>. It won't be nearly as bad as you think it's going to be. <u>Honest</u>.

## Be Imaginative

There are two tricky things about the speaking assessment — one is <u>what to say</u>, and the other is <u>how to say it</u>. No matter how good your French is, it won't shine through if you can't think of anything to say.

Say you're asked to talk about your <u>daily routine</u> (or to imagine someone else's daily routine). It would be easy to give a list of things you do when you get in from school:

> *"Je fais mes devoirs. Je regarde la télé. Je mange. Je vais au lit."*

> = I do my homework. I watch TV. I eat. I go to bed.

It makes sense, but the problem is, it's all a bit <u>samey</u>...

1) Try to think of when this <u>isn't</u> the case, and put it into a **DIFFERENT TENSE**:

> *"Mais demain ce sera différent, parce que je jouerai au hockey après le collège."*

> = But tomorrow it will be different, because I will play hockey after school.

2) Don't just talk about yourself. Talk about <u>OTHER PEOPLE</u> — even if you have to imagine them.

> *"J'ai regardé la télé avec mon frère, mais il n'aime pas les mêmes émissions que moi."*

> = I watched TV with my brother, but he doesn't like the same programmes as me.

3) Give loads of <u>OPINIONS</u> and <u>REASONS</u> for your opinions.

> *"J'aime finir mes devoirs avant de manger. Puis je peux me détendre plus tard."*

> = I like to finish my homework before eating. Then I can relax later on.

## A couple of 'DON'T's...

1) <u>DON'T</u> try to <u>avoid</u> a topic if you find it difficult — that'll mean you won't get <u>any</u> marks at all for that bit of the assessment. You'll be surprised what you can muster up if you stay calm and concentrate on what you <u>do</u> know how to say.

2) <u>DON'T</u> make up a word in the hope that it exists in French unless you're really, really stuck. Try one of the tricks on the next page first. However, if it's your <u>last resort</u>, it's worth a try.

## Have Confidence

1) Believe it or not, the teacher isn't trying to catch you out. He or she <u>wants</u> you to do <u>well</u>, and to be dazzled by all the excellent French you've learnt.

2) Speaking assessments can be pretty <u>daunting</u>. But remember it's the same for <u>everyone</u>.

3) <u>Nothing horrendous</u> is going to happen if you make a few slip-ups. Just try and focus on showing the teacher how much you've <u>learnt</u>.

# Imagine there's no speaking assessment...

It's easy if you try. But that's not going to get you a GCSE. The main thing to remember is that it's much better to have too much to say than too little. Bear in mind the <u>3 ways</u> to make your answers more <u>imaginative</u>. This will give you an opportunity to show off your <u>beautiful French</u>.

# Hints for Speaking

Nothing in life ever goes completely according to plan. So it's a good idea to prepare yourself for a few <u>hiccups</u> in the speaking assessment. (Nothing to do with glasses of water.)

## Try to find another way of saying it

There may be a particular word or phrase that trips you up. There's always a <u>way round it</u> though.

1) If you can't <u>remember</u> a French word, use an <u>alternative</u> word or try <u>describing it</u> instead.

2) E.g. if you can't remember that '<u>grapes</u>' are '<u>les raisins</u>' and you really need to say it, then describe them as 'the small green or red fruits', or 'les petits fruits verts ou rouges'.

3) You can <u>fib</u> to avoid words you can't remember — if you can't remember the word for '<u>dog</u>' then just say you've got a <u>cat</u> instead. Make sure what you're saying makes <u>sense</u> though — saying you've got a <u>pet radio</u> isn't going to get you any marks, trust me.

4) If you can't remember the word for a <u>cup</u> (la tasse) in your speaking assessment, you could say '<u>glass</u>' (le verre) instead — you'll still make yourself <u>understood</u>.

## If the worst comes to the worst, ask for help in French

1) If you can't think of a way around it, you <u>can</u> ask for help in the speaking assessment — as long as you ask for it in <u>French</u>.

2) If you can't remember what a chair is, ask your teacher; "Comment dit-on 'chair' en français?" It's <u>better</u> than wasting time trying to think of the word.

## You may just need to buy yourself some time

If you get a bit <u>stuck</u> for what to say, there's always a <u>way out</u>.

1) If you just need some <u>thinking time</u> in your speaking assessment or you want to check something, you can use these useful phrases to help you out:

| | | | |
|---|---|---|---|
| Ben... | *Um...* | Pouvez-vous répéter, s'il vous plaît? | *Can you repeat, please?* |
| Eh bien... | *Well...* | Je ne comprends pas. | *I don't understand.* |
| Je ne suis pas sûr(e). | *I'm not sure.* | Ça, c'est une bonne question. | *That's a good question.* |

2) Another good tactic if you're a bit stuck is to say what you've <u>just said</u> in a <u>different way</u>. This shows off your <u>command of French</u>, and also it might lead onto something else, e.g.:

*"On mange en famille... Je ne mange pas seul, sauf quand mes parents travaillent tard."*

Saying the same thing a different way... leading on to another idea.

= We eat as a family... I don't eat on my own, except when my parents work late.

And don't be afraid to make mistakes — even native French speakers make 'em. Don't let a silly error shake your <u>concentration</u> for the rest of the assessment.

## One last thing — don't panic...

Congratulations — you've made it to the end of the book. And without accident or injury, I hope —paper cuts hurt more than people think... Anyway, enough of this idle chit-chat. <u>Read</u> these pages, <u>take on board</u> the information, <u>use it</u> in your GCSE, <u>do well</u> and then <u>celebrate</u> in style.

## A

la A6 f  A6 motorway
à prep (à la, à l', au, aux)  at, to, in
    à la carte  à la carte (e.g. menu)
    à cause de conj  because of
    à droite  on the right
    à gauche  on the left
    à point  medium (cooked)
    à travers prep  across
abîmer v  to damage
l' abricot m  apricot
absent(e) a  absent
absolument ad  absolutely
accepter v  to accept
accompagner v  to accompany
accro a  addicted
accueillir v  to welcome
l' achat m  purchase
acheter v  to buy
l' acteur/actrice m/f  actor/actress
les actualités fpl  news,
    current affairs
l' addition f  bill (restaurant)
l' adolescent m/f  adolescent,
    teenager
adorer v  to adore
l' adresse f  address
l' adulte m/f  adult
l' aéroport m  airport
les affaires fpl  business
l' affiche f  poster, sign
affreux/affreuse a  awful
l' Afrique f  Africa
agacer v  to annoy
l' âge m  age
âgé(e) a  old, aged
l' agence de voyages f  travel agency
l' agent de police m  policeman/
    woman
agité(e) a  restless
agréable a  pleasant
agresser v  to attack
agricole a  agricultural
aider v  to help
l' ail m  garlic
aimable a  likeable, friendly
aimer v  to like, love
aîné(e) a  older (e.g. sister)
ainsi ad  in this way
l' air m  air, appearance
    avoir l'air (de)  to seem
    en plein air ad  outdoors
l' aire de repos f  motorway services
ajouter v  to add
l' alcool m alcohol
les alentours mpl surroundings
l' Algérie f  Algeria
(l') algérien(ne) a/m/f  Algerian
l' alimentation f food, groceries
l' Allemagne f  Germany
l' allemand m  German (language)
(l') allemand(e) a/m/f  German
aller v  to go
    aller bien/mieux  to be well/better
l' aller-retour m  return ticket
l' aller simple m  single ticket
allô interj  hello
    (when answering phone)
alors ad  then
les Alpes fpl  Alps
l' alpinisme m  mountaineering
l' ambiance f  atmosphere
l' ambulance f  ambulance
améliorer v  to improve
aménagé(e) a  flexible (e.g. working
    hours)
l' amende f  fine
(l') américain(e) a/m/f  American
l' Amérique f  America
l' ami(e) m/f  friend
amical(e) a  friendly, amicable
amicalement ad  in a friendly way
l' amitié f  friendship
amitiés  best wishes
l' amour m  love
amoureux/amoureuse a  in love
amusant(e) a  amusing, fun
amuser v  to amuse
    s'amuser vr  to enjoy oneself
l' an m  year
l' ananas m  pineapple

ancien(ne) a  old, former
l' anglais m  English (language)
(l') anglais(e) a/m/f  English,
    English person
l' Angleterre f  England
l' animal m  animal
l' animateur/animatrice m/f
    presenter
animé(e) a  lively, animated
l' année f  year
l' anniversaire m  birthday
l' annonce f  advertisement
l' annuaire m  phone book
annuler v  to cancel
l' anorak m  anorak
l' antenne f  aerial
l' antenne parabolique f
    satellite dish
(l') août m  August
à l' appareil  on the telephone
l' appareil-photo m  camera
l' appartement m  flat, apartment
l' appel m  call
appeler v  to call
    s'appeler vr  to be called
l' appétit m  appetite
apporter v  to bring
apprécier v  to appreciate
apprendre v  to learn
l' apprenti(e) m/f  apprentice
l' apprentissage m  apprenticeship
(s') approcher de v (r)  to approach
après prep  after
après-demain ad  the day after
    tomorrow
l' après-midi m/f  afternoon
l' arbitre m  referee
l' arbre m  tree
l' argent m  money
l' argent de poche m  pocket
    money
l' armoire f  wardrobe
l' arrêt m  stop
l' arrêt d'autobus m  bus stop
arrêter v  to stop (something)
    s'arrêter vr  to stop
les arrhes fpl  deposit (money)
l' arrivée f  arrival
arriver v  to arrive
l' arrondissement m
    district (e.g. in Paris)
arroser v  to water
l' art dramatique m  drama
l' artisan m  craftsman
l' ascenseur m  lift
l' assassin m  murderer
s' asseoir vr  to sit down
    assieds-toi! sit down! (informal)
    asseyez-vous! sit down! (polite)
assez ad  quite, enough
l' assiette f  plate
l' assurance f  insurance
l' atelier m  workshop
l' athlétisme m  athletics
(l') atlantique a/m  Atlantic
    attaquer v  to attack
    attendre v  to wait
l' attention f  attention
    faire attention  to be careful
atterrir v  to land
au = à le — see à
    au bord de la  alongside
    au bout de prep  at the end of
    au dehors de ad  outside of
    au fond de ad
        at the bottom of
    au milieu de prep
        in the middle of
    au revoir interj  goodbye
    au secours! interj  help!
l' auberge de jeunesse f
    youth hostel
aucun(e)  any
    ne ... aucun(e) a
        no .../none...
augmenter v  to increase
aujourd'hui ad  today
auparavant ad  before
aussi ad  too, as well, as
aussi ... que ad  as ... as
l' Australie f  Australia

(l') australien(ne) a/m/f  Australian
l' auto f  car
l' autobus m  bus
l' automne m  autumn
l' automobiliste m/f  motorist
l' autoroute f  motorway
autour (de) prep  around
autre a  other
autrement dit  in other words
l' Autriche f  Austria
(l') autrichien(ne) a/m/f  Austrian
aux = à les — see à
avaler v  to swallow
en avance ad  early
    à l'avance a  in advance
avant prep  before, in front of
l' avanta)ge m  advantage
avant-hier ad
    the day before yesterday
avec prep  with
    avec plaisir  gladly
l' avenir m  future
    à l'avenir ad  in the future
l' aventure f adventure
l' avenue f  avenue
l' averse f  shower (of rain)
l' avion m  plane
    en avion ad  by plane
l' avis m  opinion
avoir v  to have
    avoir besoin de  to need
    avoir hâte de  to be eager to
    avoir lieu  to take place
    avoir raison  to be right
    avoir tort  to be wrong
l' avril m  April

## B

le baby-sitting m  babysitting
    faire du baby-sitting
        to babysit
le bac(calauréat) m  baccalauréat
    (equivalent of A-levels)
les bagages mpl  luggage
la bague f  ring
la baguette f  baguette, stick
se baigner vr  to bathe
la baignoire f  bath
le bain m  bath
le bal m  ball (dancing)
la balade f  walk
le balcon m  balcony, circle (at
    theatre)
la balle f  ball
le ballon m  ball (big, e.g. football)
la banane f  banana
la bande f  group
la bande dessinée f  comic strip
la banlieue f  suburbs
la banque f  bank
le bar m  bar
    barbant(e) a  boring
la barbe f  beard
    bas(se) a  low
    en bas ad downstairs
    en bas de prep
        at the bottom of
le basket m  basketball
les baskets fpl  trainers
le bateau m  boat
le bâtiment m  building
la batterie f  drum kit
battre v  to beat
bavard(e) a  talkative
bavarder v  to chat / gossip
beau/belle a  beautiful
    il fait beau  it's nice weather
beaucoup ad  a lot
beaucoup (de) a  lots of, many
le beau-fils m  son-in-law, stepson
le beau-frère m  brother-in-law,
    stepbrother
le beau-père m  father-in-law,
    stepfather
le bébé m  baby
(le/la) belge a/m/f  Belgian
la Belgique f  Belgium
la belle-fille f  daughter-in-law,
    stepdaughter
la belle-mère f  mother-in-law,
    stepmother

la belle-sœur f  sister-in-law,
    stepsister
les béquilles fpl  crutches
le besoin m  need
    avoir besoin de  to need
bête a  stupid
la bêtise f  mistake
le béton m  concrete
le/la beur m/f  second generation
    North African immigrant
le beurre m  butter
la bibliothèque f  library
le bic m  biro
bien ad  well
    bien cuit a  well done (meat)
    bien payé(e) a  well paid
    bien sûr ad  of course
bientôt ad  soon
    à bientôt interj  see you soon
la bienvenue f  welcome
la bière f  beer
le bifteck m  steak
le bijou m  jewel, gem
la bijouterie f  jewellery
le billet m  ticket, banknote
la biologie f  biology
le biscuit m  biscuit
la bise f  kiss
    faire la bise  to kiss someone on
        both cheeks
blaguer v  to joke
blanc(he) a  white
blessé(e) a  wounded
bleu(e) a  blue
blond(e) a  blond(e)
le blouson m  jacket
le bœuf m  beef
bof! interj  huh! (shrug)
boire v  to drink
le bois m  wood
    en bois a  made of wood
la boisson (gazeuse) f  drink (fizzy)
la boîte f  tin, can, box
la boîte aux lettres f  postbox
le bol m  bowl
bon(ne) a  good
    bon anniversaire interj
        happy birthday
bon appétit interj
    enjoy your meal
bon marché a  cheap
bon voyage interj
    have a good journey
bon week-end interj
    have a good weekend
le bonbon m  sweet
le bonheur m  happiness
bonjour interj  good day, hello
bonne année interj
    Happy New Year
bonne chance interj  good luck
la bonne couleur  the right colour
bonne fête interj
    have a good party
bonne idée interj  good idea
bonne nuit interj  good night
bonnes vacances interj
    enjoy your holiday
bonsoir interj  good evening
le bord m  edge
    au bord de la mer  by the sea
la bouche f  mouth
le/la boucher/bouchère m/f  butcher
la boucherie f  butcher's
le bouchon m  cork, traffic jam
bouclé(e) a  curly
la boucle d'oreille f  earring
le/la boulanger/boulangère m/f  baker
la boulangerie f  baker's
les boules fpl  bowls (ball game)
le boulevard m  boulevard
bouleverser v  to disrupt
le boulot m  work, job
la boum f  party
la bouteille f  bottle
la boutique f  small shop
le bowling m  bowling
le bras m  arm
bravo interj  bravo, well done
le brevet (BEPC) m  equivalent of
    GCSEs

le bricolage m  DIY
briller v  to shine
la brique f  brick
    en brique a  made out of brick
(le/la) britannique a/m/f  British, British
    person
la brochure f  booklet, brochure
se bronzer vr  to sunbathe
la brosse à dents f  toothbrush
se brosser les dents/les cheveux
    vr  to brush one's teeth/hair
le brouillard m  fog
    faire du brouillard  to be foggy
le bruit m  noise
brûler v  to burn
la brume f  mist
brun(e) a  brown
Bruxelles  Brussels
bruyant(e) a  noisy, loud
le buffet m  sideboard, buffet
le bureau m  office, desk
le bureau de change m  bureau de
    change, money exchange
le bureau des objets trouvés m  lost
    property office
le bureau de renseignements m
    information service
le bureau de tabac m  tobacconist's
le bus m  bus

## C

c'est  it is
c'est-à-dire conj  that is to say
c'est quoi?  what is it?
c'était  it was
ça pron  that
ça dépend  that depends
ça fait combien?
    how much does that come to?
ça me fait rire  that makes me
    laugh
ça ne me dit rien
    that doesn't mean anything to me
ça s'écrit comment?
    how do you spell that?
ça va(?)  I'm okay, how are you?
    ça ne va pas  I'm not great
ça vaut  it's worth
la cabine téléphonique f  phone box
le cadeau m  present
cadet(te) a  younger (e.g. sister)
le cadre m  frame
le café m  coffee, café
le café-crème m  white coffee
le cahier m  notebook, exercise book
la caisse f  counter, checkout
le/la caissier/caissière m/f  cashier
le calcul m  calculation, arithmetic
la calculatrice f  calculator
calme a  calm
le camion m  lorry
cambrioler v  to burgle
la caméra f  camera
    (used for filming TV
    programmes or films)
le caméscope m  video camera
la campagne f  countryside,
    campaign
le camping m  campsite
    faire du camping
        to go camping
le Canada m  Canada
(le/la) canadien(ne) a/m/f  Canadian
le canapé m  sofa, open sandwich
le cancer m  cancer
le/la candidat(e) m/f  candidate
la cantine f  canteen, dining hall
car conj  because, since
le car m  coach
le car de ramassage m  school bus
la caravane f  caravan
le carnet m  notebook, book of tickets
la carotte f  carrot
carré(e) a  square
    à carreaux a  squared, checked
le carrefour m  crossroads
la carrière f  career
le cartable m  schoolbag, satchel
la carte f  map, card, menu
    la carte bancaire f  bank card

---

nouns — **m**: masculine   **f**: feminine   **pl**: plural        **v**: verb        **vr**: reflexive verb    **a**: adjective

la carte de crédit f credit card
la carte d'identité f ID card
la carte postale f postcard
la carte routière f road map
le carton m cardboard
la case f square, box
le casier m locker
le casque m helmet
la casquette f baseball cap
le casse-croûte m snack, lunch
casse-pieds a pain in the neck
casser v to break
la casserole f saucepan
la cassette f cassette tape
le cassis m blackcurrant
la cathédrale f cathedral
causer v to cause, to chat
la caution f guarantee (money), deposit
la cave f cellar
le CD m CD
le CDI (centre de documentation et d'information) m school library
ce, cet, cette, ces pron this
la ceinture de sécurité f safety belt
cela pron that (i.e. that thing)
célèbre a famous
célibataire a single (not married)
(le) cent a/m hundred
le centime m centime (French equivalent of penny)
le centimètre m centimetre
le centre m centre
le centre commercial m shopping centre
le centre de loisirs m leisure centre
le centre de recyclage m recycling centre
le centre sportif m sports centre
le centre-ville m city centre
cependant conj however
les céréales fpl cereal
la cerise f cherry
certainement ad certainly
le certificat m certificate
le CES = collège d'enseignement secondaire m secondary school
ceux pron these — see ce
la chaîne m TV channel
la chaîne stéréo f hi-fi system
la chaise f chair
la chaleur f heat
la chambre f bedroom
la chambre individuelle/double/de famille f single/double/family room
la chambre pour une personne f room for one person
la chambre d'hôte f bed and breakfast
le champ m field
le champignon m mushroom
la chance f luck, chance
avoir de la chance to be lucky
par chance ad luckily
changer v to change
la chanson f song
chanter v to sing
le/la chanteur/chanteuse m/f singer
le chapeau m hat
chaque a each
la charcuterie f delicatessen, pork butcher's
chargé(e) a loaded, laden
le chariot m trolley
le chat m cat
châtain(e) a chestnut coloured
le château m castle, palace
chaud(e) a warm, hot
avoir chaud to be hot
il fait chaud it's warm
le chauffage central m central heating
chauffé(e) a heated
le chauffeur m driver, chauffeur
la chaussette f sock

la chaussure f shoe
le/la chef m/f boss/chef
le/la chef de cuisine m/f head chef
le chemin de fer m railway
la chemise f shirt
le chèque (de voyage) m (traveller's) cheque
cher/chère a, cher ad dear, expensive
chercher v to search for, to look for
le cheval m horse
les cheveux mpl hair
la cheville f ankle
chez prep chez moi/toi at my/your house
chic a stylish
le chien m dog
les chiffres mpl numbers, figures
la chimie f chemistry
la Chine f China
(le/la) chinois(e) a/m/f Chinese, Chinese person
les chips mpl crisps
le chocolat m chocolate
le chocolat chaud m hot chocolate
choisir v to choose
le choix m choice
le chômage m unemployment
la chose f thing
le chou m cabbage
le chou-fleur m cauliflower
(le/la) chrétien(ne) a/m/f Christian
le cidre m cider
le ciel m sky, heaven
la cigarette f cigarette
le cinéma m cinema
(le) cinq a/m five
cinquante a/m fifty
cinquième a fifth
en cinquième in year 8
la circulation f traffic
le cirque m circus
la cité f housing estate, city
le citron m lemon
la civière f stretcher
clair(e) a light (colour), clear
la classe f class
classer v to file
le clavier m keyboard
la clé, clef f key
le/la client(e) m/f customer
le climat m climate
cliquer v to click
le club m club
le club des jeunes m youth club
le coca m Coca-Cola®
cocher v to tick
le cochon d'Inde m guinea-pig
la cochonnerie f disgusting food
le code postal m postal code
le cœur m heart
le/la coiffeur/coiffeuse m/f hairdresser
le coin m corner
la colère f anger
le colis m parcel
collectionner v to collect
le collège m school (secondary)
le/la collègue m/f colleague
la colline f hill
la colonie de vacances f holiday camp
combien ad how much, how many
c'est combien? how much is it?
la comédie f comedy
comique a funny
commander v to order
comme prep like
comme ci comme ça ad so-so
commencer v to start
pour commencer to start with, to begin with
comment (?) ad/interj how, (pardon?)
comment dit-on ... en français?
how do you say ... in French?
le commerce m business

le/la commerçant(e) m/f shopkeeper
commerçant(e) a commercial
le commissariat m police station
comparer v to compare
complet/complète a full, complete
compléter v to complete
compliqué(e) a complicated
comporter v to consist of
composer v to compose
composé(e) de composed of
composter v to stamp (ticket)
compréhensif/compréhensive a understanding
comprendre v to understand
le comprimé m tablet (to swallow)
compris(e) a inclusive
non compris(e) a not included
le/la comptable m/f accountant
le compte m account
compter (sur) v to count (on)
concerner v to concern
en ce qui concerne... as far as ... is concerned
le concert m concert
le concours m competition
le/la conducteur/conductrice m/f driver
conduire v to drive
la confiance f confidence
confirmer v to confirm
la confiserie f sweetshop
la confiture f jam
le confort m comfort
confortable a comfortable
le congé m holiday
congeler v to freeze
la connaissance f knowledge
connaître v to know (e.g. a person)
se consacrer à vr to devote oneself to
le conseil m advice
le conseiller (d'orientation) m (careers) advisor
la consigne (automatique) f left luggage (lockers)
la consommation f consumption
construire v to build
contacter v to contact
content(e) a happy
le contenu m contents
continuer v to continue
(le) contraire a/m opposite
le contrat m contract
contre prep against
le contrôle m test
convenir à v to suit
le/la copain/copine m/f friend
copier v to copy
le corps m body
correct(e) a correct
la correspondance f connection
le/la correspondant(e) m/f correspondent, penfriend
corriger v to correct
la Corse f Corsica
la côte f coast
le côté m side
à côté de prep next to
le coton m cotton
en coton a made of cotton
le cou m neck
la couche d'ozone f ozone layer
se coucher vr to go to bed
la couleur f colour
le couloir m corridor
le coup m knock, blow
le coup de feu m (gun) shot
le coup de poing m punch
le coup de soleil m sunburn
le coup de téléphone m phone call
couper v to cut
la cour f yard, playground
couramment ad fluently
courir v to run
le courrier (électronique) m post, (email)
le courrier du cœur m problem page
le cours m lesson
le cours de change m exchange rate

la course f running
les courses fpl shopping
faire les courses to go shopping
court(e) a short
le/la cousin(e) m/f cousin
le couteau m knife
coûter v to cost
la couture f sewing
couvert(e) a overcast (weather)
couvrir v to cover
la cravate f tie
le crayon m pencil
la crème f cream
la crème solaire f suncream
la crêpe f pancake
crevé(e) a burst, punctured
la crise cardiaque f heart attack
critiquer v to criticize
croire v to believe
le croissant m croissant
le croque-monsieur m cheese and ham toastie
cru(e) a raw
les crudités fpl raw salad items
la cuiller, cuillère f spoon
la cuillerée f spoonful
le cuir m leather
la cuisine f kitchen
la cuisinière f (à gaz / électrique) stove, cooker (gas / electric)
la cuisse f thigh
cultiver v to cultivate, to grow
le cyclisme m cycling

# D

d'abord ad first (of all)
d'accord inter OK, I agree
d'habitude ad normally, usually
d'occasion a used, secondhand
d'origine (africaine) f native, of (African) origin
la dame f lady
le danger m danger
dangereux/dangereuse a dangerous
dans prep in, into
dans le bon ordre in the right order
danser v to dance
la date f date (of year)
de prep (du, de la, de l', des) of, from, some
de bonne heure ad early
de chaque côté ad from each side
de l'autre côté on the other side
de la part de qui? Who's it from?
de rien don't mention it
de temps en temps ad from time to time
de tous côtés ad from all sides
débarquer v to get off (e.g boat)
débarrasser v to clear
se débrouiller vr to get on with, to manage
le début m start, début
(le) décembre m December
les déchets mpl rubbish
déchiré(e) a torn
décider v to decide
décoller v to take off
décrire v to describe
décrocher v to pick up (telephone)
déçu(e) a disappointed
dedans ad inside
défense (f) de fumer no smoking
le défilé m procession
dégoûtant(e) a disgusting
le degré m degree
dehors ad outside
déjà ad already
le déjeuner m lunch,
déjeuner v to have lunch
délicieux/délicieuse a delicious
demain ad tomorrow
à demain interj see you tomorrow
demander v to ask
déménager v to move house
demi(e) a half

deux heures et demie half past two
le demi-frère m half-brother
la demi-pension f half-board
le/la demi-pensionnaire m/f day pupil
la demi-sœur f half-sister
démodé(e) a old-fashioned
démuni(e) a destitute
le denim m denim
la dent f tooth
le dentifrice m toothpaste
le/la dentiste m/f dentist
dépanner v to fix, repair
le départ m departure
le département m department (equivalent of county)
dépassé(e) a old-fashioned
dépasser v to go past
dépêcher v to send
se dépêcher vr to hurry
dépenser v to spend
le dépliant m leaflet
déposer v drop off, put down
depuis prep since, for
déranger v to disturb
dernier/dernière a last, previous
derrière prep behind
des = de les — see de
dès prep from
désagréable a unpleasant, disagreeable
le désavantage m disadvantage
descendre v to go down
se déshabiller vr to get undressed
désirer v to desire
désolé(e) a sorry
le dessert m dessert
le dessin m art, drawing
le dessin animé m cartoon
dessiner v to draw
la destination f destination
le détail m detail
détester v to hate
le détritus m litter
détruire v to destroy
(le) deux a/m two
deuxième a second
devant prep in front of
devenir v to become
la déviation f diversion
devoir v to have to
les devoirs mpl homework
le dialogue m dialogue
la différence f difference
différent(e) a different
difficile a difficult
la difficulté f difficulty
(le) dimanche m Sunday
dîner v to dine
le dîner m supper
le diplôme m degree
dire v to say
ça (te/vous) dit quelque chose? does that mean anything to you?
direct(e) a direct
le/la directeur/directrice m/f headteacher, manager
la direction f direction, management
la discipline f discipline
la disco(thèque) f disco
discuter v to discuss, to talk
disparaître v to disappear
la disparition f disappearance
en voie de disparition a endangered (e.g. species)
disponible a available
la dispute f quarrel
se disputer vr to argue
le disque m record
le disque compact m compact disc
la distance f distance
distribuer v to distribute
le distributeur (automatique) de billets m cashpoint
divorcé(e) a divorced
(le) dix a/m ten
dix-sept a/m seventeen
dix-huit a/m eighteen
dix-neuf a/m nineteen

la dizaine f  *about ten, ten or so*
le docteur m  *doctor (academic)*
le documentaire m  *documentary*
le doigt m  *finger*
le domicile m  *home*
le dommage m  *shame, pity*
donc ad  *therefore*
donner v  *to give*
donner un coup de main  *to lend a hand*
dont pron  *of which, of whom*
dormir v  *to sleep*
le dortoir m  *dormitory*
le dos m  *back*
la douane f  *customs*
doubler v  *to repeat a year, to overtake*
la douche f  *shower*
doué(e) a  *gifted*
la douleur f  *pain*
Douvres  *Dover*
doux, douce a  *soft, mild (weather)*
la douzaine f  *dozen, about twelve*
le douze a/m  *twelve*
le drapeau m  *flag*
la drogue f  *drug(s)*
drogué(e) a  *drugged, on drugs*
se droguer vr  *to take drugs*
droit(e) a  *straight, right*
tout droit ad  *straight on*
la droite f  *right*
tournez à droite  *turn right*
drôle a  *funny*
du = de le — *see de*
dur(e) a/ad  *hard, harsh*
à durée déterminée ad  *for a fixed period of time*
durer v  *to last*

## E

l' eau f  *water*
l'eau minérale f  *mineral water*
l'eau potable / non potable f  *drinking water / non-drinking water*
l' échange m  *exchange*
échanger v  *to exchange, to swap*
les échecs mpl  *chess*
échouer (à) v  *to fail (at)*
l' éclaircie f  *sunny spell*
l' école f  *school*
l'école primaire f  *primary school*
les économies fpl  *savings*
faire des économies  *to save money*
(l') écossais(e) a/m/f  *Scottish, Scot*
l' Écosse f  *Scotland*
écouter v  *to listen*
l' écran m  *screen*
écraser v  *to crush*
écrire v  *to write*
s'écrire vr  *to write to each other, to be spelt*
comment ça s'écrit?  *how is that spelt?*
l' Édimbourg  *Edinburgh*
l' éducation physique f  *P.E.*
l' effet de serre m  *greenhouse effect*
effrayant(e) a  *frightening*
égal(e) a  *equal*
ça m'est égal  *I don't mind*
l' égalité f  *equality*
l' église f  *church*
égoïste a  *selfish*
l' électricien(ne) m/f  *electrician*
électrique a  *electric*
électronique a  *electrical, electronic*
l' élève m/f  *pupil*
l' emballage m  *package, packaging*
embarquer v  *to embark*
l' embouteillage m  *traffic jam*
l' émission f  *programme (e.g. TV)*

l' émission jeunesse f  *children's programme*
l'émission musicale f  *music programme*
l'émission sportive f  *sports programme*
emmener v  *to take (along)*
empêcher (de faire) v  *to prevent (from doing)*
l' emplacement m  *pitch (for tent)*
l' emploi m  *job*
l' emploi du temps m  *timetable, schedule*
l' employé(e) m/f  *employee*
emprunter v  *to borrow*
en prep  *in, to, by (e.g. by plane), made of (e.g. of wool)*
enchanté(e) a  *delighted (e.g. to meet someone)*
encore ad  *still, yet, another*
encore du/de la a  *more*
encore une fois ad  *once more*
pas encore ad  *not yet*
encourager v  *to encourage*
s'endormir vr  *to go to sleep*
l' endroit m  *place, area*
l' énergie f  *power*
l'énergie nucléaire f  *nuclear power*
énerver v  *to annoy*
s'énerver vr  *to get annoyed*
l' enfant m/f  *child*
enfin ad  *at last*
ennuyeux/ennuyeuse a  *boring, annoying*
enregistrer v  *to record*
enrichissant(e) a  *enriching*
enrhumé(e) a  *having a cold*
l' enseignement m  *teaching*
ensemble ad  *together*
l'ensemble m  *whole*
dans l'ensemble  *on the whole*
ensoleillé(e) a  *sunny*
ensuite ad  *next*
entendre v  *to hear*
s'entendre vr  *to get on*
entendu(e) a  *understood, agreed*
enthousiaste a  *enthusiastic*
l' entorse f  *sprain*
entre prep  *between*
l' entrée f  *entrance, admission, first course*
entrer v  *to go in*
l' entrevue f  *interview, discussion*
l' enveloppe f  *envelope*
l' envie f  *want, desire*
avoir envie de  *to want to*
environ ad  *around*
l' environnement m  *environment*
envoyer v  *to send*
l' épaule f  *shoulder*
épeler v  *to spell*
l' épicerie f  *grocery*
l' épicier/épicière m/f  *grocer*
éplucher v  *to peel*
épouser v  *to marry*
l' épouvante f  *fear, terror*
l' épreuve f  *test*
l' EPS = éducation physique et sportive f  *P.E.*
épuiser v  *to exhaust*
équilibré(e) a  *balanced*
l' équipe f  *team*
l' équitation f  *riding (horses)*
l' erreur f  *mistake*
l' escalier m  *staircase*
l' escrime f  *fencing (sport)*
l' espace m  *space*
l' Espagne f  *Spain*
l' espagnol m  *Spanish (language)*
(l')espagnol(e) a/m/f  *Spanish, Spaniard*
l' espèce f  *species*
espérer v  *to hope*
l' espoir m  *hope*
essayer (de) v  *to try (to)*
l' essence f  *petrol*
essuyer v  *to wipe*
l' est m  *east*
est-ce que...?  *is ... ?*

l' estivant(e) m/f  *summer holidaymaker*
l' estomac m  *stomach*
et conj  *and*
l' établissement m  *establishment*
l' étage m  *storey, floor*
l' étagère f  *shelf*
l' état m  *state*
les États-Unis mpl  *United States*
l' été m  *summer*
éteindre v  *to turn off, put out*
l' étoile f  *star*
étonné(e) a  *surprised*
étonner v  *to surprise*
à l'étranger ad  *abroad*
être v  *to be*
étroit(e) a  *narrow*
l' étude f  *study*
l' étudiant(e) m/f  *student*
étudier v  *to study*
l' euro m  *euro*
l' Europe f  *Europe*
l' événement m  *event*
l' évier m  *sink*
éviter v  *to avoid*
exact(e) a  *exact*
exactement ad  *exactly*
l' examen m  *exam*
excellent(e) a  *excellent*
l' excursion f  *trip, excursion*
l'excursion scolaire f  *school trip*
s'excuser vr  *to apologise*
l' exemple m  *example*
par exemple  *for example*
expérimenté(e) a  *experienced*
expliquer v  *to explain*
l' exposition f  *exhibition*
exprès ad  *on purpose*
extra a  *fantastic*

## F

fabriquer v  *to make*
la fac f  *university*
en face (de) ad/prep  *opposite*
fâché(e) a  *angry*
facile a  *easy*
le/la facteur/factrice m/f  *postman/woman*
facultatif/facultative a  *optional*
la faculté f  *faculty, department*
faible a  *weak*
la faim f  *hunger*
avoir faim  *to be hungry*
faire v  *to do, make*
faire correspondre  *to match up*
faire du lèche-vitrine  *to go window-shopping*
faire le ménage  *to do the housework*
le fait divers m  *(short) news item*
familial(e) a  *family, domestic*
la famille f  *family*
(le/la) fana a/m/f  *fanatical, fan*
fantastique a  *fantastic*
la farine f  *flour*
fatigant(e) a  *tiring*
fatigué(e) a  *tired*
faut  *see il faut*
la faute f  *fault*
le fauteuil m  *armchair*
faux/fausse a  *false, wrong*
favori(e) a  *favourite*
les félicitations fpl  *congratulations*
féliciter v  *to congratulate*
la femme f  *woman*
la femme de chambre f  *chambermaid, housekeeper*
la fenêtre f  *window*
le fer m  *iron*
férié  *see jour férié*
la ferme f  *farm*
fermé(e) a  *closed*
fermer v  *to shut*
la fermeture (annuelle) f  *closing, closure (for holidays)*
la fermeture éclair f  *zip*
le fermier/fermière m/f  *farmer*
la fête f  *party, feast, saint's day*

fêter v  *to celebrate*
le feu m  *fire*
le feu d'artifice m  *firework*
le feu rouge m  *red light*
les feux mpl  *traffic lights*
le feuilleton m  *soap opera*
(le) février m  *February*
les fiançailles fpl  *engagement*
la fiche f  *sheet, form*
fier / fière a  *proud*
la fièvre f  *fever*
la filière (scientifique) f  *(scientific) course of study*
la fille f  *girl, daughter*
le film m  *film*
film d'aventures m  *adventure film*
film comique m  *comedy*
film d'amour m  *love story*
film d'épouvante m  *horror film*
film de guerre m  *war film*
film d'horreur m  *horror film*
film policier m  *detective film*
film de science-fiction m  *science fiction film*
le fils m  *son*
la fin f  *end*
finir v  *to finish*
la Finlande f  *Finland*
(le/la) finlandais(e) a/m/f  *Finnish, Finn*
le flash m  *flash, news flash*
le fléau m  *curse, pest*
la flèche f  *arrow*
la fleur f  *flower*
le fleuve m  *river*
le flic m  *cop, police officer*
la foire f  *fair, market*
la fois f  *time*
foncé(e) a  *dark*
le fond m  *bottom*
au fond de prep  *at the bottom, back of*
le foot(ball) m  *football*
la forêt f  *forest*
la formation f  *training*
formation continue f  *further (vocational) education*
formation permanente f  *continuing education*
la forme f  *shape*
être en forme  *to be fit*
formidable a  *great*
le formulaire m  *form*
fort(e) a  *strong, loud*
le four m  *oven*
le four à micro-ondes m  *microwave*
la fourchette f  *fork*
fournir v  *to supply*
le fournisseur m  *supplier*
frais/fraîche a  *fresh*
la fraise f  *strawberry*
la framboise f  *raspberry*
le franc m  *franc*
le français m  *French (language)*
(le/la) français(e) a/m/f  *French, French person*
la France f  *France*
franchement ad  *frankly, honestly*
francophone a  *French-speaking*
frapper v  *to hit, strike*
le frein m  *brake*
le frère m  *brother*
le frigo m  *fridge*
frisé(e) a  *curly (e.g. hair)*
les frites fpl  *chips*
froid(e) a  *cold*
avoir froid  *to be cold*
il fait froid  *it's cold*
le fromage m  *cheese*
le fruit m  *fruit*
les fruits de mer mpl  *seafood*
la fumée f  *smoke*
fumer v  *to smoke*
(le/la) fumeur/fumeuse m/f  *smoker*
fumeur/fumeuse a  *smoking*

## G

gâcher v  *to spoil, to waste*
gagner v  *to win, to earn*

le gallois m  *Welsh (language)*
(le/la) gallois(e) a/m/f  *Welsh, Welsh person*
la gamme f  *range, scale*
le gant m  *glove*
le garage m  *garage*
le garçon m  *boy*
Garçon! interj  *Waiter!*
le garçon de café m  *waiter*
garder v  *to keep*
la gare f  *station*
la gare routière f  *coach station*
la gare maritime f  *port*
garer v  *to park*
le gâteau m  *cake*
gâter v  *to spoil*
(la) gauche f/a  *left*
tournez à gauche  *turn left*
le gaz m  *gas*
le gaz carbonique m  *carbon dioxide*
les gaz d'échappement mpl  *exhaust fumes*
le gazon m  *grass, lawn*
geler v  *to freeze*
le/la gendarme m/f  *policeman/woman*
gêner v  *to bother*
en général ad  *generally, usually*
généralement ad  *generally*
généreux/généreuse a  *generous*
génial(e) a  *great, of genius*
le genou m  *knee*
le genre m  *type, kind, sort*
les gens mpl  *people*
gentil(le) a  *nice, kind*
la géographie f  *geography*
le gigot d'agneau m  *leg of lamb*
le gîte m  *self-catering cottage*
la glace f  *ice cream*
le golf m  *golf*
la gomme f  *rubber*
la gorge f  *throat*
le gosse m  *kid*
le goût m  *taste*
goûter v  *to taste*
le goûter m  *tea, snack*
les graffiti mpl  *graffiti*
le gramme m  *gram*
grand(e) a  *big, great*
le grand magasin m  *department store*
la grande surface f  *hypermarket*
les grandes vacances fpl  *summer holidays*
la Grande-Bretagne f  *Great Britain*
la grand-mère f  *grandmother*
le grand-père m  *grandfather*
les grands-parents mpl  *grandparents*
gras(se) a  *fatty*
le gratin dauphinois m  *potatoes with cheese topping*
gratuit(e) a  *free (no cost)*
grave a  *serious*
(le/la) grec/grecque a/m/f  *Greek*
la Grèce f  *Greece*
le grenier m  *attic*
la grève f  *strike (industrial)*
griffé(e) a  *designer*
la grille f  *gate, grid*
la grippe f  *flu*
gris(e) a  *grey*
gros(se) a  *fat, big*
le groupe m  *group*
guérir v  *to cure*
la guerre f  *war*
le guichet m  *ticket office*
la guitare f  *guitar*
le gymnase m  *gymnasium*
la gymnastique f  *gymnastics*

## H

habile a  *skilful*
s' habiller vr  *to get dressed*
l' habitant(e) m/f  *inhabitant*
habiter v  *to live in*
l' habitude f  *habit*

---

nouns — **m**: *masculine*   **f**: *feminine*   **pl**: *plural*        **v**: *verb*        **vr**: *reflexive verb*        **a**: *adjective*

*French–English Dictionary*

d'habitude *usually*
comme d'habitude *as usual*
s' habituer vr *to get used to*
haïr v *to hate, to detest*
le hamburger m *hamburger*
le hamster m *hamster*
le handball m *handball*
le haricot vert m *green bean*
haut(e) a *high*
en haut ad *upstairs*
en haut de prep
*at the top of*
la hauteur f *height*
hélas interj *alas*
hésiter v *hesitate*
l' heure f *hour*
à l'heure ad *on time*
à quelle heure?
*at what time?*
de bonne heure ad *early*
l'heure d'affluence f
*rush hour*
l'heure du déjeuner f
*dinner time*
heurter v *to collide*
heureux/heureuse a *happy*
hier ad *yesterday*
la hi-fi f *hi-fi, stereo*
l' histoire f *history, story*
historique a *historical*
l' hiver m *winter*
le/la HLM m/f = habitation à
loyer modéré *council flat/*
*house*
le hockey m *hockey*
(le/la) hollandais(e) a/m/f
*Dutch, Dutch person*
la Hollande f *Holland*
l' homme m *man*
la honte f *shame*
l' hôpital m *hospital*
l' horaire m *timetable*
l' horreur f *horror*
avoir horreur de
*to loathe, to detest*
l' hors-d'œuvre m *starter*
l' hospitalité f *hospitality*
l' hôtel m *hotel*
l' hôtel de ville m *town hall*
l' hôtesse de l'air f *air hostess*
l' huile f *oil*
(le) huit a/m *eight*
humide a *damp (weather)*
l' hypermarché m *hypermarket*

**I**

ici ad *here*
l' idée f *idea*
identifier v *to identify*
idiot(e) a *idiot, idiotic*
il faut *(we) must,*
*it is necessary to*
il manque (un bouton)
*(a button) is missing*
il me faut *I need*
il me reste *I've got ... left*
il me reste 3 euros *I've got 3*
*euros left*
il n'y a pas *there isn't/aren't*
il s'agit de *it's about, it's a*
*question of*
il y a *there is, there are*
il y a trois ans *three years ago*
il y avait *there was, there were*
l' île f *island*
l' illustration f *illustration*
l' image f *picture*
l' immatriculation f
*registration, enrolment*
l' immeuble m *building, flats*
l' immigré(e) m/f *immigrant*
impatient(e) a *impatient*
imper(méable) m *raincoat*
impoli(e) a *impolite*
important(e) a *important*
importer v *to import,*
*to matter*
n'importe quel(le) a *any*
n'importe qui pron *any person*
l' imprimante f *printer*
imprimer v *to print*

inadmissible a *intolerable,*
*unacceptable*
l' incendie m *fire*
l' inconnu(e) m/f *stranger,*
*unknown (person)*
l' inconvénient m *disadvantage*
l' Inde f *India*
l' indicatif m *indicative (verb form)*
(l') indien(ne) a/m/f *Indian*
indiquer v *to indicate*
individuel(le) a *individual*
industriel(le) a *industrial*
l' infirmier/infirmière m/f *nurse*
l' informaticien(ne) m/f *computer*
*scientist*
les informations (les infos) fpl *news*
l' informatique f *computer science*
l' ingénieur m *engineer*
l' inondation f *flood*
inquiet/inquiète a *worried*
s'inquiéter vr *to worry*
l' insolation f *sunstroke*
l' insonorisation f *sound-proofing*
l' instant m *moment*
l' instituteur/institutrice m/f *primary*
*school teacher*
l' instruction civique f *citizenship*
intelligent(e) a *intelligent*
interdit(e) a *prohibited*
intéressant(e) a *interesting*
intéresser v *to interest*
s'intéresser à vr *to be interested in*
introduire v *to introduce*
inutile a *useless*
l' invitation f *invitation*
inviter v *to invite*
(l') irlandais(e) a/m/f *Irish, Irish*
*person*
l' Irlande f *Ireland*
l' Irlande du Nord f *Northern*
*Ireland*
l' Italie f *Italy*
(l') italien(ne) a/m/f *Italian*
l' IUT m *polytechnic,*
*technical school*
ivre a *drunk*

**J**

j'en ai marre
*I've had enough, I'm fed up*
jaloux/jalouse a *jealous*
jamais — ne...jamais ad *never*
la jambe f *leg*
le jambon m *ham*
(le) janvier m *January*
le Japon m *Japan*
(le/la) japonais(e) a/m/f
*Japanese, Japanese person*
le jardin m *garden*
le jardin zoologique m *zoological*
*garden*
le jardinage m *gardening*
jaune a *yellow*
je ne sais pas *I don't know*
je veux bien *I'm happy to*
le jean m *jeans*
jeter v *to throw (away)*
le jeu m *game*
jeu de cartes m *card game*
jeu de société m *board game*
jeu vidéo m *video game*
(le) jeudi m *Thursday*
jeune a *young*
le job m *job*
le jogging m *tracksuit, jogging*
joli(e) a *pretty*
jouer v *to play*
jouer + à = *sport*
jouer + de = *instrument*
le jouet m *game, toy*
le jour m *day*
le jour de congé m *day off (leave)*
le jour férié m *public holiday*
le journal m *newspaper*
la journée f *day*
joyeux/joyeuse a *happy*
le judo m *judo*
le/la juge m/f *judge*
juif/juive a *Jewish*
(le) juillet m *July*
(le) juin m *June*

jumelé(e) a *twin, twinned*
la jupe f *skirt*
le jus m *juice*
le jus de fruit m *fruit juice*
le jus d'orange m *orange juice*
jusqu'à prep *until, as far as*
juste a *just, fair*

**K**

le kilo m *kilo(gram)*
le kilomètre m *kilometre*
à ... kilomètres *...kilometres*
*away*

**L**

là ad *there*
là-bas ad *over there*
le laboratoire m *laboratory*
le lac m *lake*
laid(e) a *ugly*
la laine f *wool*
laisser v *to leave*
le lait m *milk*
laitier/laitière a *dairy*
la laitue f *lettuce*
la lampe f *lamp*
la langue f *language, tongue*
les langues vivantes fpl
*modern languages*
le lapin m *rabbit*
large a *wide, broad*
le lavabo m *washbasin*
laver v *to wash*
se laver vr *to wash oneself*
le lave-vaisselle m *dishwasher*
la leçon f *lesson*
le lecteur m *reader, scanner*
le lecteur DVD m *DVD player*
le lecteur MP3 m *mp3 player*
la lecture f *reading*
léger/légère a *light*
le légume m *vegetable*
le lendemain m *the next day*
lent(e) a *slow*
lentement ad *slowly*
les lentilles de contact fpl *contact*
*lenses*
la lessive f *washing powder,*
*washing*
la lettre f *letter*
la levée f *collection*
*(postal)*
lever v *to raise*
se lever vr *to get up*
la librairie f *bookshop*
libre a *free*
licencier v *to dismiss,*
*to make redundant*
le lieu m *place*
avoir lieu *to take place*
la ligne f *line*
la limonade f *lemonade*
lire v *to read*
la liste f *list*
le lit m *bed*
le grand lit m *double bed*
faire le lit *to make the bed*
le litre m *litre*
le livre m *book*
la livre sterling f *pound sterling*
livrer v *to deliver*
le local m *premises*
la location f *rental, hire*
la location de voitures f
*car rental*
le logement m *accommodation*
loger v *to stay*
loin (de) ad/prep *far (from)*
le loisir m *leisure*
Londres *London*
long(ue) a *long*
le long de prep *along*
longtemps ad *for a long time*
la longueur f *length*
le look m *look, image, style*
louer v *to hire*
le loyer m *rent*
la lumière f *light*
(le) lundi m *Monday*
les lunettes fpl *glasses*

les lunettes de soleil fpl
*sunglasses*
lutter (contre) v *to fight (against)*
le lycée m *secondary school*
le lycée technique m *secondary*
*school for vocational training*

**M**

le machin m *thing, contraption*
la machine f *machine*
la machine à laver f *washing*
*machine*
Madame f *Mrs, madam*
Mademoiselle f *Miss*
Mademoiselle! interj *Waitress!*
le magasin m *shop*
le magazine m *magazine*
(le/la) maghrébin(e) a/m/f *North*
*African*
le magnétoscope m *video recorder*
magnifique a *magnificent*
(le) mai m *May*
maigre a *thin*
le maillot m *vest*
le maillot de bain m
*swimming costume*
la main f *hand*
maintenant ad *now*
la mairie f *town hall*
mais conj *but*
la maison f *house*
la maison des jeunes (MJC —
la maison des jeunes et de la
culture) f *youth club*
la maison individuelle f
*detached house*
la maison jumelée f
*semi-detached house*
la maison de la presse f
*newsagent's*
le maître nageur m *swimming*
*instructor*
le mal m *pain, evil*
avoir mal à *to have a pain in*
mal ad *badly*
mal payé(e) a *badly paid*
(le/la) malade a/m/f *ill, ill person*
la maladie f *illness*
malheureusement ad
*unfortunately*
malheureux/malheureuse a
*unhappy, unlucky*
la maman f *mum*
la Manche f *the Channel*
manger v *to eat*
la manifestation f *demonstration*
le mannequin m *model (person),*
*mannequin*
manquer v *to miss*
le manteau m *coat*
le maquillage m *make-up*
le/la marchand(e) m/f *shopkeeper*
le marché m *market*
marcher v *to walk, to work*
(le) mardi m *Tuesday*
la marée f *tide*
le mari m *husband*
le mariage m *marriage*
marié(e) a *married*
se marier vr *to get married*
le marketing m *marketing*
le Maroc m *Morocco*
(le/la) marocain(e) a/m/f *Moroccan*
la marque f *brand, label*
marquer v *to mark, write down*
marron a *brown (eyes, hair)*
(le) mars m *March*
le Massif Central m *mountainous*
*region near the centre of France*
le match m *match (sport)*
la maternelle f *reception class*
les maths fpl *maths*
la matière f *subject*
les matières grasses fpl *fat content*
le matin m *morning*
matinal(e) a *morning*
être matinal(e)
*to be a morning person*
la matinée f *morning*
faire la grasse matinée
*to have a lie-in*

mauvais(e) a *bad*
il fait mauvais
*the weather's bad*
la mauvaise taille f *the wrong*
*size*
le/la mécanicien(ne) m/f *mechanic*
méchant(e) a *nasty, naughty*
le médecin m *doctor*
le médicament m *medicine*
la Méditerranée f *Mediterranean*
*Sea*
meilleur(e) a *better*
meilleurs vœux *best wishes*
le membre m *member, limb*
même ad *even*
même a *same*
le ménage m *household,*
*housework*
mener v *to lead*
la mentalité f *mentality, attitude*
mentir v *to lie*
le menu m *set menu*
menu à 15 euros m
*set menu at 15 euros*
menu à prix fixe m
*fixed-price menu*
menu touristique m
*tourist menu*
la mer f *sea*
merci interj *thank you*
(le) mercredi m *Wednesday*
la mère f *mother*
la merguez f *spicy sausage*
merveilleux/merveilleuse a
*marvellous*
le message m *message*
mesurer v *to measure*
le métal m *metal*
la météo f *weather forecast*
le métier m *job, profession*
le mètre m *metre*
à ... mètres *... metres away*
le métro m *underground (tube)*
le metteur en scène m *director (of*
*a play or film)*
mettre v *to put*
mettre à la poste *to post*
mettre dans le bon ordre
*to put in the right order*
(se) mettre en route
*to start up, to take to*
*the road*
le meuble m *piece of furniture*
le midi m *midday*
le Midi m *South of France*
mieux ad *better*
mignon(ne) a *cute, sweet, nice*
le milieu m *middle*
au milieu de prep
*in the middle of*
le million m *million*
mi-long(ue) a *shoulder-length*
*(hair)*
mince a *slim*
le minuit m *midnight*
la minute f *minute*
à ... minutes *in ... minutes'*
*time*
le miroir m *mirror*
la mi-trimestre f *half-term*
mixte a *mixed (e.g. school)*
la mobylette f *moped*
moche a *ugly, rotten*
la mode f *fashion*
à la mode a *in fashion,*
*fashionable*
moderne a *modern*
à moi a *mine*
moins ... que *less ... than*
au moins *at least*
le mois m *month*
la moitié f *half*
le/la môme m/f *kid*
le moment m *moment, time*
en ce moment ad *at the*
*moment*
mon Dieu! interj *my God!*
le monde m *world*
le moniteur m *instructor, computer*
*monitor*

---

**ad**: adverb    **prep**: preposition    **pron**: pronoun    **interj**: interjection    **conj**: conjunction

*French–English Dictionary*

la monnaie f *change (money)*
monoparental(e) a *single-parent (family)*
Monsieur m *Mr / sir*
la montagne f *mountain*
monter v *to rise*
la montre f *watch*
montrer v *to show*
le monument m *monument*
la moquette f *fitted carpet*
le moral m *morale, spirit*
le morceau m *piece*
la mort f *death*
mort(e) a *dead*
le mot m *word*
le moteur m *motor*
la moto f *motorbike*
le/la motocycliste m/f *motorcyclist*
le mouchoir v *handkerchief*
mouillé(e) a *wet*
mouiller v *to get wet*
mourir v *to die*
la moutarde f *mustard*
le mouton m *sheep*
moyen(ne) a *medium*
la moyenne f *average*
le mur m *wall*
le musée m *museum*
la musique f *music*
   musique pop/rock/classique f *pop/rock/classical music*
(le/la) musulman(e) a/m/f *Muslim*

## N

la N7 f *the N7 (French A-road)*
nager v *to swim*
la naissance f *birth*
la natation f *swimming*
la nationalité f *nationality*
nautique a *nautical*
né(e) le *born on*
ne ... jamais *never*
ne ... pas *not*
ne ... personne *no one*
ne ... plus *no longer*
ne ... rien *nothing*
nécessaire a *necessary*
négatif/négative a *negative*
la neige f *snow*
neiger v *to snow*
nettoyer v *to clean*
(le) neuf a/m *nine*
neuf/neuve a *new*
le neveu m *nephew*
le nez m *nose*
ni... ni... *neither... nor...*
la nièce f *niece*
le niveau m *level*
les noces fpl *wedding*
(le) Noël m *Christmas*
noir(e) a *black*
le nom m *name*
le nombre m *number*
non interj *no*
non plus ad *neither, either (e.g. I haven't any either)*
non-fumeur/non-fumeuse a *non-smoking*
le nord m *north*
normalement ad *normally*
la Normandie m *Normandy*
la note f *mark, grade*
noter v *to note*
la nourriture f *food*
nouveau/nouvelle a *new*
le Nouvel An m *New Year*
(le) novembre m *November*
le nuage m *cloud*
nuageux/nuageuse a *cloudy*
la nuit f *night*
nul(le) a *useless*
le numéro m *number*
le numéro de téléphone m *telephone number*

## O

l' obésité f *obesity*
les objets trouvés mpl *lost property*
obligatoire a *compulsory*
l' occasion f *opportunity (to)*
occupé(e) a *engaged, busy*

(l') octobre m *October*
l' odeur f *smell, fragrance*
l' œil m (pl. les yeux) *eye*
l' œuf m *egg*
l' office de tourisme m *tourist office*
l' offre f *offer*
l' offre d'emploi f *job offer*
l' oignon m *onion*
l' oiseau m *bird*
ombragé(e) a *shaded*
l' omelette f *omelette*
on pron *one, you*
   on se retrouve à quelle heure? *what time shall we meet?*
l' oncle m *uncle*
(l') onze a/m *eleven*
l' opinion f *opinion*
optimiste a *optimistic*
l' option f *option*
l' or m *gold*
l' orage m *storm*
orageux/orageuse a *stormy*
orange a *orange (colour)*
l' orange f *orange (fruit)*
l' orangina m *orangina*
l' orchestre m *orchestra*
ordinaire a *ordinary*
l' ordinateur m *computer*
l' ordonnance f *prescription*
les ordures fpl *rubbish*
l' oreille f *ear*
organiser v *to organise*
l' os m *bone*
ou conj *or*
où pron/ad *where*
   d'où? *where from?*
oublier v *to forget*
l' ouest m *west*
oui interj *yes*
ouvert(e) a *open*
ouvrir v *to open*

## P

la page f *page*
le pain m *bread*
le pain grillé m *toast*
la paire f *pair*
paisible a *quiet, peaceful*
en panne a *broken down*
le panneau m *sign, notice*
le pantalon m *trousers*
le papa m *dad*
le papier m *paper*
   en papier a *made of paper*
   le papier peint m *wallpaper*
(les) Pâques m/fpl *Easter*
le paquet m *parcel, packet*
par prep *by, per*
   par chance ad *luckily*
   par contre ad *on the other hand*
   par hasard ad *by chance, on the off-chance*
   par ici/là ad *this way/that way*
   par terre *on the ground*
paraître v *to appear*
le parapluie m *umbrella*
le parc m *park*
   le parc d'attractions m *amusement park*
parce que conj *because*
pardon interj *excuse me*
le pare-brise m *windscreen*
pareil(le) a *the same*
les parents mpl *parents*
paresseux/paresseuse a *lazy*
parfait(e) a *perfect*
parfois ad *sometimes*
le parfum m *flavour, perfume*
la parfumerie f *perfume shop*
le parking m *car park*
parler v *to talk*
la parole f *word*
à part *on one side, separately, except for*
partager v *to share*
le/la partenaire m/f *partner*
la partie f *part*
partir v *to depart, leave*
   à partir de prep *from*
partout ad *everywhere*
pas — ne...pas ad *(...) not*

pas de — je n'ai pas de... *I have no ...*
pas du tout ad *not at all*
pas encore ad *not yet*
pas grand-chose *not much*
pas mal de a *quite a few*
passable a *acceptable*
le passage à niveau m *level crossing*
le/la passant(e) m/f *passer-by*
le passé m *past*
le passeport m *passport*
passer v *to pass*
   passer l'aspirateur *to vacuum*
   passer un examen *to take an exam*
   passer le temps à *to spend time doing*
se passer vr *to happen*
le passe-temps m *hobby*
la passion f *passion*
passionnant(e) a *exciting*
les pastilles fpl *lozenges*
le pâté m *pâté*
les pâtes fpl *pasta*
patient(e) a *patient*
patienter v *to wait*
le patin à roulettes m *roller skate*
le patinage m *skating*
patiner v *to skate*
la patinoire f *ice rink*
la pâtisserie f *cake/pastry shop*
le/la patron(ne) m/f *boss*
la pause f *break, pause*
   la pause-café f *coffee break*
   la pause de midi f *lunch break*
   la pause-déjeuner f *lunch break*
   la pause-thé f *tea break*
pauvre a *poor*
payer v *to pay*
le pays m *country*
le paysage m *countryside*
le pays de Galles m *Wales*
le PC m *computer*
le PDG (président-directeur général) m *chairman and managing director*
le péage m *toll*
la peau f *skin*
la pêche f *fishing, peach*
se peigner vr *to comb one's hair*
la peine f *sadness, difficulty*
   ce n'est pas la peine *don't bother, there's no point*
à peine a *barely*
la peinture f *painting*
la pellicule f *(camera) film*
la pelouse f *lawn*
pendant (+ que) prep (conj) *during, while*
pénible a *hard, tiring*
penser v *to think*
la pension f *board*
la pension complète f *full board*
perdre v *to lose*
le père m *father*
perfectionner v *to perfect, to improve*
le périphérique m *ring road*
permettre v *to allow*
le permis (de conduire) m *permit, (driving) licence*
la permission f *permission*
la personnalité f *personality*
la personne f *person*
la perte f *loss*
peser v *to weigh*
pessimiste a *pessimistic*
petit(e) a *small, short*
le/la petit(e)-ami(e) m/f *boyfriend/girlfriend*
le petit déjeuner m *breakfast*
le petit-fils m *grandson*
la petite-fille m *granddaughter*
les petits pois mpl *peas*
le pétrole m *oil, petroleum*
peu ad *little, few*
   un peu de a *a little*
la peur f *fear*
   avoir peur *to be scared*
peut-être ad *perhaps*

le phare m *lighthouse, headlight*
la pharmacie f *pharmacy*
le/la pharmacien(ne) m/f *pharmacist*
la photo f *photo*
la photocopie f *photocopy*
la phrase f *sentence*
la physique f *physics*
le piano m *piano*
la pièce f *piece, coin, room*
la pièce de théâtre f *play*
la pièce d'identité f *proof of identity*
le pied m *foot*
   à pied a *on foot*
(le/la) piéton(ne) m/f/a *pedestrian*
piquant(e) a *spicy*
le pique-nique m *picnic*
piquer v *to sting*
la piqûre f *bite, sting*
la piscine f *swimming pool*
la piste f *track, trail*
   la piste cyclable f *cycle lane, cycle track*
pittoresque a *picturesque, vivid*
la pizza f *pizza*
le placard m *cupboard*
la place f *square, room, space, seat*
le plafond m *ceiling*
la plage f *beach*
se plaindre vr *to complain*
plaire (+ à) v *to please*
le plaisir m *pleasure*
le plan m *plan, map*
le plan de la ville m *map of the town*
la planche à voile f *windsurfing*
la plante f *plant*
le plastique m *plastic*
   en plastique a *made of plastic*
le plat m *dish*
le plat du jour m *dish of the day*
le plat principal m *main course*
la platine laser f *laser disc player*
plein(e) a *full*
   faire le plein *to fill the car up*
   plein de vie a *full of life*
pleurer v *to cry*
pleuvoir v *to rain*
le plombier m *plumber*
plonger v *to dive*
le/la plongeur/plongeuse m/f *diver*
la pluie f *rain*
plus ad *more*
   plus tard ad *later*
   plus ... que *more ... than*
plusieurs pron *several*
pluvieux/pluvieuse a *rainy*
le pneu m *tyre*
la poche f *pocket*
le poids (lourd) m *(heavy) weight*
à point a *medium (cooked)*
la pointure f *size (of shoe)*
la poire f *pear*
le poisson m *fish*
   le poisson rouge m *goldfish*
le poivre m *pepper*
poli(e) a *polite*
la police f *police*
la police-secours f *emergency services*
le/la policier/policière m/f *policeman/ woman*
pollué(e) a *polluted*
la pollution f *pollution*
la Pologne f *Poland*
(le/la) polonais(e) a/m/f *Polish, Polish person*
la pomme f *apple*
la pomme de terre f *potato*
le pont m *bridge*
populaire a *popular*
le porc m *pork, pig*
le port m *harbour, port*
le portable m *mobile phone*
la porte f *door*
   la porte d'entrée f *front door*
le portefeuille m *wallet*
le porte-monnaie m *purse*
porter v *to carry, wear*
la portière f *door (of car, train)*
(le/la) portugais(e) a/m/f *Portuguese, Portuguese person*
le Portugal m *Portugal*

poser v *to pose, to place*
   poser des questions *to ask questions*
   poser sa candidature *to apply (for a position)*
positif/positive a *positive*
possible a *possible*
la poste f *post office*
le poster m *poster*
le pot m *jar, pot, carton*
potable/non potable ad *drinkable/ undrinkable*
le potage m *soup, broth*
la poubelle f *dustbin*
le poulet m *chicken*
le poumon m *lung*
pour prep *for*
le pourboire m *tip*
pourquoi ad/conj *why*
pousser v *to push*
pouvoir v *to be able to*
pratique a *practical*
pratiquer v *to practise*
la préférence f *preference*
préférer v *to prefer*
premier/première a *first*
   au premier étage ad *on the first floor*
   en premier a *first of all*
prendre v *to take*
le prénom m *first name*
préparer v *to prepare*
près (+ de) ad (prep) *near, close (to)* tout près *very near*
présent(e) a *present (here)*
présenter v *to present*
le préservatif m *condom*
presque ad *almost*
pressé(e) a *busy*
la pression f *pressure*
prêt(e) a *ready*
prêter v *to lend*
la prévention routière f *road safety*
les prévisions fpl *weather forecast*
prévu(e) a *expected*
le printemps m *spring (season)*
priorité à droite *give way to the right (on road signs)*
la prise f *catch, hold*
privé(e) a *private*
le prix m *price*
le prix fixe m *fixed price (e.g. menu)*
le problème m *problem*
prochain(e) a *next*
proche a *near, close*
le produit m *product*
le professeur m *teacher*
la profession f *profession*
profiter de v *to profit from, to take advantage of*
profond(e) a *deep*
le programme m *programme*
le/la programmeur/ programmeuse m/f *programmer*
les progrès mpl *progress*
le projet m *project*
la promenade f *walk*
   faire une promenade *to go for a walk*
promener v *to walk (e.g. a dog)*
se promener vr *to go for a walk*
la promotion f *promotion*
   en promotion ad *in a sale*
proposer v *to propose, suggest*
propre a *clean, own (e.g. my own room)*
le/la propriétaire m/f *owner*
la protection f *protection*
protéger v *to protect*
en provenance de a *coming from*
la Provence m *Provence*
la proximité f *closeness*
   à proximité a *close, nearby*
la prune f *plum*
public/publique a *public*
la publicité f *publicity, advertisement(s)*
puis ad *then, next*

---

**nouns — m**: *masculine*   **f**: *feminine*   **pl**: *plural*        **v**: *verb*        **vr**: *reflexive verb*        **a**: *adjective*

*French–English Dictionary*

le pull (over) m *jumper*
la purée f *mashed potato*
le pyjama m *pyjamas*
les Pyrénées fpl *Pyrenees*

## Q

le quai m *platform*
la qualité f *quality*
quand(?) conj/ad/interj *when(?)*
la quantité f *quantity*
(le) quarante a/m *forty*
le quart m *quarter*
le quartier m *district, part of town*
(le) quatorze a/m *fourteen*
(le) quatre a/m *four*
quatre-vingts a/m *eighty*
quatre-vingt-dix a/m *ninety*
quatrième a *fourth*
en quatrième a *in year 9*
que conj/pron *that, than*
le Québec m *Quebec*
quel, quelle, quels, quelles pron *which*
quelque(s) a *some*
quelque chose pron *something*
quelqu'un pron *someone*
quelquefois ad *sometimes*
qu'est-ce que / qu'est-ce qui *what, who (in questions)*
qu'est-ce que c'est? *what is it?*
qu'est-ce qu'il y a? *what is there, what is it?*
la question f *question*
la queue f *tail, queue*
que veut dire ... en anglais? *what does ... mean in English?*
qui(?) pron/interj *who, that, which*
(le) quinze a/m *fifteen*
(les) quinze jours mpl *fortnight*
quitter v *to leave (e.g. a place)*
quoi(?) pron interj *what(?)*
le quotidien m *everyday life, the daily newspaper*
quotidien(ne) a *daily*

## R

raccrocher v *to hang up (e.g. phone)*
raconter v *to tell*
la radio f *radio*
raid a *straight*
le raisin m *grape*
le raisin sec m *raisin*
la raison f *reason*
avoir raison *to be right*
ralentir v *slow down*
la randonnée f *hike*
ranger v *to tidy (e.g. a bedroom)*
(le) rapide a/m *quick, express train*
rapidement ad *quickly*
le rappel m *recall, reminder*
rappeler v *to call back*
se rappeler vr *to recall, to remember*
les rapports mpl *relationships*
rare a *rare*
se raser vr *to shave*
ravi(e) a *delighted*
rayé(e) a *striped*
le rayon m *shelf, department (of a department store)*
la réaction f *reaction*
le/la réalisateur/réalisatrice m *director (of film)*
récemment ad *recently*
récent(e) a *recent*
la réception f *reception*
recevoir v *to receive*
être reçu(e) *to be received*
le réchaud m *stove*
le réchauffement m *warming (up)*
le réchauffement de la planète m *global warming*
recommander v *to recommend*
reconnaissant(e) a *grateful*
la récréation f *leisure, recreation, break(time)*
le reçu m *receipt*
recycler v *to recycle*

le rédacteur/rédactrice m/f *editor*
redoubler v *to repeat a year*
la réduction f *reduction*
réduit(e) a *reduced*
réfléchir v *to reflect, think*
refuser v *to refuse*
regarder v *to look at, to watch*
le régime m *diet*
la région f *region*
la règle f *rule, ruler*
le règlement m *ruling, guideline*
regretter v *to be sorry*
se relaxer vr *to relax*
religieux/religieuse a *religious*
la religion f *religion*
remarquer v *to notice*
rembourser v *to reimburse, to give back*
remercier v *to thank*
la remise f *discount*
remplir v *to fill (in)*
remporter (un prix) v *win (a prize)*
(se) rencontrer v(r) *to meet (up)*
le rendez-vous m *meeting*
renoncer à v *to give up*
renouvelable a *renewable*
les renseignements mpl *information*
la rentrée f *start of school year*
rentrer v *to return*
renverser v *to knock over, to reverse*
le repas m *meal*
repasser v *to iron*
répéter v *to repeat*
le répondeur m *answerphone*
répondre v *to reply*
la réponse f *reply*
se reposer vr *to rest*
reprendre v *to start again*
le RER (réseau express régional) m *regional train network*
la réservation f *reservation*
réserver v *to reserve*
respecter v *to respect, to observe*
respiratoire a *breathing*
la responsabilité f *responsibility*
ressembler v *to look like, resemble*
se ressembler vr *to look alike*
la ressource f *resource*
les ressources naturelles fpl *natural resources*
le restaurant m *restaurant*
rester v *to stay*
le résultat m *result*
le retard m *delay*
en retard a *late*
la retenue f *deduction, detention*
retirer v *to take out*
le retour m *return (journey)*
retourner (à) v *to return (to)*
la retraite f *retirement*
rétrécir v *to shrink, to make narrower*
la réunion f *meeting, gathering*
réussir v *to succeed*
le réveil m *alarm clock*
se réveiller vr *to wake up*
revenir v *to come back*
rêver v *to dream*
réviser v *to revise*
revoir v *to see/meet again*
au revoir interj *goodbye*
la revue f *magazine*
le rez-de-chaussée m *ground floor*
le Rhin m *Rhine (river)*
le Rhône m *Rhone (river)*
le rhume m *cold*
riche a *rich*
le rideau m *curtain*
ridicule a *ridiculous*
rien pron *nothing*
rigolo(te) a *funny*
rire v *to laugh*
le risque m *risk*
la rivière f *river*
le riz m *rice*
la robe f *dress*
le robinet m *tap*
le rock m *rock (music)*

le roman m *novel*
le roman-photo m *graphic novel, comic*
rond(e) a *round*
le rond-point m *roundabout*
rose a *pink*
rôti(e) a *roast*
la roue f *wheel*
rouge a *red*
le rouge à lèvres m *lipstick*
rouler v *to go (car)*
la route f *road*
la route nationale f *A-road*
le routier m *lorry driver*
roux/rousse a *red (hair)*
le Royaume-Uni m *United Kingdom*
la rue f *street*
le rugby m *rugby*

## S

s'il te plaît/s'il vous plaît *please*
le sable m *sand*
le sac m *bag*
le sac à main m *handbag*
le sac de couchage m *sleeping bag*
le sac en plastique m *plastic bag*
sage a *wise, good (child)*
saignant(e) a *bleeding, rare (meat)*
sain(e) a *healthy*
la Saint-Sylvestre f *New Year's Eve*
la Saint-Valentin f *Valentine's Day*
la saison f *season*
la salade f *salad*
le salaire m *salary*
sale a *dirty*
salé(e) a *salted, savoury*
la salle f *room*
la salle à manger f *dining room*
la salle d'attente f *waiting room*
la salle de bain(s) f *bathroom*
la salle de classe f *classroom*
la salle de séjour f *living room*
le salon m *living room*
salut interj *hi, bye*
(le) samedi m *Saturday*
le SAMU m *mobile emergency medical service*
la sandale f *sandal*
le sandwich m *sandwich*
le sang m *blood*
sans prep *without*
sans doute ad *without doubt*
sans plomb a *unleaded*
sans-souci a *carefree*
sans travail a *unemployed*
la santé f *health*
en bonne santé a *in good health*
les sapeurs-pompiers mpl *fire service*
satisfaire v *to satisfy, to live up to*
la sauce f *sauce*
la saucisse f *sausage*
le saucisson m *cold sausage*
sauf prep *except (for)*
le saumon m *salmon*
sauter v *to jump*
sauvage a *wild, undomesticated*
sauvegarder v *to protect, to save*
sauver v *to save*
savoir v *to know (e.g. how to do something)*
je ne sais pas *I don't know*
le savon m *soap*
la science-fiction f *science fiction*
les sciences fpl *science*
scolaire a *school*
la scolarisation f *schooling*
le/la SDF (sans domicile fixe) m/f *homeless person*
la séance f *showing (e.g. of film)*
sec/sèche a *dry*
secondaire a *secondary*
la seconde f *second (period of time)*
en seconde ad *in year 11*
le secours m *help*
au secours! interj *help!*
le/la secrétaire m/f *secretary*
la section (d'anglais) f *(English)*

section, *department*
la sécurité f *security, safety*
séduisant(e) a *attractive*
(le) seize a/m *sixteen*
le séjour m *stay*
le sel m *salt*
la semaine f *week*
sembler v *to seem*
le sens de l'humour m *sense of humour*
à sens unique a *one-way*
sensass a *sensational*
sensible a *sensitive*
sentir v *to feel, smell*
se sentir vr *to feel*
se sentir bon/mauvais *to feel good/ill*
séparé(e) a *separated*
(le) sept a/m *seven*
(le) septembre m *September*
la série f *set, series*
sérieux/sérieuse a *serious*
serré(e) a *tight*
le/la serveur/serveuse m/f *waiter/waitress*
le service m *service*
la serviette f *towel, napkin*
servir v *to serve*
seul(e) a/ad *only, alone*
tout(e) seul(e) *all alone*
à moi seul(e) *by myself*
seulement ad *only*
sévère a *strict*
le shampooing m *shampoo*
le shopping m *shopping*
le short m *shorts*
si conj *if*
le sida m *AIDS*
signer v *to sign*
le silence m *silence*
simple a *simple, single*
le sirop m *syrup (medicine)*
le site m *site*
situé(e) a *situated*
(le) six a/m *six*
sixième a *sixth*
en sixième *in year 7*
le skate m *skateboarding*
le ski m *skiing*
faire du ski *to go skiing*
faire du ski nautique *to go water skiing*
SNCF (Société nationale des chemins de fers français) f *French national railway*
la sœur f *sister*
la soif f *thirst*
avoir soif *to be thirsty*
soigner v *to care for*
le soin m *care*
le soir m *evening*
la soirée f *evening*
(le) soixante a/m *sixty*
(le) soixante-dix a/m *seventy*
le/la soldat(e) m/f *soldier*
les soldes mpl *sales*
le soleil m *sun*
il fait du soleil *it's sunny*
le son (et lumière) m *sound and lighting, a type of show*
le sondage m *survey*
sonner v *to ring*
la sorte f *sort, kind (of)*
la sortie f *exit*
la sortie de secours f *emergency exit*
sortir v *to go out*
le souci m *worry*
soudain ad *suddenly*
souffrir v *to suffer*
souhaitable a *desirable*
souligner v *to underline*
la soupe f *soup*
sourire v *to smile*
la souris f *mouse*
sous prep *under*
sous-marin(e) a *underwater*
le sous-sol m *basement*
sous-titré(e) a *subtitled*
souterrain(e) a *underground*

le souvenir m *souvenir, memory*
souvent ad *often*
les spaghettis mpl *spaghetti*
le sparadrap m *sticking plaster*
spécial(e) a *special*
la spécialité (locale) f *(local) speciality*
le spectacle m *show*
le/la spectateur/spectatrice m/f *spectator*
splendide a *splendid*
le sport m *sport*
faire du sport *to do sport*
les sports d'hiver mpl *winter sports*
les sports nautiques mpl *water sports*
sportif/sportive a *sporty*
le stade m *stadium*
le stage (en entreprise) m *work experience*
la station f *station, stop*
la station balnéaire f *seaside resort*
la station de ski f *ski resort*
le stationnement m *parking*
stationner v *to park*
la station-service f *petrol station, service station*
le steak m *steak*
strict(e) a *strict*
le studio m *studio apartment*
stupide a *stupid*
le stylo m *pen*
le sucre m *sugar*
sucré(e) a *sweetened*
le sud m *south*
suffisamment a *sufficiently, enough*
la Suisse f *Switzerland*
(le/la) suisse a/m/f *Swiss*
suivant(e) a *following, next*
suivre v *to follow*
super a *great*
le supermarché m *supermarket*
le supplément m *extra, supplement*
supporter v *to put up with*
sur prep *on, on top of*
sur le point de *about to*
sur (vingt) *out of (twenty)*
sûr(e) a *sure*
surcharger v *to overload*
le surf m *surfing*

le surf des neiges m *snowboarding*
la surpopulation f *overpopulation*
la surprise f *surprise*
la surprise-partie f *surprise party*
surtout ad *especially*
le/la surveillant(e) m/f *guard, supervisor*
surveiller v *to watch*
le sweat-shirt m *sweatshirt*
sympa(thique) a *nice, friendly*
le syndicat m *union, association*
le syndicat d'initiative m *tourist information office*

## T

le tabac m *newsagent, tobacco*
la table f *table*
le tableau m *picture*
la taille f *size*
se taire vr *to be quiet*
la Tamise f *Thames*
tant ad *(so) much*
tant mieux *good, that's better*
tant pis *never mind, too bad*
la tante f *aunt*
taper v *to type, to knock*
taper à la machine *to type*
le tapis m *carpet*
tard ad *late*
le tarif m *tarif, rate*
le tarif réduit m *reduced tarif*
la tarte au citron f *lemon tart*
la tasse f *cup*
le tatouage m *tattoo*
le taux (d'alcool) m *(alcohol) percentage, level (of alcohol)*

---

**ad**: adverb    **prep**: preposition    **pron**: pronoun    **interj**: interjection    **conj**: conjunction

*French–English Dictionary*

le taxi m  taxi
le/la technicien(ne) m/f  technician
la technologie f  technology
la télécarte f  phonecard
le téléphone m  telephone
le téléphone portable m  mobile
téléphoner v  to phone
le/la téléspectateur/téléspectatrice m/f  television viewer
la télévision f  television
le témoin m  witness
la température f  temperature
la tempête f  storm
le temps m  weather, time
de temps en temps ad  from time to time
en même temps ad  at the same time
à temps partiel a  part-time
le tennis m  tennis
la tente f  tent
en terminale ad  in upper 6th
terminer v  to terminate, end
le terrain m  ground
la terrasse f  terrace
terrible a  terrible, dreadful
la tête f  head
le texte m  text
le texto m  text message
le TGV (train à grande vitesse) m  high-speed train
le thé m  tea
le théâtre m  theatre
faire du théâtre to act, be a stage actor
le ticket m  ticket
à la tienne interj  cheers!
le timbre m  stamp
timide a  shy
tirer v  to pull
le (gros) titre m  headline
le toast  m toast
les toilettes fpl  toilets
le toit m  roof
la tomate f  tomato
tomber v  to fall
tomber amoureux (de) to fall in love (with)
la tonalité f  dialling tone
tondre v  to cut, to mow
le tort m  fault, wrong
avoir tort v  to be wrong
tôt ad  early
la touche f  key, button, touch
toucher v  to touch
toujours ad  always
la tour f  tower
le tourisme m  tourism
le/la touriste m/f  tourist
touristique a  touristy
la tournée f  tour, round
tourner v  to turn
tourner un film  to shoot a film
tous m  everyone
tous les jours ad  every day
la Toussaint f  All Saints' Day, November 1st
tousser v  to cough
tout, toute, tous, toutes pron  all
tout à coup ad  all of a sudden
à toute à l'heure interj  see you later
tout de suite ad  immediately
tout droit ad  straight ahead
tout le monde pron  everyone
tout près m  close by
toutes directions fpl  all directions (on road sign)
toutes les cinq minutes  every five minutes
le train m  train
être en train de faire quelque chose  to be in the process of doing something
le train-train m  daily routine
le traitement de texte m  word-processing
traiter de v  to deal with
le trajet m  journey
la tranche f  slice

tranquille a  quiet
les transports en commun mpl  public transport
le travail m (pl. les travaux)  work
travailler v  to work
travailleur/travailleuse a  hard-working
traverser v  to cross (e.g. street)
(le)  treize a/m thirteen
le tremblement de terre m  earthquake
tremper v  to soak
la trentaine f  about thirty, thirty or so
(le)  trente a/m thirty
très ad  very
le tricot m  jumper
le trimestre m  term
triste a  sad
(le)  trois a/m three
troisième a  third
en troisième ad  in year 10
le troisième âge m  retirement years
se tromper vr  to make a mistake
se tromper de numéro  to dial the wrong number
trop ad  too, too much
le trottoir m  pavement
le trou m  hole
la trousse de premiers secours f  first-aid kit
trouver v  to find
se trouver  to be (situated)
le truc m  thing, trick
la truite f  trout
le T-shirt m  T-shirt
le tube m  tube, hit song
tuer v  to kill
la Tunisie f  Tunisia
(le/la) tunisien(ne) a/m/f  Tunisian
typique a  typical

## U

l' UE (Union européenne) m  EU (European Union)
un/une/des art/a  a, one, some
la une f  the front page
l' uniforme m  uniform
uni(e) a  plain, smooth
unique a  only
l' université f  university
l' usine f  factory
utile a  useful
utiliser v  to use

## V

les vacances fpl  holiday, vacation
la vache f  cow
la vague f  wave
la vaisselle f  washing-up
faire la vaisselle  to wash up
valable a  valid
la valeur f  value
la valise f  suitcase
la vallée f  valley
le vandalisme m  vandalism
la vanille f  vanilla
varié(e) a  varied
variable a  variable, unsettled
le veau m  veal
la vedette f  star (e.g. film star)
(le/la) végétarien(ne) a/m/f  vegetarian
le véhicule m  vehicle
le vélo m  bike
le/la vendeur/vendeuse m/f  shop assistant
vendre v  to sell
(le) vendredi m  Friday
venir v  to come
le vent m  wind
il fait du vent  it's windy
le ventre m  stomach
le verglas m  (black) ice
vérifier v  to check, verify
la vérité f  truth
le verre m  glass
en verre a  made of glass
vers prep  around, about, towards

la version française f  film dubbed into French
la version originale f  film in the original language, with subtitles
le vert(e) a  green
la veste f  jacket
les vêtements mpl  clothes
le/la veuf/veuve m/f  widower, widow
la viande f  meat
vide a  empty
le vide-grenier m  car-boot sale, garage sale
la vie f  life
vieux/vieille a  old
le village m  village
la ville f  town
en ville ad  in town
le vin m  wine
le vinaigre m  vinegar
(le) vingt a/m  twenty
la vingtaine f  about twenty, twenty or so
la violence f  violence
violet(te) a  purple
le visage m  face
la visite f  visit
visiter v  to visit (a place)
la vitamine f  vitamin
vite ad  quickly, fast
la vitesse f  speed
à toute vitesse ad  at full speed
la vitrine f  window
vivre v  to live
le vocabulaire m  vocabulary
voici prep  here is, here are
la voie f  way, route
voilà prep  there is, there are
la voile f  sailing, sail
voir v  to see
se voir vr  to see each other
voisin(e) a  neighbouring
le/la voisin(e) m/f  neighbour
la voiture f  car
la voix f  voice
le vol m  flight
le volant m  steering wheel
voler v  to fly, to steal
le volet m  shutter, section
le volley m  volleyball
volontiers ad  gladly, willingly, with pleasure
vomir v  to vomit
à la vôtre interj  cheers!
vouloir v  to want
vouloir bien  to not mind, be happy to
je veux bien  I'll be happy to
le voyage m  journey
voyager v  to travel
le/la voyageur/voyageuse m/f  traveller
vrai(e) a  true
vraiment ad  really
le VTT (vélo tout-terrain) m  mountain bike
la vue f  sight, view

## W

le wagon-lit m  sleeping car
le wagon-restaurant m  restaurant car
le W.C. m  W.C., toilet
le web m  web
le web mail m  webmail
le week-end m  weekend

## X, Y

y pron  there, to it etc.
le yaourt m  yoghurt
les yeux mpl  eyes (plural of l'oeil)

## Z

(le) zéro a/m  nought
la zone f  zone
la zone piétonne f  pedestrian zone
le zoo m  zoo
zut! interj  dash it!

| KEY | |
|---|---|
| m: | masculine noun |
| f: | feminine noun |
| pl: | plural noun |
| v: | verb |
| vr: | reflexive verb |
| a: | adjective (describes a noun) |
| ad: | adverb (describes a verb/adjective) |
| prep: | preposition (connects the verb to a place, thing or person: e.g. 'to', 'for') |
| pron: | pronoun (replaces noun: e.g. 'he', 'me') |
| interj: | interjection (stands alone: e.g. 'Hello!') |
| conj: | conjunction (connects two parts of a sentence: e.g. 'and', 'because') |
| art: | article (e.g. 'the', 'a') |

# Index